Mexico's Unscripted Revolutions

Viewpoints/Puntos de Vista
Themes and Interpretations in Latin American History

Series Editor: Jürgen Buchenau

The books in this series will introduce students to the most significant themes and topics in Latin American history. Intended as supplementary textbooks, the books will also discuss the ways in which historians have interpreted these themes and topics, thus demonstrating to students that our understanding of our past is constantly changing, through the emergence of new sources, methodologies, and historical theories. Unlike monographs, the books in this series will be broad in scope and written in a style accessible to undergraduates.

Published

A History of the Cuban Revolution, Second Edition
Aviva Chomsky

Bartolomeé de las Casas and the Conquest of the Americas
Lawrence A. Clayton

Beyond Borders: A History of Mexican Migration to the United States
Timothy J. Henderson

The Last Caudillo: Alvaro Obregón and the Mexican Revolution
Jürgen Buchenau

A Concise History of the Haitian Revolution
Jeremy D. Popkin

Spaniards in the Colonial Empire: Creoles vs. Peninsulars?
Mark A. Burkholder

Dictatorship in South America
Jerry Dávila

Mothers Making Latin America: Gender, Households, and Politics Since 1825
Erin E. O'Connor

A Short History of U.S. Interventions in Latin America and the Caribbean
Alan McPherson

Latin American Cultural Objects and Episodes
William H. Beezley

Mexico's Unscripted Revolutions: Political and Social Change since 1958
Stephen E. Lewis

Forthcoming

Emancipations: Latin American Independence
Karen Racine

Mexico's Unscripted Revolutions

Political and Social Change since 1958

Stephen E. Lewis

WILEY Blackwell

Published by John Wiley & Sons, Inc., Hoboken, New Jersey.
Published simultaneously in Canada.

Library of Congress Cataloging-in-Publication Data:
Names: Lewis, Stephen E., 1967– author.
Title: Mexico's unscripted revolutions : political and social change since 1958 / Stephen E. Lewis, California State University.
Other titles: Political and social change since 1958
Description: Hoboken, New Jersey : Wiley-Blackwell, [2024] | Series: Viewpoints / Puntos de vista : themes and interpretations in Latin American history | Includes bibliographical references and index.
Identifiers: LCCN 2023048965 (print) | LCCN 2023048966 (ebook) | ISBN 9781444337600 (paperback) | ISBN 9781119719106 (adobe pdf) | ISBN 9781119719120 (epub)
Subjects: LCSH: Mexico–History–1946– | Mexico–Politics and government–20th century. | Mexico–Politics and government–21st century. | Social change–Mexico–History–20th century. | Social change–Mexico–History–21st century.
Classification: LCC F1235 .L45 2024 (print) | LCC F1235 (ebook) | DDC 972.08/2–dc23/eng/20231101
LC record available at https://lccn.loc.gov/2023048965
LC ebook record available at https://lccn.loc.gov/2023048966

Cover Design: Wiley
Cover Image: © Sipa US/Alamy Stock Photo

Set in 10.5/13.5pt Minion by Straive, Pondicherry, India

Contents

Series Editor's Preface

Each book in the "Viewpoints/Puntos de Vista" series introduces students to a significant theme or topic in Latin American history. In an age in which student and faculty interest in the Global South increasingly challenges the old focus on the history of Europe and North America, Latin American history has assumed a prominent position in undergraduate curricula.

Some of these books discuss the ways in which historians have interpreted these themes and topics, thus demonstrating that our understanding of our past is constantly changing, through the emergence of new sources, methodologies, and historical theories. Others offer an introduction to a particular theme by means of a case study or biography in a manner easily understood by the contemporary, non-specialist reader. Yet others give an overview of a major theme that might serve as the foundation of an upper-level course.

What is common to all of these books is their goal of historical synthesis. They draw on the insights of generations of scholarship on the most enduring and fascinating issues in Latin American history, and through the use of primary sources as appropriate. Each book is written by a specialist in Latin American history who is concerned with undergraduate teaching, yet has also made his or her mark as a first-rate scholar.

The books in this series can be used in a variety of ways, recognizing the differences in teaching conditions at small liberal arts colleges, large public universities, and research-oriented institutions with doctoral programs. Faculty have particular needs depending on whether they teach large lectures with discussion sections, small lecture or discussion-oriented classes, or large lectures with no discussion sections, and whether they teach on a semester or trimester system. Recently, and especially since the COVID-19 pandemic, online teaching has also gained greater prominence. The format adopted for this series fits all of these different parameters.

The 11th book in this series, Stephen E. Lewis's expertly crafted *Mexico's Unscripted Revolutions: Political and Social Change since 1958*, is an example of a work that is both great and timely. Serendipitously, a project that began some years ago as an effort to synthesize Mexico's postrevolutionary history since 1940 has become the best explanation of Mexico's current "Fourth Transformation," spearheaded by the controversial populist president, Andrés Manuel López Obrador, or AMLO for short. It is not often that historians can explain the present, but that is precisely what this book does, in pithy chapters that include both political and social transformations since 1958, the year before the Cuban Revolution. The author tells the intertwined stories of a number of "unscripted revolutions," which collectively reshaped Mexican politics and society in even more consequential ways than the "big" revolution of 1910, which ended in 1917, 1920, 1929, 1940, or 1946, depending on the historian.

Seven cohesive chapters tell Professor Lewis's story. The first two chapters are chronological, tracing Mexico's political and social history in the long sixties and into the 1980s, covering issues such as neopopulism, neoliberalism, and democratization. The next three chapters examine three specific unscripted revolutions: the rethinking of race and ethnicity, religious movements, and women's roles, respectively. The final two chapters return to a chronological examination of recent events in Mexico, covering the 2000s all the way to the AMLO presidency (2018–2024). This is a tour de force through high and low politics, with examples from many of Mexico's regions, and due attention—especially—to the subaltern segments of Mexican society. The book will surely attract a wide readership for years to come.

Jürgen Buchenau
Dowd Term Chair of Capitalism Studies
Professor of History and Latin American Studies
University of North Carolina, Charlotte

Acknowledgments

Many thanks to series editor Jürgen Buchenau, who proposed this project to me and guided it from start to finish. He wisely recommended that I structure the book as a series of linked, thematic essays. Other projects, obligations, and family commitments prevented me from completing the job sooner, but Jürgen stood by me, for which I am deeply grateful.

Shannon Mattiace guided my attempts to understand and interpret contemporary Mexican politics. She also read the manuscript from start to finish. Chapters 2, 6, and 7 especially benefited from her wise, subtle interventions. Another longtime friend, Susie Porter, gave a close read to Chapter 4. Tanalís Padilla helped me think through Chapter 3. Federico Morales Barragán has been a generous host and friend. He may disagree with my assessment of AMLO's "Fourth Transformation," which ensures that we will have plenty to debate in the coming years! Mariam Yitani Baroudi, Margarita Sosa Suárez, and Martín González Solano have also informed my thinking about contemporary Mexico.

Jürgen Buchenau, an anonymous Wiley reviewer, and Jessica Vandehoven read the entire manuscript and made additional valuable comments and suggestions. I am wholly responsible for any remaining errors and oversights.

I would like to dedicate this book to the thousands of Chico State students who have taken Latin American history classes with me over the years. They have humored my fascination with modern Mexico, asked good questions, and shared smart insights. My most engaged students have shaped my thinking in more ways than they realize. To those students past, present, and future, this book is for you.

Stephen E. Lewis
California State University, Chico

List of Abbreviations

ACG	Asociación Civil Guerrerense (Guerrerense Civic Association)
AMLO	Andrés Manuel López Obrador
ACNR	Asociación Cívica Nacional Revolucionaria (National Revolutionary Civic Association)
CDI	Comisión Nacional para el Desarrollo de los Pueblos Indígenas (National Commission for the Development of Indigenous Peoples)
CFE	Comisión Federal de Electricidad (Federal Electricity Commission)
CNDH	Comisión Nacional de Derechos Humanos (National Commission on Human Rights)
CONAPO	Consejo Nacional de Población (National Council on Population)
CONAPRED	Consejo Nacional para Prevenir la Discriminación (National Council to Prevent Discrimination)
CTM	Confederación de Trabajadores de México (Confederation of Mexican Workers)
DFS	Dirección Federal de Seguridad (Federal Security Directorate)
EZLN	Ejército Zapatista de Liberación Nacional (Zapatista National Liberation Army)
FNALIDM	Frente Nacional por la Liberación y los Derechos de las Mujeres (National Front for Women's Rights and Liberation)

IFE	Instituto Federal Electoral (Federal Electoral Institute)
IMF	International Monetary Fund
INAI	Instituto Nacional de Transparencia, Acceso a la Información y Protección de Datos Personales (National Freedom of Information Institute)
INE	Instituto Nacional Electoral (National Electoral Institute)
INI	Instituto Nacional Indigenista (National Indigenist Institute)
INPI	Instituto Nacional de Pueblos Indígenas (National Institute of Indigenous Peoples)
IPN	Instituto Politécnico Nacional (National Polytechnic Institute)
MAS	Mujeres en Acción Solidaria (Women in Solidarity Action)
MLM	Movimiento de Liberación de la Mujer (Women's Liberation Movement)
MORENA	Movimiento Regeneración Nacional (National Regeneration Movement)
MURO	Movimiento Universitario de Renovadora Orientación (University Movement of Renovating Orientation)
NAFTA	North American Free Trade Agreement
NGO	Non-Governmental Organization
PAN	Partido Acción Nacional (National Action Party)
PDLP	Partido de los Pobres (Party of the Poor)
PEMEX	Petroleos Mexicanos (Mexico's national petroleum industry)
PNR	Partido Nacional Revolucionario (National Revolutionary Party)
PRD	Partido de la Revolución Democrática (Party of the Democratic Revolution)
PRM	Partido de la Revolución Mexicana (Party of the Mexican Revolution)

PRI	Partido Revolucionario Institucional (Institutional Revolutionary Party)
PT	Partido del Trabajo (Labor Party)
PVEM	Partido Verde Ecologista de México (Mexican Green Party)
SEDENA	Secretaría de la Defensa Nacional (National Defense Ministry)
SEP	Secretaría de Educación Pública (Ministry of Public Education)
SIL	Summer Institute of Linguistics
TEPJF	Tribunal Electoral del Poder Judicial de la Federación (Electoral Tribunal of the Federal Judiciary)
UNAM	Universidad Nacional Autónoma de México (National Autonomous University of Mexico)

Introduction

When most people think of revolution in Mexico, they are drawn to the Revolution of 1910, and with good reason. What started as a political rebellion against an aging dictator devolved into a full-blown civil war in 1913, followed by a constitutional convention and two decades of postrevolutionary state and nation building.[1] We think of Francisco Madero's quixotic call for electoral democracy, Emiliano Zapata's relentless pursuit of land reform, and the photos of Pancho Villa and Zapata in the National Palace in late 1914, Villa enjoying himself immensely while Zapata looks like a trapped animal, expecting an ambush at any moment.

Mexico's Revolution of 1910 is still regarded as the country's most important single event since independence. But what if Mexicans experienced more meaningful change *decades after* the Revolution with a capital R?

This book proposes just that. It looks at Mexico's unscripted, unheralded, relatively understudied "revolutions" that have unfolded since 1958. What historians now call the Long 1960s brought generational change as many young Mexicans joined a global rebellion against patriarchy, religion, and government authority. By the late

Mexico's Unscripted Revolutions: Political and Social Change since 1958,
First Edition. Stephen E. Lewis.

1970s, Mexico's democratic transition was underway. Initiated by the hegemonic official party, it was pushed forward at crucial moments by ordinary citizens who joined social movements, opposition parties, and even armed insurgencies. Meanwhile, Mexican feminists challenged traditional gender roles. They were propelled forward by economic crises that forced them into the formal workplace as never before. Mexican society was in flux, and some of the ideological assumptions of the postrevolutionary state were challenged and cast aside. Not even the Catholic Church was immune to Mexico's unscripted revolutions, as the faithful increasingly sought alternative religious expressions. By 2000, a tenuous, thin democratic transition seemed complete, but democratic *consolidation* was hobbled by the persistence of inequality and corruption and a chilling spike in violence. The man who won the presidential election in 2018, populist Andrés Manuel López Obrador (AMLO), promised Mexico's "Fourth Transformation" but attacked the institutions that had presided over the democratic transition. This left some to wonder if, in fact, Mexico risked reverting to its authoritarian past.

The Mexican Revolution in Context

The Revolution of 1910 and the Constitution of 1917 cast long shadows over more recent Mexican history. The Revolution's first major protagonist, Francisco I. Madero, is remembered as the "apostle" of democracy. When he called for a national uprising in November 1910 against President Porfirio Díaz, who had just had himself reelected for a seventh time, he famously unleashed a tiger that he could not control. President Madero was betrayed and murdered by his most important general in 1913, but his antireelectionist crusade against Díaz left its mark. Four years after his demise, delegates at the constitutional convention in Querétaro enshrined his campaign slogan, "effective suffrage, no reelection," into law. Article 83 of the Constitution of 1917 limited presidents to a single four-year term. Mexico's Institutional Revolutionary Party (*Partido Revolucionario Institucional,* or PRI) later made a mockery of Madero's legacy by controlling the presidency and every congressional and statewide political post for decades, but antireelectionism prevented any single individual from remaining in power indefinitely.

The 1917 Constitution also had important consequences for peasants and industrial workers and for Church-state relations. Article 27 codified Emiliano Zapata's call for land reform, even though Zapata was not invited to the constitutional convention and was, in fact, later assassinated by the faction that signed the new constitution into law. Article 123 granted workers the right to form unions and go on strike and gave the Mexican state a role in mediating between capital and labor. Articles 3 and 130 limited the Catholic Church's role in education and politics. These two articles, and others, reflected the surprising intensity of anticlerical sentiment in revolutionary Mexico. In the 1920s, President Plutarco Elías Calles brought the long-simmering Church-state conflict to a boil. He declared himself "the enemy of the political priest, the scheming priest, the priest as exploiter, the priest who intends to keep our people in ignorance, the priest who allies with the *hacendado* (hacienda owner) to exploit the *campesino* (peasant), and the priest allied with the industrialist to exploit the worker."[2] When Calles enforced some of the Constitution's anticlerical provisions, the Catholic Church hierarchy suspended Mass for three years. Catholic guerrillas, meanwhile, fought the armies of the federal government to a draw. In time, the Church learned to coexist with a Mexican state that remained fiercely anticlerical, at least on paper.

Ordinary Mexicans made their greatest gains in the immediate postrevolutionary period during the presidency of Lázaro Cárdenas (1934–1940). Cárdenas lived up to the promise of Article 3 of the Constitution by investing in public education and endorsing a popular curriculum that celebrated revolutionary heroes like Madero, Zapata, and Villa. He put some teeth to the nationalist provisions in Article 27 and nationalized the oil fields operated by U.S. and British companies. His sweeping land reform redistributed nearly fifty million acres to landless peasants. The Cárdenas administration also gave new life to

Article 123 by supporting most industrial strikes and grouping together over 3000 unions to form the Confederation of Mexican Workers (*Confederación de Trabajadores de México*, or CTM).

The Cárdenas administration also looked poised to clarify an issue that the Constitution of 1917 had not directly addressed—voting rights for women. In late 1937, after many years of suffragist activism, Cárdenas called on Congress to amend the Constitution to give women the right to vote in federal elections and to hold public office. The proposed constitutional amendment sailed through the Senate and the Chamber of Deputies; statehouses then prepared to ratify the amendment. But legislators found a loophole and failed to publish the vote counts in the Congressional Record. The amendment was stopped in its tracks. Perhaps Cárdenas himself feared that the women's vote might jeopardize his ability to manage the upcoming 1940 elections. In 1958, twenty years after Congress had passed the original amendment, women were finally allowed to cast votes for president.[3]

After President Cárdenas left office, the one-party state consolidated its control over both workers and peasants and entered a *modus vivendi* with the Catholic Church. By the 1950s, the much-celebrated Revolution of 1910 had lost its punch for ordinary Mexicans. Textbooks continued to celebrate state-sanctioned heroes and urban planners still named streets after Madero and Zapata. But some of the great conquests of the Revolution had not worn well. The pace of land reform slowed, and workers bristled under the control of corrupt union bosses. The PRI-government perfected the pageantry of holding elections regularly while remaining in almost complete control of the results.

When I was in graduate school, in the 1990s, my cohort and I spent many long hours in seminars, libraries, archives, and in informal gatherings discussing the Revolution of 1910 and its immediate aftermath. In part, we were responding to (and inspired by) the pathbreaking work of historians who had published grand narratives of the Mexican Revolution in the 1980s. Alan Knight's monumental two-volume study focused on the internal causes of the Revolution and argued that the *process* was revolutionary even if the *outcome* was not; John Hart argued persuasively that the Revolution was largely a nationalist rebellion against foreign (and especially United States) capitalism. Ramón Ruíz, for his part, claimed that the Revolution was not a revolution at all, but rather a "great rebellion."[4] Knight's book and articles had the greatest impact on my generation. Many of us wrote dissertations that took regional and state-level approaches to measure the impact of the Revolution on ordinary people. Inspired by the work of Mary Kay Vaughan and Adrian Bantjes,[5] among others, we zeroed in on the immediate postrevolutionary period, the 1920s and 1930s.[6] Few of us ventured beyond the mid-1940s.

To me, at least, the period after midcentury seemed relatively uninteresting. I dismissed it as a time when the hegemonic party successfully managed an economic "miracle" and kept workers, peasants, and the middle class under its thumb. My ignorance stemmed in part from the fact that the PRI-government restricted access to many important archives, making historical research on more recent decades difficult, if not impossible. Fortunately, graduate students nipping at our heels gained access to newly available archival collections and began to push into the middle decades of the twentieth century, revealing the fascinating complexity and effervescence of this period. Their publications provide the foundation for the early chapters of this book.

Overview of This Book

Mexico since 1958 is not a standard textbook. It does not aim to cover everything that has happened in Mexico over the last several decades. Instead, it can be read as a series of linked essays that discuss the rebellious Long Sixties, the democratic transition, the rejection of the cult of mestizaje, Mexico's religious diversity, the revolution in women's lives, and the country's democratic transition and consolidation in historical and contemporary terms. The early chapters draw heavily from historical work, but the latter chapters become more contemporary and pull increasingly from anthropology, sociology, political science, and journalism.

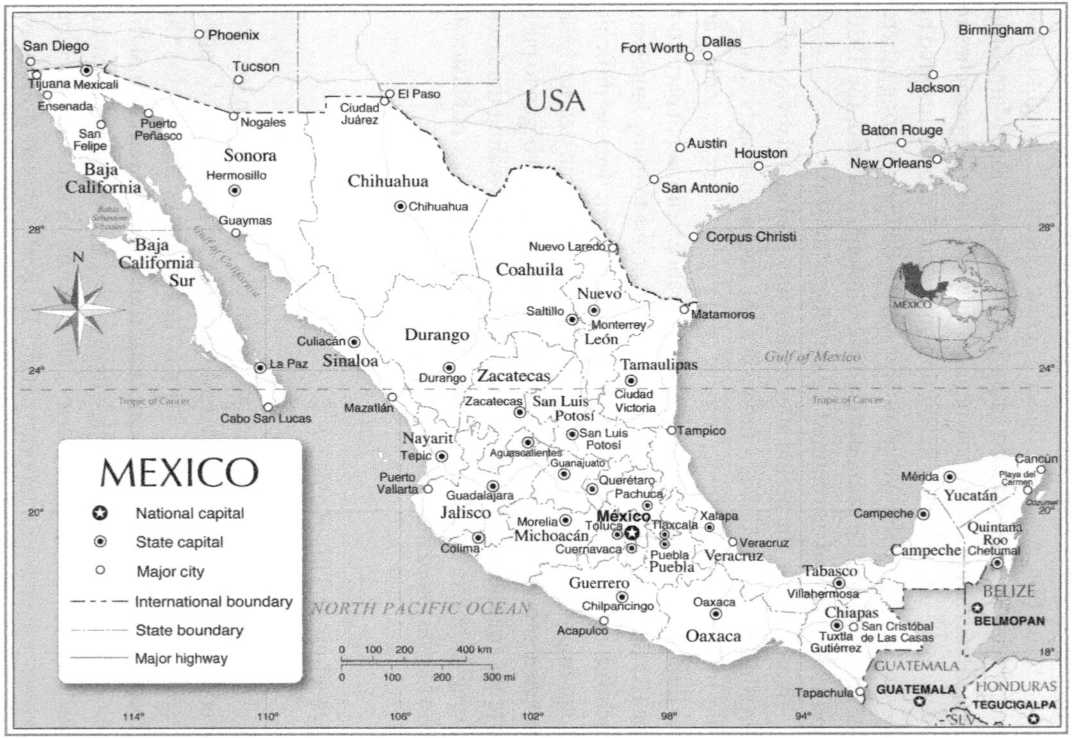
MEXICO
National capital
State capital
Major city
International boundary
State boundary
Major highway
USA
San Diego
Phoenix
Tucson
Tijuana
Mexicali
Ensenada
San Felipe
Puerto Peñasco
Nogales
El Paso
Ciudad Juárez
Fort Worth
Dallas
Birmingham
Jackson
Baton Rouge
New Orleans
Austin
Houston
San Antonio
Corpus Christi
Baja California
Baja California Sur
Sonora
Hermosillo
Guaymas
Chihuahua
Chihuahua
Coahuila
Nuevo Laredo
Nuevo León
Saltillo
Monterrey
Matamoros
Gulf of California
Gulf of Mexico
Durango
Durango
Culiacán
Sinaloa
La Paz
Cabo San Lucas
Mazatlán
Zacatecas
Zacatecas
Tamaulipas
Ciudad Victoria
San Luis Potosí
San Luis Potosí
Tampico
Tropic of Cancer
Tropic of Cancer
Nayarit
Tepic
Puerto Vallarta
Aguascalientes
Guanajuato
Querétaro
Pachuca
Guadalajara
Jalisco
Colima
Morelia
Michoacán
Toluca
México
Tlaxcala
Xalapa
Cuernavaca
Puebla
Puebla
Veracruz
Veracruz
Guerrero
Chilpancingo
Acapulco
Oaxaca
Oaxaca
NORTH PACIFIC OCEAN
Mérida
Yucatán
Cancún
Playa del Carmen
Cozumel
Campeche
Campeche
Quintana Roo
Chetumal
Tabasco
Villahermosa
Chiapas
Tuxtla Gutiérrez
San Cristóbal de Las Casas
Tapachula
BELIZE
BELMOPAN
GUATEMALA
GUATEMALA
HONDURAS
TEGUCIGALPA
SLV
MEXICO
N
0 100 200 400 km
0 100 200 300 mi
28°
24°
20°
18°
114°
110°
106°
102°
98°
94°

Chapter 1 begins with the paradoxes of Mexico at midcentury. The PRI-government presided over a growing economy and growing inequalities. Mexican workers and peasants challenged the PRI to live up to the promises enshrined in the Constitution of 1917. They tested the limits of a government famous for co-opting and negotiating with its opposition. Inspired by the tumult of the Global Sixties, students in Mexico City challenged government authoritarianism and paid a steep price at Tlatelolco in October 1968, just days before the opening ceremonies of the Mexico City Summer Olympic Games. The likely architect of the Tlatelolco massacre, Luis Echeverría, became president in 1970. He would spend the next six years trying to shore up the agonizing PRI-government.

Chapter 2 mixes history with political science as it explores Mexico's remarkable and protracted democratic transition. The process was unique to Mexico and garnered international headlines. It focused on national elections and strengthened political parties but left key elements of the authoritarian state intact. In 1997, the PRI lost its majority in the Chamber of Deputies and conceded the presidency to the opposition National Action Party (*Partido Acción Nacional*, or PAN) in 2000. Had Mexico become a democracy without qualifying adjectives like "emerging," "partial," "fragile," and "thin?" Time would soon render its verdict.

Chapter 3 draws on history, sociology, and journalism to explore how Mexicans resisted and refashioned two of the foundational ideologies of the postrevolutionary Mexican state—*mestizaje*, or biological and cultural mixing, and *indigenismo*, which celebrated Mexico's Indigenous past but called for their "improvement" and integration into the national mainstream. These two ideologies seemed to offer a place at the table to the mestizo majority and gave a conditional welcome to the Indigenous. In practice, however, Mexicans with dark complexions remained the country's poorest and most marginalized citizens. In the 1990s, Indigenous Mexicans emphatically rejected attempts to "incorporate" them into a homogenous nation of mestizos. But they and other dark-skinned Mexicans still struggle to overcome Mexico's pigmentocracy, which makes them invisible in the media and more likely to experience poverty, incarceration, and violence. Some analysts are hopeful that Mexico can more honestly confront its racist and classist legacy now that the ideologies of mestizaje and indigenismo have been overturned.

Religious life in Mexico has also undergone revolutionary changes, as explored in Chapter 4. The Catholic Church, so steeped in tradition, is also now remarkably diverse. Since the late 1960s, several important ideological, theological, geographic, and ethnic expressions have emerged *within* Mexican Catholicism. Meanwhile, alternative devotions have emerged. Some are tolerated by the Church hierarchy while others—like the Santa Muerte (Saint Death)—are not. Outside of the Catholic Church, Protestant and especially Evangelical denominations are making steady inroads. Other Mexicans consider themselves agnostics or practice no religion at all. The incredible dynamism and fluidity of spiritual life in Mexico today often go unnoticed but are key to understanding how most Mexicans make sense of their existence.

The lives of Mexican women have been fundamentally transformed over the last several decades, as discussed in Chapter 5. The "second wave" of Mexican feminism took off in the 1970s and became popularized in the 1980s. Meanwhile, the federal government launched family planning initiatives that succeeded in halving Mexican fertility rates within a generation. During the 1990s, women took advantage of democratic openings to push for greater political opportunities. Gender quotas were first introduced at the party level, and then mandated at the federal and state levels. Today, remarkably, there is gender parity in Mexico's Senate and Chamber of Deputies and in state legislatures. Mexican women exercise more control over their lives and their bodies today than ever before and are flexing their political muscles at the highest levels.

Chapter 6 draws from political science and journalism as it considers Mexico's precarious democratic consolidation. The first sign of serious trouble came in the aftermath of the hotly disputed 2006 presidential election. The declared winner of that election, Felipe Calderón, sought to bolster his legitimacy by declaring war on the country's drug-trafficking organizations. The results were disastrous and defined his presidency. The return of the PRI to national power in 2012 ushered in an especially venal form of politics. Several PRI governors ended up behind bars. Meanwhile, the violence continued unabated. By 2018, most Mexicans regarded the two main parties of the democratic transition, the PRI and the PAN, with disgust. AMLO and his new party, Morena, swept the 2018 election with promises to destroy the old regime and initiate Mexico's "Fourth Transformation," following Mexico's independence from Spain (1810–1821), the period of Liberal reforms, known as *la Reforma* (1854–1876), and the Revolution (1910–1920).

The final chapter draws heavily from Mexican scholars and journalists as it assesses President López Obrador and his "Fourth Transformation." Was AMLO's movement truly transformative? Did it live up to its brash billing? Because a recurring suggestion in this book is that in recent Mexican history, the most meaningful transformations have taken place at the grassroots, outside of the political arena, where ordinary Mexicans have struggled and often prevailed against authoritarian political and cultural practices, tradition, and patriarchy.

Notes

1 See, among others, Mary Kay Vaughan and Stephen E. Lewis, eds., *The Eagle and the Virgin: Nation and Cultural Revolution in Mexico, 1920–1940* (Durham: Duke University Press, 2006).

2 Quoted in Jürgen Buchenau, *Plutarco Elías Calles and the Mexican Revolution* (Lanham, MD: Rowman and Littlefield Publishers, 2007), 127.

3 Stephanie Mitchell, "Revolutionary Feminism, Revolutionary Politics: Suffrage under Cardenismo," *The Americas* 72:3 (July 2015), 439–468; and Jocelyn Olcott, *Revolutionary Women in Postrevolutionary Mexico* (Durham: Duke University Press, 2005), 2, 234.

4 See Alan Knight, *The Mexican Revolution* 2 vols. (New York: Cambridge University Press, 1986); John M. Hart, *Revolutionary Mexico: The*

Coming and Process of the Mexican Revolution (Berkeley: University of California Press, 1987); and Ramón E. Ruiz, *The Great Rebellion: Mexico, 1905–1924* (New York: Norton, 1980).

5 Mary Kay Vaughan, *Cultural Politics in Revolution: Teachers, Peasants, and Schools in Mexico, 1930–1940* (Tucson: University of Arizona Press, 1997); and Adrian Bantjes, *As If Jesus Walked on Earth: Cardenismo, Sonora, and the Mexican Revolution* (Wilmington, DE: Scholarly Resources, Inc., 1998).

6 Many of us later turned our dissertations into books. An incomplete list includes Christopher Boyer, *Becoming Campesinos: Politics, Identity, and Agrarian Struggle in Postrevolutionary Michoacán* (Palo Alto: Stanford University Press, 2003); Alexander S. Dawson, *Indian and Nation in Revolutionary Mexico* (Tucson: University of Arizona Press, 2004); Ben Fallaw, *Cárdenas Compromised: The Failure of Reform in Postrevolutionary Yucatán* (Durham: Duke University Press, 2001); Stephen E. Lewis, *The Ambivalent Revolution: Forging State and Nation in Chiapas, 1910–1945* (Albuquerque: University of New Mexico Press, 2005); Rick A. López, *Crafting Mexico: Intellectuals, Artisans, and the State after the Revolution* (Durham: Duke University Press, 2010); and Patience A. Schell, *Church and State Education in Revolutionary Mexico City* (Tucson: University of Arizona Press, 2003).

1

Revolution or Bust? The Long Sixties in Mexico

Until recently, many considered the middle decades of the twentieth century in Mexico to be a time of relative peace and prosperity that ended abruptly on October 2, 1968, with the massacre of students in Mexico City. Now, as historians focus their attention on the "Long" Sixties—from about 1958 through the early 1970s—a more nuanced and paradoxical picture emerges. Was this truly a time of economic "miracles?" If so, for whom? Was this a time of PRIísta peace marred only by the bloody crackdown at Tlatelolco? Or was the crackdown less of an aberration than we had once thought?

Mexico at Midcentury

It was the best of times, it was the worst of times. On the one hand, Mexico was in the midst of its so-called economic miracle. Using protectionism and investment policies to stimulate domestic industry, the federal government oversaw a period of remarkable, sustained economic growth. The economy grew at an average annual rate of 6.4 percent from 1940 to 1970, which allowed the Mexican government to make major investments in education, public health, and social security. As modern health care services extended into the countryside,

Mexico's Unscripted Revolutions: Political and Social Change since 1958,
First Edition. Stephen E. Lewis.

life expectancy increased dramatically. Literacy rates also increased during this period, from 44 percent in 1940 to 66 percent in 1970. The federal government had also begun investing in public housing projects, including the Tlatelolco complex in Mexico City, just north of the historic downtown. Mexicans were living longer and better, especially in urban, industrial areas and in the northern and central regions of the country.

Figure 1.1 Mexico's National Indigenist Institute (INI) built coordinating centers in Indigenous regions in the 1950s and early 1960s and launched controversial development and assimilation programs. These boys from Chamula, Chiapas, had just been vaccinated by INI nurses. Photographer unknown. Fototeca Nacho López, Comisión Nacional para el Desarrollo de los Pueblos Indígenas. Circa 1955.

The ruling PRI-government presided over all of this. One of the keys to its success was corporatism, the incorporation of various political and economic actors, like the Confederation of Mexican Workers (*Confederación de Trabajadores de México*, or CTM) and the National Peasant Confederation (*Confederación Nacional Campesina*, or CNC). Another key was clientelism, the deeply rooted patron–client relationships that permeate Mexican life. The PRI-government combined near-absolute control with the outward appearance of democratic participation. It was, as Peruvian novelist Mario Vargas Llosa stated on Mexican television in 1990, "the perfect dictatorship."

Some historians have embraced the term "*dictablanda*"—"soft" dictatorship—to describe Mexico at midcentury.[1] They argue that the PRI-government was a hybrid regime that combined elements of authoritarianism and democracy. It ruled through tactical negotiation and the deft application of co-optation and repression. Perhaps the strength of the government was its weakness; perhaps the need to negotiate its rule required flexibility and pragmatism that, in turn, allowed it to remain hegemonic for so long. The PRI-government could not hold onto power through brute force. The Mexican army was small, at about two soldiers per thousand citizens, and its share of the budget actually declined over the period.[2] Nor could the PRI dominate the country through largesse; Mexico's tax structure was heavily regressive, meaning that those who had the most paid the least relative to their income. Tax evasion was easy. This "limited the state's capacity for authoritarianism, corporatism, or even cultural hegemony," writes Benjamin Smith.[3]

Co-optation and repression were at the heart of PRI rule. Nobody mastered these tactics better than Fidel Velázquez, who dominated and tamed organized labor in Mexico from 1941 until his death in 1997. In the 1920s, Velázquez worked at a milk factory in Mexico City, making deliveries by mule. He became the union representative of the Union of Dairy Industry Workers. He joined the CTM in 1936. When the CTM's founder fell out of favor with the revolutionary elite, Velázquez became secretary general, a position he would hold for all but three of the next 56 years.

Pragmatism allowed Velázquez to survive at the pinnacle of organized labor in Mexico for so long. He was committed to realizing the Revolution's egalitarian goals, within reason. He was careful never to threaten the established order. His ideology—a mix of anticommunism and conservative nationalism—fit perfectly in Cold War Mexico. He also delivered the goods to his co-opted clients. CTM members had seats at the table in the PRI and in the Mexican Congress. Pliant union bosses, known as *charros*, often enjoyed lavish lifestyles so long as they kept the rank and file in line. They helped Velázquez preside over most of the country's labor unions even at times when workers' wages failed to keep pace with the cost of living.[4]

Co-optation offered material advantages to those who temporarily or permanently shelved their grievances. Michael Snodgrass argues that Mexico's much-maligned *charros* "delivered considerable benefits to rank-and-file workers" from the mid-1940s to the mid-1970s. By the 1960s, some industrial workers could purchase modern appliances and cars and enjoyed "greater job security and material progress than any generation of Mexican workers experienced before or since."[5] Co-optation also worked in rural Mexico, where *campesinos* produced cheap food for the industrializing cities. In the restive state of Morelos—home to legendary Emiliano Zapata and his steadfast disciple, Rubén Jaramillo—most sugar growers chose to remain loyal to the PRI. One historian chalks it up to "a combination of co-option, divide and rule among popular groups, the narrowing of protest channels, and the strategic deployment of repression."[6] In any case, the cost of continued resistance was high. Jaramillo ran for governor twice and took up arms three times to protest electoral fraud and repression. In 1961, he finally won approval for an agrarian community that combined Zapatista and Cardenista principles. But the PRI-government grew tired of trying to co-opt the irrepressible agrarian leader. In May 1962, the federal army kidnapped and assassinated Jaramillo, his wife, and three sons. Their bloody demise, writes Tanalís Padilla, "demonstrates the extent to which state terror undergirded Mexico's 'perfect dictatorship.'"[7]

A *Pax PRIísta*?

The fate of Rubén Jamarillo notwithstanding, PRI apologists spoke glowingly of a *Pax PRIísta* (PRIísta peace) during these years. Militaries elsewhere in Latin America cycled in and out of office during the Cold War, typically toppling governments deemed to be "communist." Mexico, by contrast, seemed remarkably calm. Apart from some meddling in the 1952 presidential election, the military had gained a reputation for political neutrality. It stayed out of national politics; instead, ambitious generals focused on getting rich. They won lucrative construction contracts, grafted from the army budget, owned gambling dens and cantinas, and smuggled liquor and sometimes drugs. Given Mexico's rowdy past, the country at midcentury seemed exceptionally stable. But the fact that the Mexican military was small and maintained a low profile does not mean that it was not used. Unable to defend the national territory in the event of a U.S. invasion, the Mexican armed forces were used to police Mexicans.

For all of the talk of a Pax PRIísta, there was trouble brewing. In 1958, three massive strikes signaled the limits of PRI corporatism. Teachers and telegraph and railroad workers struck for better pay and more democratic union representation. Students defended their institutions of higher learning. And in the early 1960s, a cross-class coalition of citizens in Guerrero pushed the authorities to live up to the promises enshrined in the Constitution of 1917.

The most militant working-class organization in postrevolutionary Mexico was the railroad workers' union. Members worked for the government-owned Railroads of Mexico (*Ferrocarriles de México*, or FNM). In 1947, the federal government imprisoned the leadership of this powerful union and called an election for secretary general. The winner was an electrician named Jesús Díaz de León, the original *charro*. This nickname was a nod to his enthusiasm for *charrería* (Mexican equestrian) and his fondness for wearing cowboy attire. (The derisive term "charro" has been applied to pliant union leaders ever since.) After the union rank-and-file voted him out, El Charro—with support from President Miguel Alemán—led a violent takeover of union headquarters. For the next ten years, charro leadership in the railroad workers' union froze wages to keep freight rates low for agribusiness and strategic industries like mining and textiles. Mexico's railroad workers (*rieleros*) saw a steep decline in their real wages. Inflation, a peso devaluation, and rising prices eroded their modest purchasing power.

In 1958, Demetrio Vallejo led two strikes to sidestep the union's charro leadership. The first strike ended with a face-to-face meeting with outgoing Mexican president Adolfo Ruiz Cortines, who granted a generous wage increase. Two months later, rieleros went on strike again to democratize their union. The government-owned railroad company agreed to a new election for secretary general, which Vallejo won in a landslide.

The twin victories of summer 1958 encouraged the rank-and-file to push for another wage hike plus housing and medical subsidies for family members. Federal authorities declared the resulting February 1959 strike illegal, meaning that strikers could be arrested. At this critical moment, however, the new president, Adolfo López Mateos, intervened and agreed to the workers' demands. The union had won its third major victory in less than a year.

The 100,000-plus railroad workers' union had become the vanguard of a movement to democratize Mexico's most powerful unions. This threatened CTM boss Fidel Velázquez. Were the movement to grow unchecked, it could weaken the PRI's control of organized labor and potentially destabilize the regime. In March 1959, when railroad workers at four *private* rail companies demanded the same wage hikes and benefits granted to the workers at the national railway, rieleros at the national railroad supported them in solidarity. Perhaps the union had overplayed its hand. Fidel Castro's takeover of Cuba in January and growing expressions of radical politics in Mexico compelled the López Mateos government to act swiftly against the rieleros. Soldiers occupied union buildings, took over railroad operations, and led thousands of union members to military camps and then prisons. Vallejo himself was indicted under Article 145 of the Federal Penal

Code, the so-called social dissolution (sedition) law. The Mexican Congress initially approved this law during World War Two to fight internal subversion. But President Alemán had expanded Article 145 to include acts that weakened the general economy or paralyzed basic industrial or public services. Vallejo and fellow rielero Valentín Campa were sentenced to over eleven years in prison.[8]

The PRI-government had beaten down a formidable challenger, but others rose in its place to further test the regime's co-optive capabilities. Students in Mexico City declared strikes and took radical action to democratize their campuses in the late 1950s. The "Mexican Miracle" was experienced differently at the schools of the working-class Polytechnic Institute (IPN) and those of the middle-class National Autonomous University of Mexico (UNAM). The economic boom favored the middle class, but inequalities emerged and real wages began to decline for workers and peasants. In 1956, IPN students had called for the resignation of their director, seen as being too close to the government and the United States, and demanded more say in how their campus was governed. To call public attention to their demands, they devised strategies that became ubiquitous in the better-known student movement a dozen years later, in 1968, seizing buses and occupying classrooms, dormitories, and administrative offices. The authorities sent in a hated riot squad known as the *granaderos*, paid professional thugs to intimidate students, and arrested strike leaders under the social dissolution law. Later, the Army occupied the schools of the IPN. UNAM students (*universitarios*) remained on the sidelines.

Two years later, however, universitarios initiated a short-lived movement to protest inadequate public transportation, the fading economic miracle, and *charrismo* in the bus union. Mexican students began to see themselves as a collective that transcended class differences. Their mobilization would trigger authoritarian responses from a regime no longer able or willing to co-opt its opposition.[9]

Middle-class disappointment was also on display during the 1964–1965 doctors' strike in Mexico City. Young residents and interns who had graduated from the UNAM, the IPN, and other institutions endured low pay, underemployment, and unsanitary living quarters at public hospitals. They went on strike to protest the suspension of their Christmas bonuses. For ten months, they staged protests at hospitals and clinics and even marched in their white surgical gowns through the streets of Mexico City. Mexican president Gustavo Díaz Ordaz denounced the "homicidal actions" of the striking doctors, and the media depicted the young residents as greedy, privileged, and lazy. Hundreds were fired, blacklisted, or lost their licenses to practice medicine.[10]

In rural Mexico, PRI authoritarianism was exercised more bluntly. The PRI's economic model required the countryside to provide the industrializing cities with cheap and abundant food. This would allow industrialists to hold down urban wages. The PRI also favored agribusiness through its massive irrigation projects, tax breaks, and other policies that indirectly undermined small farmers. In short, the so-called "Mexican Miracle" witnessed a massive transfer of wealth and resources from the countryside to the city, and from the mostly rural South to the industrializing cities of central and northern Mexico. Agricultural production trebled during this time, but rural wages fell by 40 percent.[11] Keeping a lid on rural unrest became a priority for the regime. Historian Alexander Aviña writes that "What seemed mild authoritarianism in Mexico City appeared as state terror in the highlands of Sonora, Guerrero, Sinaloa, and Chihuahua, where army units brutally attacked rural communities throughout the 1960s and 1970s."[12]

Guerrero, a mountainous state south of Mexico City, and home to Mexico's first modern beach resort, Acapulco, produced two of the most important insurgent leaders and organizations in the Long Sixties. Both leaders were educators and organic intellectuals who pursued peaceful change before being forced to take up arms and head for the hills. Genaro Vázquez, son of a peasant leader, joined a multiclass civic movement called the Guerrerense Civic Association (ACG) to protest the abuses of the governor of Guerrero, General Raúl Caballero Aburto. The general was known for his corruption and nepotism, his regressive tax policies, and his constant violations of municipal autonomy. The general's gunmen also forcibly removed and even killed peasants who lived on land southeast of Acapulco to make way for private beaches and luxury homes.

Vázquez was a teacher and a gifted, pragmatic organizer. In October 1960, he organized a multi-class sit-in strike in Guerrero's state capital, Chilpancingo, to press for Aburto's removal. Small business owners, peasants, Zapatista veterans, homemakers, teachers, students, and even municipal governments joined the civic movement, which then called a city-wide general strike and tax strike. But the Mexican government was in no mood to negotiate with or co-opt this opposition. On December 30, 1960, the army attacked the civilians, leaving at least 23 dead and 40 wounded and ending more than two months of peaceful civic demonstrations. Soldiers also stormed the University of Guerrero in Chilpancingo, assaulting the striking students. Five days after the massacre, the Mexican Senate voted to depose Governor Aburto.[13]

Vázquez then helped turn the ACG into an opposition political party and campaigned ahead of the 1962 state elections with the help of Lucio Cabañas, a national student leader who headed the ACG's Youth Action Committee. Aviña notes that "state repression had not yet fully exhausted the widely held belief among the majority of progressives and leftists that the postrevolutionary state and the 1917 Constitution still represented the vehicle by which to achieve a more just and equitable society."[14] But the ACG's efforts in the 1962 elections were met with large-scale electoral fraud. Voters were harassed and intimidated, newborns and the deceased cast votes for the PRI, and ACG votes were simply changed to PRI votes. Later that year, when Vázquez organized an event in Iguala to commemorate the 1960 massacre in Chilpancingo, shots rang out and seven were killed (including a police officer) and 23 injured. Accused of murdering the officer, Vázquez fled, eluding the authorities for several years. Realizing that the PRI would not accept peaceful protest, he came to embrace more radical action.

Lucio Cabañas, for his part, hailed from a family of Zapatistas who participated actively in the Cardenista land reform of the 1930s. He was a charismatic student and later teacher at the rural teacher training school in Ayotzinapa, shaped by the Mexican Communist Party and inspired by the Cuban Revolution. After state police forces carried out two separate massacres of peasants in 1967, Cabañas traveled through the mountains of the Costa Grande region of Guerrero, moving like a "fish in water" among impoverished peasant farmers, migrant agricultural laborers, rural schoolteachers and their students, trying to convince them of the need for guerrilla warfare.

By 1967, both Vázquez and Cabañas had made the decision to take up arms. State terror had radicalized what began as a relatively innocuous, democratic civic movement. Vázquez founded the National Revolutionary Civic Association (*Asociación Cívica Nacional Revolucionaria*, ACNR), with teachers constituting the guerrilla core. Cabañas founded the Party of the Poor (*Partido de los Pobres*, PDLP), with a military wing called the Peasant Brigade of *Ajusticiamiento* that meted out peasant justice on abusive rural bosses known as *caciques*. Self-defense militias morphed into revolutionary movements that fought to establish alternative forms of state power into the late 1960s and early 1970s.

Youth Culture in the Long Sixties

Of all the trends that we can document in Mexico during the Long Sixties, nothing changed as dramatically as youth culture. At midcentury, family life was hierarchical and patriarchal. The idealized family was led by a stern father, a maternal mother, and obedient, well-groomed children. Gender roles were strictly prescribed for boys and girls, men and women, and the Catholic Church loomed large. This began to change in the late 1950s when a perceived crisis in the family coincided with the strikes that erupted across the country. The 1960s became a "cumulative crisis of patriarchal values," writes Eric Zolov. The slang word *desmadre*, or "unmothering," came to connote social chaos. Mexican youth embraced rock and roll—both foreign and Mexican—because of its "unmothering" tendencies. Rock and roll also led to more individualistic dance styles in which males no longer had to lead. "Thus even the fundamental structure of dance was disappearing, in which girls no longer had to wait for a boy's invitation and individualism prevailed over partnership."[15]

By 1966, student dissent was a global phenomenon, and it cut across class differences just as it transcended national boundaries. In Mexico, a full-fledged, rebellious countercultural movement known as *La Onda* was manifesting itself in music, literature, language, and fashion, especially on high school and college campuses. Young men started to wear their hair long, while many young women wore pants or miniskirts. A "filthy language revolution" spread across Mexican campuses, as words like *cabrón* and *chingar*, along with *desmadre*, infected students' argot. This kind of speech was anathema to traditional polite society, which of course made it all the more attractive to rebellious youth.

Many students across Latin America were inspired by the idealized image of Ernesto "Che" Guevara, the Argentine doctor who joined Fidel Castro's successful bid to overthrow the Fulgencio Batista dictatorship in Cuba. Both Guevara and Castro were university-educated, middle-class revolutionaries, and they seemed to provide a blueprint for students who wanted to launch revolutions and topple corrupt, authoritarian regimes. Guevara was killed in October 1967 in Bolivia, and his martyrdom further inspired idealistic youth. Many students were drawn to alternative philosophies and religions and began to question the centrality of marriage. This threatened to destabilize the pillars of traditional Mexican society. But "the overwhelming majority of leftist students did not want to overthrow the government or implement a socialist regime in Mexico," writes historian Jaime Pensado. Rather, their calls for revolutionary change "were overwhelmingly 'moderate' and 'cultural' in nature."[16] They wanted "*una revolución, pero sin fusil*"—a revolution, but without rifles.

Rural schoolteachers, on the other hand, were more inclined to take up arms against the regime. Mexico's rural teacher training schools, known as *escuelas normales rurales*, had been established in the 1920s and 1930s when the federal government supported agrarianism and saw teachers as agents of state consolidation. *Normalistas* in the 1960s were inspired by the Cuban Revolution and radicalized by the precarious conditions at their boarding schools. Their training taught them to be at the vanguard of agrarian struggles that the PRI-government no longer supported. In 1964, *normalistas* in Chihuahua led scores of land invasions and, one year later, led peasants in a suicidal attack on the military barracks in Ciudad Madera that bore similarities with Castro's attack on the Moncada barracks in Cuba in 1953. "The very schools the revolutionary government had once designed to create a loyal citizenry were now producing its most militant foes."[17]

But not all young Mexicans embraced La Onda. Some, in fact, actively and even violently opposed it. Conservative students on high school and university campuses were mobilized by the spirit of the times. Rightist student groups opposed foreign influences, specifically the Cuban Revolution, the changes associated with the Second Vatican Council (1962–1965), and the liberal cultural influences of the United States. They especially rejected alternative religions, feminism, psychoanalysis, and international cinema. They targeted Judaism, communism, and hippies. Several right-wing student organizations espoused violence and deployed nationalist homophobic rhetoric to tout their virility and condemn their adversaries as "women," *malinchistas* (traitors), or "degenerate homosexuals." The most important of these groups, the militant Catholic organization MURO, joined Mexican president Gustavo Díaz Ordaz (1964–1970) in condemning leftist authorities at Mexico's flagship university, the UNAM.[18]

The Student Movement of '68

Viewed in its proper context, then, the 1968 student movement in Mexico City did not happen in a vacuum. Important sectors of the Mexican population had been disaffected if not openly rebellious for years, and now the urban middle class (and its children) was involved in the upheaval. Important, irreversible cultural transformations added fuel to the fire. Mexican president Gustavo Díaz Ordaz seemed to epitomize the stern father figure of an earlier age. He lacked the "charm, rhetorical skills, and cosmopolitan spirit" of his predecessor, López Mateos. "Irony, contempt, and antipatriarchal cultural rebellion were rapidly whittling away at the symbolic infrastructure of the PRI's hegemony," writes Zolov.[19]

The 1968 student movement had relatively innocuous origins. On July 22, a street brawl broke out between rival groups of students. Neighborhood gangs and government-sponsored provocateurs joined in. The next day, as the clashes continued, the authorities sent in the hated *granaderos* to restore order. They swung their clubs indiscriminately at students, teachers, and other school employees. Days later, students participated in two rival demonstrations. *Politécnicos* mobilized to protest police brutality, while leftist *universitarios* marched to commemorate the fifteenth anniversary of Fidel Castro's attack on the Moncada army barracks. Both marches had been declared legal by city authorities, but police, army infantry, and government-sponsored student agitators attacked them anyway. After one week of disturbances, countless students and granaderos had been injured, hundreds had been sent to prison, and at least one young man had died.

As more young people mobilized to protest police brutality, the authorities sent tanks and armored vehicles to clear out all the secondary schools that had been taken over by students. On July 28–29, *universitarios* and *politécnicos* joined forces at the IPN to combat the police and the army. Paratroopers fired an explosive bazooka round to break down the baroque wooden door at the UNAM-affiliated San Ildefonso High School, where students had taken refuge. Some undoubtedly died. This invasion violated the school's autonomy and prompted the UNAM's president, Javier Barros Sierra, to lead a peaceful march of at least 80,000 students and faculty.

Why had the government overreacted? Why this disproportionate use of force? It is important to note that Mexico would host the 1968

Summer Olympics in October. It would be the first Latin American country to host the Games and the first from the developing world. The PRI planned to use the Olympics to showcase the "Mexican Miracle," and it was not about to be embarrassed by rebellious students. This raised the stakes for both the students and the government as October drew closer and international media began to turn their attention to Mexico.

In early August, *politécnicos* and *universitarios* declared themselves on strike. Faculty and administrators supported them. On August 8, students formed a National Strike Committee, representing more than 150 public and private high schools, colleges, vocational schools, and universities. Members were elected democratically by their respective schools. The Strike Committee had a rotating directorship to prevent both the co-optation and repression of its leadership. It articulated six rather modest demands:

1. Liberty for all political prisoners;
2. Abolition of the granaderos;
3. Dismissal of Mexico City's chiefs of police;
4. Elimination of Article 145 (the sedition law) from the Penal Code;
5. Indemnification for the victims of repression; and
6. Justice against those responsible for the acts of repression.[20]

None of these demands was explicitly political. The students did not call for Díaz Ordaz's resignation, the cancellation of the Olympic Games, or even clean, truly democratic elections. Instead, they echoed familiar demands made during the Long Sixties. They also called for direct, public dialogue with the president, implying that there was no path forward with the rubber-stamp Mexican Congress. So, while their demands were not *explicitly* political, *implicitly* they were because they called out a self-proclaimed revolutionary government for its authoritarianism.

The National Strike Committee organized two massive marches in August to the Zócalo, the historic center of Mexico City. The first drew roughly 200,000 participants and the second about 400,000. The atmosphere at these marches was "jovial, multitudinous, and, at times, violent," writes Pensado. "A festive attitude of '*desmadre*'—in the form of offensive *corridos* (revolutionary folk songs) insulting government authorities … spontaneous street plays mimicking the granaderos, and the commandeering of transportation buses—offered students opportunities for the direct exercise of freedom and solidarity."[21] At the August 27 march and demonstration, some students entered the National Cathedral, rang the bells, and placed an image of Che Guevara on one of the altars, while others ran up the anarchists' red and black flag in front of the adjacent National Palace. This helped feed the government's narrative that the entire movement was the work of outside agitators.

In his annual address to the nation on September 1, President Díaz Ordaz demanded the students' submission. He warned of dire consequences if the unrest continued. In defiance, students organized the Great Silent March on September 13. They marched through the heart of downtown Mexico City with their mouths taped shut. They also changed out their placards of Che Guevara and Mao Zedong with iconic posters of Villa, Zapata, Jaramillo, and Vallejo. "This decision was profoundly significant, for it reflected a direct challenge to the PRI's monopoly of the symbolism of Mexico's revolutionary heritage," writes Zolov. "The nation's revolutionary heroes were being used against the government itself."[22]

By the middle of September, the battle lines had hardened as the Olympic Games drew near. Díaz Ordaz remained aloof, seemingly incapable of meeting this new kind of challenge. Attempts to start a dialogue with Interior Minister Luis Echeverría had run into roadblocks and had probably run out of time. As public support for the students waned, Díaz Ordaz ordered the military occupation of the UNAM and the schools of the IPN. Hundreds of arrests were made at the UNAM; at the IPN, students fought pitched battles and resisted for ten hours.

Figure 1.2 Students are escorted by soldiers after being arrested during a demonstration on September 23, 1968, in Mexico City. Photographer unknown. AFP/Getty Images

Figure 1.3 Mexican soldiers just outside the Tlatelolco housing complex one day before the October 1968 massacre. The spire of Santiago Tlatelolco church is seen in the background. Mario De Biasi; Sergio Del Grande/Mondadori/Getty Images

On October 2, the National Strike Committee met at the Plaza of the Three Cultures at the Tlatelolco public housing project to plot its next move. A march had been planned that day to protest the continued occupation of the IPN, but it was cancelled at the last minute after organizers learned that the army had massed its forces along the planned protest route. Government repression was taking its toll. After the meeting started, a helicopter flew overhead and dropped flares into the crowd. Moments later, government-sponsored snipers perched on rooftops began firing indiscriminately into the crowd. Soldiers and granaderos who had been sent to arrest the main leaders of the National Strike Committee returned fire. After roughly an hour of mayhem, at least two hundred people had been killed, thousands injured, and hundreds more had been taken to prison. The army then cordoned off hospitals and morgues to prevent an accurate body count.[23] The Olympic Games opened ten days later without a hitch.

After Tlatelolco

Luis Echeverría, probable architect of the Tlatelolco massacre, was tapped by Díaz Ordaz to become the PRI's candidate in the 1970 presidential election. The PRI was losing its grip on the country, and Echeverría knew it. After his candidacy was announced, he embarked on a vigorous, exhausting campaign and sought to distance himself from the unpopular president. The outcome of the election was, of course, never in doubt, but Echeverría campaigned as if it were. His mission was not simply to win the election but to redeem the Mexican Revolution, to restore legitimacy to the one-party state. On election day, he beat his closest rival by a margin of six to one. But only 42 percent of Mexicans bothered to vote, a historically low turnout. The high rate of abstention in states like Guerrero was deeply troubling to Echeverría. He had won the election in a landslide, yes, but he had yet to restore revolutionary luster to the PRI.[24]

Despite his likely role in the bloody events of October 1968, Echeverría had *bona fide* leftist credentials. He had married into a historically progressive family from Guadalajara; his wife, María Esther Zuno Arce, was daughter of the founder of the Universidad de Guadalajara, José Guadalupe Zuno. The presidential couple apparently first met at the home of leftist artists Diego Rivera and Frida Kahlo, with whom María Esther was friendly. Echeverría promised a "democratic opening" and deployed a leftist, nationalist rhetoric to win back disaffected sectors of the Mexican population. As president-elect, he helped procure the early release of rieleros Demetrio Vallejo and Valentín Campa; as president, he released hundreds of other political prisoners, including former leaders of the 1968 student movement. Echeverría invited leftist intellectuals into his government and warmly embraced Chile's socialist president, Salvador Allende. To win back Mexican youth, he lowered the voting age to 18 and invested heavily in higher education.

But the Corpus Christi massacre on June 10, 1971 complicated his relationship with the young. On that day, students in Mexico City marched to the Monument of the Revolution demanding university autonomy, democratic unions, and the release of political prisoners. They were attacked by the *Halcones* (Hawks), a paramilitary group trained at the Police Academy since 1968 to suppress riots. Dozens of students died and hundreds were wounded and imprisoned, but this time the repressors did not wear military uniforms. Echeverría claimed to know nothing of the Halcones, but most evidence suggests that he ordered the attack.[25]

Meanwhile, peasants in Guerrero experienced more state terror. Echeverría launched a charm offensive, sending 300 doctors, dentists, barbers, social workers, veterinarians, and others into Guerrero's Costa Grande region. But he also sent many more troops. In a series of interviews, ACNR leader Genaro Vázquez warned leftists that Echeverría's "democratic opening" was a bluff. Months later, Vázquez was killed in a car accident.

Lucio Cabañas remained in the field. His PDLP-BCA attacked state police and executed local caciques from 1969–1972, then ambushed Mexican military forces from 1972–1974. Dozens of soldiers were killed and the guerrillas captured high-powered weapons and ammunition. This triggered another round of brutal counterinsurgency. The military limited the transport of food and medicine into Guerrero's Costa Grande region to "starve out" the guerrilla fighters and punish their civilian supporters. "Torture, rape, disappearance, death flights, strategic hamlets, the rationing of food and medicine, and the razing of villages turned coastal Guerrero into a counterinsurgent war zone," writes Aviña.[26] The PDLP-BCA was never a serious military threat; it failed to export its movement to other states and, in fact, failed to break out of Guerrero's Costa Grande. But it was a public relations nightmare for Echeverría and for the PRI, which still claimed the legacy of Zapata as its own.

In May 1974, the PDLP-BCA kidnapped a wealthy federal senator (and candidate for governor), Rubén Figueroa. The guerrillas demanded the removal of the military from four Costa Grande municipalities and a ransom payment of 50,000 pesos. The Mexican

Figure 1.4 A self-defense militia group in Temalacatzingo, Guerrero commemorates the 47th anniversary of Lucio Cabañas's murder in 2021. NurPhoto/Getty Images

military managed to free Figueroa and finally caught up with Cabañas in December. Whether he was killed in combat or committed suicide is a matter of speculation. Nearly 600 inhabitants of the Costa Grande region remain "disappeared," most likely tortured and executed at military camps or thrown out of airplanes stationed near the port of Acapulco. Fishing communities north of the port reported that the sea "vomited" human remains, clothes, and sandals from the end of 1973 to 1975.[27]

The Echeverría presidency failed to resurrect the PRI, and the Long Sixties in Mexico ended on an unsettled note. The Mexican Miracle was over, and the countryside was increasingly impoverished and restless. Twenty-nine guerilla organizations operated in Mexico in the 1970s; most were based in the countryside and counted rural *normalista* teachers and graduates among their leaders, militants, and support networks.[28] Despite its pro-worker rhetoric, the Echeverría administration actually approved fewer strikes than the Díaz Ordaz administration. Northern industrialists were angry, university campuses were infiltrated and under strict surveillance, and students remained highly dubious of Echeverría and the PRI.

Conclusion: Remembering the Long Sixties in Mexico

During the Long Sixties, things were not as they once seemed. The PRI-government trumpeted its rule as a time of consensus, peace, and prosperity, but the reality is much more complicated. Consensus was often produced by the selective use of co-optation and repression; peace was relative; and prosperity was increasingly limited to skilled workers and the middle classes residing in the cities of central and northern Mexico. The regime's development policy squeezed the countryside, and its management of labor relied on *charros*. Peasants in Guerrero and working-class laborers and students in the cities tested the limits of the PRI's negotiating capacity. Historians will continue to debate whether the PRI-government during this time was more *dictablanda* than *dictadura*. But Padilla cautions that this debate "sets up a false dichotomy for a regime that was both staunchly repressive *and* remarkably flexible."[29]

Until recently, it was common to read that the massacre at Tlatelolco was a watershed moment that signaled the end of the Mexican Revolution and "unmasked" the authoritarianism of the one-party state. This chapter proposes that the regime was unmasked well before 1968. The 1968 student movement was important, but it never achieved a truly popular dimension, as did the more radical student uprisings in Europe and the United States. It failed in its outreach to other sectors of society, and the six points articulated by the strike committee were not particularly novel. The movement was mostly confined to Mexico City. Elsewhere in Mexico, "1968" had already happened in 1961 (San Luis Potosí), 1964 (Puebla), and 1965 (Chihuahua).[30] In the end, the Olympic Games went forward, and Luis Echeverría received a promotion. The hegemonic PRI retained control of all three branches of the federal government for another 29 years, belying the casual, oft-repeated claim that the student movement marked the start of Mexico's transition to democracy. The massacre at Tlatelolco was a terrible, scarring event that left its mark on a generation of urban youth, but it did not change much in concrete terms. Rather than the *parteaguas* (watershed) that many have claimed, perhaps it was not much more than a *partemadres* (skull-breaker).[31]

Misperceptions about the history of the '68 student movement can be traced back to its authors, the middle-class, male protagonists of the movement. "This group of elite leftists has not only been in charge of cultural production in Mexico for the last fifty years but also has published most of the history of student activism," writes Pensado.[32] Working-class students at the IPN, high school students, progressive PRIístas and Catholics, granaderos, conservatives, and those who refused to join the movement have been quite literally written out of this history.

So, too, have female students. Women participated as cooks and *brigadistas*, addressing passengers on public buses, handing out flyers and collecting money. Deemed apolitical and nonthreatening, they easily slipped in and out of occupied universities in full view, delivering messages and safely transporting leaders. They called spontaneous meetings in the markets and on street corners, pitching the cause to other women and men. One group of women *brigadistas* from the National School of Anthropology distributed flyers in cantinas, where women were not allowed. "They would enter very quickly and distribute flyers while the waiters or the boss told them 'Get out, get out, you can't be here!' And the drunks would yell, 'Let them stay!'"[33] (The prohibition on women in cantinas was finally lifted in 1981.)

Leslie Jo Frazier and Deborah Cohen write that the male leadership's prison experience in the months and years following the massacre shaped the way that the events of summer and early fall of 1968 have been remembered—and forgotten. Their memoirs and histories celebrated traits of middle-class masculinity. Female participants mostly dropped out of view. Frazier and Cohen conducted interviews in 1989 with former female participants who felt that their participation did not warrant historical study because they were not leaders. But they claimed that their relationships with men changed that summer. One participant, named Rosa, said, "We shared the risks… The guys had to change. And they did change their attitude toward us. Before, they were conquerors. After, they talked about relationships based on friendship, companionship, and solidarity."[34] These young women began to see themselves as activists. It led many of them to defy patriarchal control at home and participate in feminist movements in the coming years, as we will explore in Chapter 5.

Notes

1 *Dictablanda: Politics, Work, and Culture in Mexico* eds. Paul Gillingham and Benjamin T. Smith (Durham: Duke University Press, 2014). The scholarly anthology *México Beyond 1968: Revolutionaries, Radicals, and Repression during the Global Sixties and the Subversive Seventies* eds. Jaime M. Pensado and Enrique Ochoa (Tucson: University of Arizona Press, 2018) may be read as a rebuttal to *Dictablanda*'s main argument.

2 Paul Gillingham, *Unrevolutionary Mexico: The Birth of a Strange Dictatorship* (New Haven: Yale University Press, 2021), 245–247; and Thomas Rath, *Myths of Demilitarization in Postrevolutionary Mexico, 1920–1960* (Chapel Hill: University of North Carolina Press, 2013), 170.

3 Benjamin T. Smith, "Building a State on the Cheap: Taxation, Social Movements, and Politics," in *Dictablanda*, 256.

4 Joseph U. Lenti, *Redeeming the Revolution: The State and Organized Labor in Post-Tlatelolco Mexico* (Lincoln: University of Nebraska Press, 2017), 35–40.

5 Michael Snodgrass, "The Golden Age of Charrismo: Workers, Braceros, and the Political Machinery of Postrevolutionary Mexico," in *Dictablanda*, 186.

6 Gladys McCormick, "The Forgotten Jaramillo: Building a Social Base of Support for Authoritarianism in Rural Mexico," in *Dictablanda*, 211.

7 Tanalís Padilla, *Rural Resistance in the Land of Zapata: The Jaramillista Movement and the Myth of the Pax Priísta, 1940–1962* (Durham: Duke University Press, 2008), 7.

8 Robert F. Alegre, *Railroad Radicals in Cold War Mexico: Gender, Class, and Memory* (Lincoln: University of Nebraska Press, 2013); and Eric Zolov, *The Last Good Neighbor: Mexico in the Global Sixties* (Durham: Duke University Press, 2020), 2-3.

9 Jaime M. Pensado, *Rebel Mexico: Student Unrest and Authoritarian Political Culture During the Long Sixties* (Stanford: Stanford University Press, 2013), 132.

10 Gabriela Soto Laveaga, "Médicos, hospitales y servicios de inteligencia: el movimiento médico mexicano de 1964–1965," *Salud Colectiva* 7:1 (January–April 2011); and Louise Walker, *Waking from the Dream: Mexico's Middle Classes after 1968* (Stanford: Stanford University Press, 2013), 13.

11 Paul Gillingham and Benjamin T. Smith, "Introduction: The Paradoxes of Revolution," in *Dictablanda*, 2; and John W. Sherman, "The Mexican Miracle and its Collapse," in *The Oxford History of Mexico*, 2nd ed., eds. William H. Beezley and Michael C. Meyer (New York: Oxford University Press, 2010 [2000]), 552–554.

12 Alexander Aviña, *Specters of Revolution: Peasant Guerrillas in the Cold War Mexican Countryside* (New York: Oxford University Press, 2014), 13.

13 Aviña, 59–66.

14 Aviña, 78.

15 Eric Zolov, *Refried Elvis: The Rise of the Mexican Counterculture* (Berkeley: University of California Press, 1999), 105.

16 Pensado, *Rebel Mexico*, 151.

17 Tanalís Padilla, "Rural Education, Political Radicalism, and *Normalista* Identity in Mexico after 1940," in *Dictablanda*, 356.

18 Jaime M. Pensado, "'To Assault with the Truth': The Revitalization of Conservative Militancy in Mexico During the Global Sixties," *The Americas* 70:3 (January 2014): 489-521.

19 Zolov, *The Last Good Neighbor*, 281–283, 288.

20 Pensado, *Rebel Mexico*, 206.

21 Pensado, *Rebel Mexico*, 207.

22 Zolov, *Refried Elvis*, 127.

23 Elena Poniatowska, *La noche de Tlatelolco: testimonios de historia oral* (México D.F.: Ediciones Era, 1971).

24 Lenti, 72, 79.

25 Pensado, *Rebel Mexico*, 236.

26 Aviña, 174.

27 Alexander Aviña, "A War against Poor People," in *México Beyond 1968*, 146.

28 Tanalís Padilla, *Unintended Lessons of Revolution: Student Teachers and Political Radicalism in Twentieth-Century Mexico* (Durham: Duke University Press, 2021), 224–228.

29 Padilla, *Unintended Lessons*, 14–15.

30 Aviña, *Specters of Revolution*, 109.

31 Pensado, *Rebel Mexico*, 232, citing Barry Carr.

32 Pensado in *Dictablanda*, 362.

33 Marta Lamas, "Del 68 a hoy: la movilización política de las mujeres," *Revista Mexicana de Ciencias Políticas y Sociales* 63:234 (septiembre-diciembre de 2018): 273.

34 Lessie Jo Frazier and Deborah Cohen, "Mexico '68: Defining the Space of the Movement, Heroic Masculinity in the Prison, and 'Women' in the Streets," *Hispanic American Historical Review* 83:4 (November 2003), 653.

2

Twilight of the "Perfect Dictatorship"

The Democratic Transition, 1977–2000

Mexico's recent political history has been truly exceptional. For most of the twentieth century—a time of highly volatile politics in most of Latin America—the Institutional Revolutionary Party (PRI) dominated Mexico and the military stayed out of the political spotlight. When the PRI finally conceded a presidential election in 2000, it had held power longer than any other political party in the world. Improbably, this same hegemonic ruling party also initiated a transition to democracy. The transition proceeded in fits and starts, with a series of electoral reforms and counter-reforms. It culminated in the 1997 midterm election, when the PRI lost its traditional absolute majority in the Mexican Congress, and in the 2000 presidential election, when it conceded to Vicente Fox of the opposition National Action Party (PAN).

How did the first country to launch a twentieth-century social revolution end up with a hegemonic one-party state? Once established, why would it ever agree to fair, transparent elections? What role did civil society and opposition parties play to propel the process forward at key moments?

Mexico's Unscripted Revolutions: Political and Social Change since 1958,
First Edition. Stephen E. Lewis.

Origins of the Perfect Dictatorship

Mexico's ruling party emerged out of the chaos of the immediate postrevolutionary period. During the 1920s, Mexico held three presidential elections, and each one triggered a military insurrection. In 1920, General Álvaro Obregón and his supporters in Sonora rose in rebellion against his former battlefield ally, outgoing president Venustiano Carranza, who was preparing to impose a puppet successor. Within weeks, Obregón controlled the country and Carranza was dead. Obregón won a landslide election that fall. Three years later, as another election loomed, another former ally, Adolfo de la Huerta, declared himself in revolt when Obregón indicated that his sidekick, Plutarco Elías Calles, would succeed him. Other disgruntled generals and tens of thousands of troops and civilians supported the revolt, which dragged on for months and cost tens of thousands of lives. In the aftermath, Obregón took the opportunity to purge and execute several key generals who had deserted him.

There was more trouble in 1927, on the eve of another presidential election. After Obregón's allies in the Senate voted to amend the Constitution of 1917 to allow nonconsecutive reelection, Obregón announced that he would run for a second term. Politically ambitious generals were furious with this cynical manipulation of Madero's antireelectionist legacy. But these generals were cut down one by one. After his opposition literally vanished from the political scene, Obregón was elected unopposed.[1]

Less than two weeks later, a young Catholic radical assassinated Obregón at an outdoor restaurant. Calles, who was still president, stepped into the breach and announced that Mexico would transition from a "country of one man" to a "nation of institutions and laws." He called for the creation of a single revolutionary party that could peacefully reconcile political differences and ambitions. After an interim president was selected, Calles loyalists announced the creation of the National Revolutionary Party (*Partido Nacional Revolucionario*, or PNR).[2] Regional parties applied for PNR affiliation and sent delegates to a party convention, as did the two main labor and peasant parties.

As if to underscore the need for a broad-based party that might incorporate and subdue restless generals, delegates at the convention learned that Obregón protégé General José Gonzalo Escobar had launched yet another costly, dangerous rebellion. After the dust settled, the fledgling PNR took charge of nominating its candidate for the 1930 presidential election and making sure that he won.

The PNR also began to tout itself as the inheritor of a reimagined, unifying historical tradition. Without a hint of irony, it promoted the notion of a "revolutionary family," with Calles as the grand patriarch. This "family" included everyone who had fought in the conflict, especially leaders such as Madero, Zapata, Villa, Carranza, and Obregón. Turning a vicious civil war into a unifying experience required some fancy historical revisionism, some selective remembering and forgetting. After all, Madero and Zapata became bitter enemies; Zapata and Villa both fought Carranza and Obregón, together and separately, for years; Carranza ordered Zapata's ambush and murder (1919); and Obregón probably ordered the murders of both Carranza (1920) and Villa (1923). With the passing of time, it became easier for the ruling party to cherry-pick aspects of each man's legacy in official discourse and in public school textbooks. In 1938, Mexico City's Monument to the Revolution, honoring all participants, was inaugurated.[3]

The emergence of the PNR coincided with a repeal of the constitutional amendment that had allowed nonconsecutive reelection of the president. In 1933, this anti-reelectionist principle was extended to the federal and state legislatures. The prohibition on reelection forced a periodic turnover of all elected positions. This opened the possibility that politically ambitious party members could win office by working patiently *within* the system instead of working to overthrow it. On the surface, this would seem to promote Mexican democracy. But antireelectionism could also *undermine* democracy because it made officeholders more loyal to their party than to their constituents.

The institutionalization of Mexico's ruling party took a further step in 1938. President Lázaro Cárdenas called a party convention to reform the internal structure of the PNR and consolidate the progressive gains of his administration. The restructured government party was now called the Party of the Mexican Revolution (*Partido de la Revolución Mexicana*, or PRM). It consisted of four sectors: organized labor (including the CTM and other industrial unions); the peasantry (including the CNC); the "popular" sector, which included the middle class and government bureaucrats, teachers, students, and women's groups; and the military. In 1946, Cárdenas's successor, Manuel Ávila Camacho, dropped the military from the party's corporatist structure and gave the party the name that it retains to this day, the Institutional Revolutionary Party, or PRI.

Paradoxically, Mexico's PRI-government combined an imperial presidency with the trappings of mass participation. The president exercised extraordinary control over the party and dominated the national legislature and the federal judiciary. He decided who ran for governor in each of Mexico's 31 states (plus Mexico City) and chose the candidates for the Senate and the Chamber of Deputies, often tapping corporatist allies in the CTM and the CNC. This ensured a docile, pliant Congress that rubber-stamped presidential initiatives. The president kept a lid on party infighting and intrigue by choosing his successor in an elaborate political ritual known as the *destape*, or unveiling. The candidates to succeed the president were invariably men who had been part of the president's cabinet. In the months before the destape, they strutted about like peacocks, calling media attention to their achievements. The man who received the presidential "finger tap"—the *dedazo*—received immediate congratulations from the disappointed men who had not. Party discipline was maintained at all costs. These men then worked with the party to make sure that the Chosen One prevailed in the formal presidential election.[4]

At election time, PRI candidates held several significant advantages over their rivals. Since the government and the party were one and the same, PRI candidates had almost unlimited campaign budgets. The pliant television, radio, and print media could be counted on to provide ample and glowing coverage of PRI candidates. The PRI also appropriated Mexican nationalism—its colors were the colors of the Mexican flag. A vote for another party might be construed as a vote *against* Mexico. On election day, the voter rolls were often skewed and shaved, ballot boxes were routinely stuffed, and the institutions to settle electoral conflicts were controlled by PRI politicians. Because presidents, governors, senators, legislators, and even mayors could not be reelected, the individual faces of leadership changed even if the party in power did not. Political scientists have used a variety of adjectives and terms to describe this system, variously calling it a "semi-authoritarian regime," a "restricted democracy," an "electoral autocracy" or, optimistically, an "emerging democracy."

So, why did Mexicans even both voting? Historian Paul Gillingham warns us not to assume that all elections in Mexico were rigged. Thousands of "unseen," local elections were often quite competitive and democratic. The fact that important federal elections were generally noncompetitive has led some analysts to presume that *all* Mexican elections were rigged. In fact, Mexico's democratic transition began at the municipal level, when the opposition PAN began to successfully contest elections in the northern states. "[S]ome elections, some of the time, in some places, were competitive, far more than has been traditionally appreciated," Gillingham concludes. "[P]residential elections...were more ritualistic, and the more important the election the less competitive it became."[5]

Reluctant First Steps

The PRI-government was an authoritarian hegemonic state, to be sure, but it took pains to avoid single-party elections such as those held in the former Soviet Union. This was a delicate balancing act; the PRI needed to present a democratic façade and honor democratic rituals without allowing the opposition to challenge its political monopoly. "When the opposition showed signs of disappearing (whether due to weakness or weariness), electoral reforms would offer improved competitive conditions and greater opportunities to gain new political spaces," notes José Antonio Crespo. But "when the opposition gave dangerous signs of expansion, changes in electoral law would strengthen the PRI's position."[6]

Mexico's democratic transition began after the 1976 presidential election. That year, two of the three officially registered opposition parties agreed to back the PRI's candidate, José López Portillo. The one remaining opposition party, the PAN, chose not to put forward a candidate. The PRI was forced to confront a shameful reality—its candidate would run unopposed. López Portillo won 100% of the valid votes cast in that election—an absurd outcome even by the standards of an official party that had swept to victory in every presidential election since its inception. The PRI also won all 64 seats in the Senate, 194 out of 196 seats in the Chamber of Deputies, and all but four of the country's 2500 municipalities. The apparent unanimity of this election belied the fact that Mexico in the 1970s was too plural,

Figure 2.1 José López Portillo (wearing sash) waves to the crowd after his presidential inauguration on December 1, 1976. At right is President Luis Echeverria. Rolls Press/Popperfoto/Getty Images

too complicated, and too restless—and its population too literate and savvy—to accept a one-party-state outcome.[7]

The PRI-government agreed to reforms in 1977 because it needed to put the opposition back on the political playing field. These reforms gave legal status to several opposition parties, including the Mexican Communist Party, and granted them the right to media coverage and public financing. It offered amnesty to political prisoners and fugitives in a bid to bring them into the mainstream political fold. The reform also added 100 seats elected by proportional partisan representation to the Chamber of Deputies and guaranteed that the opposition would win at least 25 percent of these seats. In the 1979 midterm election, three new parties participated; the PRI took 296 seats in the Chamber of Deputies and the opposition, 104 seats. In the next presidential election, in 1982, there were seven rival candidates for the presidency. Even though the PRI retained absolute majorities in Congress and easily won the presidential election, most analysts trace the beginning of Mexico's democratic transition to the 1977 reform.[8]

Mexico's worst economic crisis since the 1910 Revolution further drove the democratic transition. López Portillo's *sexenio* (six-year term) started well. The discovery of rich oil deposits in 1977 made Mexico the world's fourth-largest oil producer. Petroleum export revenue increased exponentially, from $500 million in 1976 to $13 billion in 1981. This led to massive spending and borrowing; López Portillo called it "administering abundance." Oil prices dropped sharply in April 1982, however, and within months, Mexico could no longer pay its creditors. Suddenly, Mexico held the dubious distinction of being the world's second-most indebted country. After first declaring that he would defend the Mexican peso "like a dog," López Portillo devalued the currency twice, causing it to lose three-fourths of its value. This triggered capital flight and prompted the president to nationalize the private banks.[9] Finally, López Portillo reluctantly agreed to IMF structural adjustment as a condition for rescheduling Mexico's debt repayments. This meant that the PRI-government would be under intense international pressure to reduce government spending, privatize the economy, and lower tariffs on imported foreign goods.

After López Portillo left office, Mexicans learned the full extent of corruption in his administration. The president had built a lavish five-mansion estate for himself on the outskirts of Mexico City, dubbed "Dog Hill" by his opponents. His longtime friend, Arturo Durazo, who became chief of the Mexico City police, had managed to build several luxury houses for himself on a government servant's salary of less than one thousand dollars a month. One of these homes, at the coastal resort town of Zihuatanejo, resembled the Greek Parthenon and featured a replica of Manhattan's famous Studio 54 discotheque.

López Portillo's successor, Miguel de la Madrid (1982–1988), had little choice but to embrace austerity and open the economy through privatization and trade liberalization, also known as neoliberalism. De la Madrid sold hundreds of state-owned companies, shut down inefficient state-owned factories, and lifted price controls. Ordinary Mexicans suffered the effects of hyperinflation and declining real wages, while de la Madrid's government slashed social spending by almost one-third. Unemployment rose, the peso was devalued again, and the country fell into a prolonged recession.[10] Mexico's middle classes also suffered after having benefited from the PRI's management of the economy for decades. "Miraculous" years of robust economic growth became distant memories.[11] The PRI began to lose what political scientists call "performance legitimacy," and its alliance with Mexico's middle classes frayed.

The devastating earthquakes that hit Mexico City in September 1985 also propelled Mexico's democratic transition. The quakes left between 10,000 and 20,000 dead, an estimated 50,000 injured, and 250,000 homeless. Compounding the tragedy was the shockingly incompetent and delayed official response. Mexico City's middle classes took to the streets for the first time since the ill-fated student protests of 1968. Many lived in the Tlatelolco housing project, the largest of its kind in Latin America and one of the areas hardest hit. Ordinary citizens dug through the rubble, made lists of survivors, and counted bodies. Soon, Tlatelolco residents began demanding an investigation into shoddy construction and maintenance practices at the Nuevo León building, which had collapsed, killing 472. Organizers from various political parties and urban social movements helped with rescue and clean-up efforts and mobilized Tlatelolco's residents politically. The result was a potent cross-class alliance of political activists that pushed for electoral democracy in Mexico.[12]

Figure 2.2 The earthquake that struck Mexico City in September 1985 registered 8.1 on the Richter scale. Political aftershocks followed. Nik Wheeler/ Getty Images

Meanwhile, in the north, Mexico's oldest opposition party took advantage of the country's ongoing political and economic crises to compete in municipal and gubernatorial elections. For decades, the right-of-center, pro-Catholic PAN was little more than a middle-class debating society. During the 1940s and 1950s, the party never held more than six seats in the Chamber of Deputies and never controlled more than a handful of municipalities. During the "lost decade" of the 1980s, however, negative economic growth rates and spiraling inflation prompted frustrated *norteño* businessmen to join the PAN. Known as *neo-PANistas*, they brought a dose of pragmatism to the party. In 1983, PAN candidates won control of all eight municipalities in the northern state of Chihuahua, including the state capital.

Three years later, in the biggest electoral showdown yet, the PAN challenged the PRI for the governorship of Chihuahua. On election day, PRI activists stuffed ballot boxes before the polls opened and forcibly removed election observers. Some rural precincts reported not a single vote for opposition candidates while voters elsewhere were forced to wait in line for hours to cast their ballots. After the fraud was consummated, PAN activists engaged in acts of civil disobedience to call national and international attention to their plight. They blocked international bridges and declared work stoppages, and Chihuahua City mayor Luis H. Álvarez went on a forty-day hunger strike. In a widely read article, Mexican political scientist Juan Molinar Horcasitas documented how the PRI-government dramatically inflated the number of registered voters in PRI strongholds while eliminating voters in opposition areas.[13] Many of Mexico's most prominent writers and intellectuals signed an open letter to protest the PRI's "dangerous obsession with unanimity" and suggested that the election be annulled. Chihuahua's bishops, led by Archbishop Adalberto Almeida, denounced the fraud and defended the citizens' right to engage in civil disobedience. Almeida then threatened to suspend all masses in his diocese. The Mexican government took the threat seriously, for it echoed the boycott of Catholic masses that kicked off the Cristero revolt in 1926. The archbishop called off the boycott only after Interior Minister Manuel Bartlett and the Vatican's delegate in Mexico, Girolamo Prigione, pressured him to reconsider.

Meanwhile, the PRI-state held firm. In an ironic move, it sent ten thousand soldiers to Chihuahua to enforce the "legitimacy" of its victory.[14] Convinced now that the Catholic middle class would increasingly vote for the PAN, the final version of the 1987 Federal Electoral Code carried heavy fines and prison sentences for any priest or minister who induced citizens to vote for a certain candidate or party or encouraged abstention. Twenty bishops signed a letter describing the law as a violation of human rights, but to no avail. De la Madrid, who began his term in 1982 with a promise to relax political controls, had reversed course.

Shortly after the PRI pulled off its messy fraud in Chihuahua, it found itself dealing with an important internal schism. In 1987, a nationalist, populist wing had emerged within the party called the Democratic Current (*Corriente Democrática*). It was led by Cuauhtémoc Cárdenas, former governor of Michoacán and son of former president Lázaro Cárdenas, and Porfirio Muñoz Ledo, former secretary general of the PRI. The Democratic Current opposed de la Madrid's technocratic neoliberalism and committed itself to a democratic revival. It proposed letting PRI party militants choose the party's candidate in the upcoming presidential election. In October 1987, a week after de la Madrid tapped neoliberal economist Carlos Salinas de Gortari to succeed him, Cárdenas announced that he would mount his own candidacy. He, Muñoz Ledo, and others left the PRI; others were expelled. Cárdenas headed into the 1988 presidential election backed by a loose alliance of leftist parties, political organizations, and social movements known as the National Democratic Front. His platform called for a rejection of neoliberalism, a moratorium on foreign debt payments, and a return to the populist, nationalist, redistributionist policies first championed by his father. Mexican peasants and workers who had languished through many years of economic crisis, unfulfilled promises, and charro union leadership pledged their support to the "son of the General." They sent Cárdenas thousands of handwritten letters, sometimes signed with their own blood.[15] Tlatelolco's earthquake survivors were also among his most committed supporters.

The Twilight of PRI Hegemony

If the 1976 presidential election was not competitive enough for the PRI, the 1988 election gave the hegemonic party more than it could handle. On election day, PRI activists tried to shape the outcome by resorting to time-worn tactics. Voters found ballot boxes filled before their polling stations opened; armed thugs stole boxes from some precincts; and many polling stations never opened at all. PRIístas were allowed to vote several times in different places. Despite this, early returns still showed Cárdenas beating PRI candidate Salinas by

Figure 2.3 Insurgent presidential candidate Cuauhtémoc Cárdenas on election night, July 1, 1988. Photo by Cindy Karp/Getty Images.

a wide margin in vote-rich Mexico City and Mexico State, as well as in Cárdenas's home state of Michoacán.

Interior Minister Manuel Bartlett, who oversaw the election, asked President Miguel de la Madrid for permission to suspend the release of more returns until rural PRI strongholds had reported. De la Madrid agreed. Bartlett announced that evening that technical problems with a brand-new, $17 million vote-tabulating computer had made the results unavailable. One week later, when the "system" came back online, it showed Salinas winning with a suspiciously slim absolute majority—50.36 percent of the vote, including a whopping 100 percent of the vote in 1700 precincts! Officially, Cárdenas came in second with 30.8 percent of the vote and the PAN's Manuel Clouthier, a millionaire businessman from Sinaloa, took 17.07 percent. In the Chamber of Deputies, the PRI held onto a slim majority, but not without a fight. The opposition unsuccessfully challenged electoral outcomes in 253 of Mexico's 300 relative majority districts. Officially, with 51.1 percent of the votes, the PRI won 260 seats; the opposition split the remaining 240 seats.[16]

The phrase "*se cayó el sistema*"—or "the system crashed"—attributed the "crashing" to no one in particular but most Mexicans were not fooled. In the ensuing weeks and months, as Mexican citizens stumbled upon the ashes of burned-up ballot boxes in back alleys and found counterfeited tally sheets in dumps, the full scale of this sloppy operation became too great to ignore. (Years later, de la Madrid admitted in his biography that the election had been fraudulent.) Cárdenas and his allies on the left decided not to contest the fraud via confrontation in the streets. Instead, they channeled their momentum to create a center-left political party, the Party of the Democratic Revolution (*Partido de la Revolución Democrática*, or PRD), in May 1989.

In the wake of the 1988 election, Salinas and the PRI leadership faced a major crisis of legitimacy. Never had PRI hegemony been so seriously challenged. To consolidate his power and fend off the PRD—and forge the two-thirds majority that he needed in Congress for constitutional reforms—Salinas courted the PAN and made it his legislative ally. Within months of taking office, he recognized the victory of PAN candidate Ernesto Ruffo Appel in Baja California's 1989 gubernatorial election. This marked the first time that the PRI-government had conceded an election for governor. Salinas also agreed to support a PAN proposal to create the Federal Electoral Institute (*Instituto Federal Electoral*, or IFE). The IFE, which remained under the control of the Interior Ministry, took the role of managing and certifying elections out of the hands of the PRI-controlled Chamber of Deputies.[17]

Salinas was also playing to an international audience, especially the United States Congress. In 1993, as Washington debated and eventually ratified his North American Free Trade Agreement, Salinas pushed another round of electoral reforms to open the Mexican Senate to pluralism by doubling the number of seats. This reform created Mexico's Senate as it is known today. In each of Mexico's thirty-one states (plus Mexico City), two seats are assigned to the party with the most votes, and one seat goes to the party with the second-highest vote share. The remaining 32 are allocated in proportion to each party's share of the total national vote for a grand total of 128. Another reform required political parties to report on their spending, and yet another established voter photo ID cards.

But Salinas was no democrat. He arbitrarily removed seventeen state governors during his *sexenio*; not since the 1930s had a president so dramatically imposed his will on the states. Of this number, seven were removed to appease the PAN through a bargaining process called *concertacesión*. After an opposition party had "lost" a close election to the PRI, it would bargain in electoral courts to get something in return. In the 1991 election for governor in the state of Guanajuato, for example, the election authorities declared the PRI's candidate, Ramón Aguirre, to be the winner. The PAN and its candidate, Vicente Fox, cried foul. Following high-level negotiations between the two parties, Aguirre stepped aside and an interim governor from the PAN, Carlos Medina Plascencia, was appointed.[18] (Fox was elected governor of Guanajuato in the next election cycle.) The

PAN actually lacked evidence of overwhelming fraud in this case, but Salinas was willing to sacrifice the PRI's gubernatorial candidate in exchange for the PAN's support for constitutional reforms designed to annul land reform (Article 27) and repair Church/state relations (Article 130). This kind of bargaining, which sacrificed local PRI interests for the sake of the short-term needs of the national PRI, caused a serious rift in the party.[19]

Concertacesiones were also hammered out at the local level, where PRD activists fought for municipal council positions. "PRD demonstrations tended to be isolated, enduring, and threatening to local governability," writes political scientist Todd Eisenstadt; PAN mobilizations, on the other hand, "tended to be centrally orchestrated, theatrical, and nonthreatening."[20] The PRD staged four times as many postelectoral challenges as the PAN but usually had to settle for minor concessions. The PRI was loath to enter informal negotiations with the PRD; its goal throughout the late 1980s and 1990s was to co-opt the PAN, the "loyal opposition," which shared its commitment to neoliberal economic policies, and suppress the uncompromising, anti-regime left. The PRI often stole local elections, baited the PRD into mounting postelectoral challenges, and then branded the leftists as confrontational and unwilling to play by democratic rules. During the Salinas sexenio, 250 PRD activists were killed in conflicts with the PRI.[21]

Events in 1994, a presidential election year, accelerated Mexico's democratic transition. On New Year's Day, a rebel group calling itself the Zapatista Army of National Liberation (*Ejército Zapatista de Liberación Nacional*, or EZLN) declared war on the PRI-government from Mexico's southernmost state, Chiapas. The Zapatistas' "Declaration of the Lancandón Jungle" condemned "traitors" and "sellouts" like Salinas and lambasted the PRI's authoritarian rule.[22] They declared themselves the defenders of the authentic Mexican nation. After twelve days of fighting in which an estimated 500 combatants and noncombatants perished, President Salinas bowed to pressure from civil society and declared a unilateral ceasefire. He likely feared that a bloodbath in Chiapas could jeopardize the success of NAFTA and his ability to control the presidential succession.

Thanks to cable television and the internet, the Zapatista uprising was an immediate sensation in Mexico and in much of the world. The rebels' spokesman, *Subcomandante Marcos*, reveled in the attention. Meanwhile, the presidential campaign of Salinas' handpicked successor, reformer Luis Donaldo Colosio, had trouble gaining traction. As he competed with the charismatic Marcos for airtime, Colosio critiqued the PRI's past practices and called for a true, authentic democracy. Then, on March 22, he was assassinated at the conclusion of a political rally in Tijuana. Months later, Salinas's former brother-in-law, PRI party secretary José Francisco Ruiz Massieu, was gunned down in broad daylight in Mexico City. The motives behind these murders have never been fully clarified.[23]

As he struggled to regain control over the final year of his sexenio, Salinas agreed to a progressive electoral reform that allowed for six "citizen councilors" on the General Council of the IFE. They would outnumber the five politicians remaining on the council. Additional reforms made it easier for individual citizens and organizations to observe the election process. All three major parties approved these reforms, including the PRD. Political scientist Guillermo Trejo has suggested that these reforms "were a direct response to the EZLN uprising."[24]

Ernesto Zedillo, Colosio's former campaign manager, became the PRI's unlikely candidate for the presidential election that was held in August 1994. He squared off against the PAN's Diego Fernández de Cevallos and the PRD's Cuauhtémoc Cárdenas. On election day, Zedillo won with 48.7 percent of the vote. This marked the first time that a PRI presidential candidate had won an election with less than an absolute majority. The PAN candidate came in second, followed by Cárdenas. The process was relatively clean, although Zedillo later admitted that the playing field had not been level—his campaign vastly outspent its rivals, bought votes, and benefitted from extensive and overwhelmingly positive media coverage.

President Zedillo took definite and unequivocal steps early in his administration to support Mexico's democratic transition. Weakened by the economic crisis that he inherited—the worst since 1929—Zedillo broke from the hyperpresidentialism that had characterized the Mexican presidency for decades. With backing from the PAN and the PRD, he introduced a reform package in 1996 that separated the IFE from the Interior Ministry, thereby giving it more autonomy. Zedillo's reforms also provided generous public funding for all of Mexico's political parties, creating the conditions for the opposition to compete against the PRI. He also made provision for residents of Mexico City to elect their own mayor; previously, Mexico's presidents had appointed a trusted loyalist to the position. Finally, constitutional reforms that year created the Federal Electoral Tribunal (the *Tribunal Federal Electoral*, now *Tribunal Electoral del Poder Judicial de la Federación*, or TEPJF) with powers to resolve all electoral disputes at the federal, state, and municipal levels.[25] Trejo believes that the ongoing Zapatista conflict and fear that the popular classes might radicalize were the motivating factors behind Zedillo's reforms. "The authoritarian elites became reformers only when faced with bayonets," he writes.[26]

The midterm election in 1997 was the culmination of Mexico's democratic transition. The PRI lost its absolute majority in the Chamber of Deputies for the first time. No longer was it a hegemonic party. And no longer did it control the federal budget; for the first time since its founding, the PRI had lost control of its principal means of maintaining party loyalty. Mexico City residents elected the PRD's Cuauhtémoc Cárdenas to be their mayor and gave his party the most seats in the city's legislative assembly. Several of the PRD's newly elected representatives had participated in the 1968 student movement. Change was also felt beyond Mexico City; following the election, 44 percent of Mexicans lived in municipalities that were governed by parties other than the PRI. Ever the party outsider, President Zedillo later announced that he would not appoint his successor in the 2000 presidential election. This seemed to signal the end of one of Mexico's most enduring political traditions, the *dedazo*. Instead, the

PRI held a fierce, sometimes violent party primary and selected Francisco Labastida Ochoa to be its candidate.[27]

An essential actor in Mexico's democratic transition was the media. During the years of the authoritarian, hegemonic PRI, print media was largely controlled through its heavy dependence on government advertising. Periodicals printed inserts disguised as bona fide news articles and adopted pliant editorial policies. In return, they received tax forgiveness, subsidized utilities and newsprint, and easy access to credit. The PRI and government ministries ensured their control over individual journalists by delivering money in paper envelopes known as *embutes* or *chayotes*. These payments padded the journalists' meager, almost symbolic, salaries. The result was a high degree of self-censorship. Most journalists "considered themselves part of the governing system and defended it against attacks," writes one specialist. "Reporting was passive and included stenographic-like transfer from press releases and speeches."[28] But recent research suggests that PRI control over the media was always far from complete, especially outside of Mexico City.[29]

The broadcast media, dominated by Televisa, was notoriously loyal to the PRI. At election time, it offered glowing coverage of PRI candidates, flat or sarcastic coverage of the PRI's challengers (like Cuauhtémoc Cárdenas in 1988), and disproportionate coverage of minor political parties in hopes of fracturing the opposition. As one political scientist notes, the hegemonic PRI's claim to political legitimacy "rested upon a peculiar combination of revolutionary heritage, state-corporatist intermediation, electoral victory, economic stewardship, and simple tradition." Television played a crucial role in transmitting this political pageantry to the Mexican public.[30]

The print media was the first to break free of the clutches of the PRI-government. This was possible in part because their limited circulation made them unthreatening. Periodicals like *Proceso* (1976), *Vuelta* (1976), and *La Jornada* (1984) introduced a new kind of independent investigative journalism that found a readership base in Mexico's politically active civil society. This readership allowed independent media to survive without government patronage. By the mid-1980s, independent media was stealing market share from "official" periodicals. By the midterm election of 1997, even Mexican television had become more independent. No longer a "private 'Ministry of Truth,'" it had become "a semi-competitive, commercially oriented medium."[31] In that election, the PRI received only 34 percent of the campaign-related television coverage, and in the historic election that followed, that of 2000, all three major candidates received roughly the same amount of coverage. The quality of the reporting had also improved, as coverage of rival parties and candidates was more equitable and less biased. This further leveled the electoral playing field for all parties.

The 2000 Elections: the End of the PRI?

The elections in 2000 were therefore historic even before the final vote tallies were announced. The PRI's Labastida, chosen through a bruising primary process, faced the PRD's Cuauhtémoc Cárdenas, who was making his third run at the presidency. The PAN's candidate was Vicente Fox Quesada, the former governor of Guanajuato and former CEO of Coca-Cola in Mexico. He understood marketing and campaigned like a folksy populist. Rather than run on the issues, he emphasized his leadership credentials and positioned himself as a change agent. He paraded his Catholic religiosity at every turn, shrewdly generating controversy that set him apart from his PRI opponent. Polls leading up to the election showed Labastida with a small but shrinking lead.

On election day, July 2, 2000, many Mexicans chose to make their vote "useful"; they opted for the candidate most likely to end the PRI's 71-year monopoly on the presidency. The *voto útil* gave Fox a decisive margin of victory. The PANista won 42.5 percent of the vote and Labastida took 36 percent, leaving Cárdenas a distant third at less than 17 percent. The PRI also lost its majority in the Senate. Indeed, the drama of that day took place not at the polling places but at PRI headquarters, where Labastida and PRI loyalists struggled to accept their loss and delayed conceding to Fox. Many analysts believe that hardline PRIístas were waiting for a signal to execute a fraud. At 11 pm that evening, the IFE's citizen president, José Woldenberg, announced the election results. "We are a country in which a change of government can be accomplished peacefully, by means of a regulated competition, without recourse to force by the loser," he proclaimed. "That is democracy." Zedillo then recognized Fox's victory. The president stood in front of the camera, stone-faced, flanked by a Mexican flag to his right and an oil painting of Benito Juárez behind him to his left.[32] He congratulated the Mexican people for an orderly, transparent, and peaceful electoral process, praised the IFE, and congratulated Fox on his victory. In the span of just twelve years, Mexicans had converted one of the most fraudulent electoral systems in the world into one of the cleanest.

Conclusions

Mexico's transition to democracy was one of the most compelling storylines in late-twentieth-century Latin America. The transition was gradual and incremental, with no shocking reversals. It did not come on the heels of a coup or the collapse of the prior regime. Elsewhere in Latin America, democratic transitions took place after military juntas gave up power when faced with economic crises and social unrest (Argentina, Brazil, and Chile, among others), or when UN-brokered peace agreements marked the end of a civil war, as in El Salvador. In Mexico, however, the transition was overseen by the incumbent, hegemonic party over the course of two decades.[33] It focused on national elections and strengthened political parties while leaving intact authoritarian legal and police institutions. Under presidents Salinas and Zedillo, the PRI "made concessions as an authoritarian ruling party in order to increase the likelihood of remaining a ruling party."[34] The incumbents divided and conquered the opposition, winning over the ideologically compatible PAN through patronage while suppressing the leftist PRD. The transition was propelled forward by economic and political crises at critical moments (1985, 1988, and 1994) and by social movements, armed insurgents, and a newly independent media. The reaction of PRI hardliners to their party's loss in the 2000 presidential election suggests that for some, the transition came too fast or should never have happened at all.

Mexico was lauded internationally for its smooth and peaceful democratic transition. Indeed, there was much to celebrate. The IFE made remarkable progress at fighting fraud, leveling the playing field, and improving the recording and counting of votes. An independent print and broadcast media that did not even exist in the middle 1970s had begun to offer equal time and fair coverage to candidates from all parties. Mexican citizens participated in the process as voters, of course, but they also ran polling places and counted votes on election night.

Yet important aspects of Mexico's authoritarian political culture remained intact, like its corporatist unions and its corrupted judicial system and security apparatus. Mexico never fully reckoned with the human rights abuses that took place during authoritarianism and never assigned responsibility for atrocities. In a country where nearly half the population lives in either poverty or extreme poverty, all political contenders practiced vote-buying and other forms of electoral alchemy. Chapter 6 will explore whether President Vicente Fox and his successors were able to eradicate the vestiges of Mexico's authoritarian past and put Mexico squarely on the path to democratic consolidation.

Notes

1 Jürgen Buchenau, *The Last Caudillo: Álvaro Obregón and the Mexican Revolution* (Malden, MA: Wiley-Blackwell, 2011), 154–158.

2 Buchenau, *Plutarco Elías Calles*, 146–148.

3 Buchenau, *Plutarco Elías Calles*, 155–156; see also see Thomas Benjamin, *La Revolución: Mexico's Great Revolution as Memory, Myth, and History* (Austin: University of Texas Press, 2000).

4 Jorge Castañeda, *Perpetuating Power: How Mexican Presidents Were Chosen* trans. Padraic Arthur Smithies (New York: The New Press, 2000 [1999]).

5 Paul Gillingham, "Mexican Elections, 1910–1994: Voters, Violence, and Veto Power," in *The Oxford Handbook of Mexican Politics* ed. Roderic Ai Camp (New York: Oxford University Press, 2012), 68.

6 José Antonio Crespo, "Party Competition in Mexico: Evolution and Prospects," in *Dilemmas of Political Change in Mexico* ed. Kevin Middlebrook (London: Institute of Latin American Studies, 2004), 59, 61.

7 José Woldenberg, *Historia mínima de la transición democrática en México* (México, D.F.: El Colegio de México, 2012), 19–25.

8 Crespo, "Party Competition in Mexico," 68–69; Todd Eisenstadt, *Courting Democracy: Party Strategies and Electoral Institutions* (New York: Cambridge University Press, 2004), 38–41; and Woldenberg, *Historia mínima*, 27–37.

9 Emily Edmonds-Poli and David A. Shirk, *Contemporary Mexican Politics* 4th ed. (Boulder: Rowman and Littlefield, 2020 [2009]), 211–212.

10 Alexander Dawson, *First World Dreams: Mexico since 1989* (New York: Zed Books, 2006), 9–11.

11 Walker, 145, 172.

12 Walker, 177–187.

13 Juan Molinar Horcasitas, "Regreso a Chihuahua," *Nexos* 1 marzo 1987.

14 Woldenberg, *Historia mínima*, 44–47.

15 Adolfo Gilly, with Rhina Roux, Gerardo Ávalos Tenorio, Felipe Arturo Ávila Espinosa, and Dagoberto Vargas Méndez, *Cartas a Cuauhtémoc Cárdenas* (México, D.F.: Ediciones Era, 1989).

16 Kathleen Bruhn, "The PRD and the Mexican Left," in *The Oxford Handbook of Mexican Politics* ed. Roderic Ai Camp (New York: Oxford University Press, 2012), 191–192; Julia Preston and Samuel Dillon, *Opening Mexico: The Making of a Democracy* (New York: Farrar, Straus and Giroux, 2004), 149–180; and Silvia Gómez Tagle, "Public Institutions and Electoral Transparency in Mexico," in Middlebrook, ed., 89.

17 Eisenstadt, *Courting Democracy*, 46–49, 133; and Woldenberg, *Historia mínima*, 68–75, 80–85.

18 Woldenberg, *Historia mínima*, 78–79.

19 Eisenstadt, *Courting Democracy*, 106–109.

20 Eisenstadt, *Courting Democracy*, 122–123.

21 Edmonds-Poli and Shirk, 4th edition, 138; and Dawson, 40.

22 *Rebellion in Chiapas: An Historical Reader* ed. John Womack, Jr. (New York: The New Press, 1999), 245–249.

23 The five-part Netflix documentary *1994: Power, Rebellion and Crime in Mexico* (2019) chronicles this chaotic year with documentary footage and interviews with prominent protagonists, like former president Carlos Salinas.

24 Guillermo Trejo, "Las calles, las montañas y las urnas (notas sobre la participación social y la transición a la democracia)," in *Los retos de la democracia: Estado de derecho, corrupción, sociedad civil* ed. Alberto Ortega Venzor et al. (México: Editorial Porrúa, 2004), 524–525; see also Woldenberg, *Historia mínima*, 93–101.

25 Crespo, 74; and Jorge Domínguez, "Mexico's Campaigns and the Benchmark Elections of 2000 and 2006," in *The Oxford Handbook of Mexican Politics*, ed. Roderic Ai Camp (New York: Oxford University Press, 2012), 526–527.

26 Trejo, 525.

27 Preston and Dillon, 17–18, 276–277; and Walker, 196. Many argue that Zedillo, in fact, favored the candidacy of Francisco Labastida, his Interior Minister. Certainly, there was no love lost between Zedillo and Labastida's principal rival, governor of Tabasco Roberto Madrazo, who had defied and humiliated Zedillo years earlier; see Castañeda, xx–xxii.

28 Sallie Hughes, "Democracy in the Newsroom: The Evolution of Journalism and the News Media," in *The Oxford Handbook of Mexican Politics*, 381.

29 Benjamin T. Smith, *The Mexican Press and Civil Society: Stories from the Newsroom, Stories from the Street* (Chapel Hill: The University of North Carolina Press, 2018), 43–80, 185–187.

30 Chappell H. Lawson, "Building the Fourth Estate: Media Opening and Democratization in Mexico," in *Dilemmas of Political Change in Mexico*, ed. Kevin J. Middlebrook (London: Institute of Latin American Studies, 2004), 378–379, 388

31 Lawson, 391.

32 Preston and Dillon, 18–27; and Domínguez, "Mexico's Campaigns," 523–526.

33 Shannan Mattiace, "Social and Indigenous Movements in Mexico's Transition to Democracy," in *The Oxford Handbook of Mexican Politics* ed. Roderic Ai Camp (New York: Oxford University Press, 2012), 399.

34 Jorge Domínguez, "Mexico's 2012 Presidential Election: Conclusions," in *Mexico's Evolving Democracy: A Comparative Study of the 2012 Elections* eds. Jorge I. Domínguez, Kenneth F. Greene, and Alejandro Moreno (Baltimore: Johns Hopkins University Press, 2015), 255.

3

Mexico's Partial Embrace of Its Dark-Skinned Majority

People watching Mexican television for the first time can hardly be blamed for thinking that the country must be located somewhere in Western Europe. Tall, light-skinned actors and actresses, news presenters, soap opera stars, and other performers dominate the sets. During commercial breaks, more light-skinned actors hawk every product imaginable to Mexico's majority dark-skinned viewing public. It is not surprising that the people that we see on television or in glossy magazines look different from the people that we see in our daily lives. But Mexico represents an extreme case. Light-skinned Mexicans also dominate the business world, academia, and beauty contests, just as surely as dark-skinned people perform manual and domestic labor and tend to fill the jails. Help-wanted ads often ask for *buena presentación*, good presentation, rather than talent or experience. At exclusive nightclubs, known as *antros*, bouncers openly discriminate according to skin tone, facial features, and clothing. They typically allow the tall and light-skinned to enter immediately; their friends with darker complexions must wait outside. Mexico is a pigmentocracy. The color of privilege is white, poverty has a darker complexion, and indigence—or extreme poverty—is Indigenous.

Mexico's Unscripted Revolutions: Political and Social Change since 1958,
First Edition. Stephen E. Lewis.

This, ironically, in a country that is world-famous for its inclusive celebration of biological and cultural mixing, known as *mestizaje*.

The Origins of Mexican Racism

Geneticists have been telling us for decades that races do not exist *per se*.[1] The idea of race is a social construction, a fiction that presumes a connection between a person's physical appearance—like the color of one's eyes, hair, and skin, and the shape of their noses and mouths—and their behavior, their character, and their intellect. Once differences became racialized, however, as they were in the latter eighteenth century, it was not necessary for race to be real for *racism* to be real. And the reality of racism leads some to believe in the reality of race.[2]

Contemporary Mexican racism is rooted in the country's colonial past. The Spaniards introduced hierarchies and social organizations based on notions of ethnicity and class. A person's *calidad* or socioracial "qualities" like ancestry, skin color and physical features, occupation, wealth, and degree of Hispanicization determined their *casta* identity. These qualities determined who would serve and who would be served. Yet this system could also be somewhat flexible since some "qualities" were elastic and could be altered or changed.[3]

Spanish explorers and conquerors invented the term "Indian" and applied it to the hundreds of often mutually antagonistic ethnic groups that they encountered in the Americas. In effect, they lumped the Indigenous together into one undifferentiated mass of tribute-payers. Indigenous people were required to become Christians, pay tribute, and provide goods and services to the Spaniards. Their "qualities" prohibited them from holding public office, carrying weapons, or becoming priests.

The first mestizos were the offspring of Spanish explorers and Indigenous women; in fact, the term *mestizo* was initially synonymous with "bastard."[4] In time, "mestizo" also became a social category used to describe those who bore the marks of assimilation and had shed their indigeneity—they had become Catholics, spoke Spanish, changed their dress, and usually lived in market centers. Although legal restrictions against mestizos, the Indigenous, and other *castas* were abolished after Mexico won its independence from Spain, the colonial legacy of hierarchy and caste left its mark. Many of independent Mexico's leading thinkers—influenced by European racist thinking—believed that mestizaje produced degenerate populations. They also disparaged living, breathing Indians, even as they ironically celebrated the mythic Indians of the pre-Colombian past and turned them into pillars of Mexican nationalism.[5]

The rehabilitation of the mestizo began in the latter nineteenth century. Prominent writers began to self-identify as mestizo and hailed the mestizo as the dynamic factor in Mexican history. Andrés Molina Enríquez's widely influential *Los grandes problemas nacionales* (1909) equated mestizaje with *Mexicanidad* (the essence of being Mexican) and argued that Mexico's future development and prosperity hinged on whether it could become integrated and ethnically homogeneous. His book inaugurated what has been called the "golden age of mestizophilia."[6]

The Cult of Mestizaje

The popular upheaval of the Mexican Revolution (1910–1920) and its immediate aftermath presented an opportunity for intellectuals, politicians, artists, educators, and social reformers to forge a new nation based on new cultural ideals. This resulted in what some scholars have called the "ethnicization" or "browning" of Mexican national identity.[7] Mestizaje was a racial counter-discourse, writes Mexican sociologist Mónica Moreno Figueroa, a direct rebuttal "to ideas of purity and 'white' hegemonic discourses emanating from European and U.S. scientific racism, social Darwinism, and eugenics."[8] Philosopher José Vasconcelos popularized the idea of a national race.

His most influential work, *La raza cósmica* (1925), promoted mestizaje as beneficial for Mexico and Spanish America.[9] This "cosmic race," writes Karin Rosemblatt, "would combine the material successes of 'white' civilization with the artistic and spiritual merits of Latin America."[10] Mestizophilia became central to the cultural and eugenic policies of the Mexican state.[11] At a time when much of the world still celebrated "pure" races, when even Argentina and Brazil still condemned miscegenation, the official embrace of mestizaje looked like progressive policy.

Figure 3.1 Philosopher José Vasconcelos directed the Ministry of Public Education from 1921 to 1924. He published his most famous work, *The Cosmic Race*, in 1925 but soon dismissed it as a "miserable little essay," lost faith in Latin America's mestizo future, and directed an ephemeral pro-Nazi magazine, *Timón*, in 1940.

To the extent that Mexican mestizophilia inverted racist thinking that had denigrated both mestizos and Indigenous peoples, it was democratic and liberating. It held out the prospect of inclusion to all those willing to assimilate. But it was still racist. It departed from the premise that certain people, particularly the Indigenous, were inferior and in need of improvement. And mestizaje was never seen as a mix of equal parts. Many prominent Mexicans—including doctors, politicians, and members of Mexico's Eugenics Society—believed that the genetic superiority of the Spaniards would, over time, prevail over Indigenous elements and thereby "improve the race."[12]

The cult of mestizaje was also exclusionary. Not everyone was invited to join the cosmic race. Both Vasconcelos and Manuel Gamio in his seminal text *Forjando patria* (1916) "disavowed Asians and Africans from participating in mestizo racial progress" and "voiced yellow-peril racism in their writings."[13] Mexican government officials crafted immigration policies that aligned with the ideology of mestizaje. In 1927, the Ministry of Foreign Relations excluded Chinese and Black immigration, citing "scientific" evidence that mixing with such populations would produce degenerate offspring.[14] Only Europeans (and fellow Latin Americans) would be invited to participate in Mexican mestizaje. But even here, Mexican policymakers had clear preferences; in 1929, the Department of Health recommended excluding certain Eastern European populations. In 1934, the Interior Ministry reaffirmed the previous bans and extended the prohibition to include Palestinians, Arabs, Turks, Bulgarians, Persians, Yugoslavs, Greeks, Albanians, Algerians, Egyptians, and Moroccans. It justified a ban on Jewish immigration because "more than any other race, it is undesirable due to its psychological and moral characteristics."[15]

The celebration and promotion of mestizaje was built on racist, exclusionary foundations, but it was touted as a generous and tolerant policy. Mexico's political and cultural leaders offered mestizaje as a way around the kind of racism that plagued its northern neighbor, with its legacy of Black enslavement and Jim Crow laws that institutionalized racist discrimination and segregation well into the 1960s. Mexico did not produce explicitly discriminatory policies and laws. Its hegemonic political ideology explained the difference between mestizos and the Indigenous in cultural, not racial, terms, and tried to assimilate and integrate differences.[16]

But equating mestizaje with Mexican national identity had the effect of silencing and rendering invisible Mexico's diverse Indigenous peoples and its Afro-descendent populations. Mestizaje fed the commonly held belief that there can be no racism in Mexico because all Mexicans are of mixed heritage. In an ironic twist, "Mexico has produced a raceless social context where people are not recognized as racialized subjects but live through the consequences and everyday presence of racism," writes Moreno Figueroa. Mestizaje claims to offer the possibility of inclusion, but "it also allows an everyday experience of racism that continues to privilege processes of whitening… and uses the national discourse, such as a 'Mexican' identity, to cover up and render invisible processes of discrimination and social exclusion."[17]

From Indigenismo to (Neo) Zapatismo

To produce mestizaje and integration in the largely Indigenous countryside, Mexico developed a complementary set of policies and practices known as indigenismo. Practitioners of indigenismo, known as *indigenistas*, were typically not Indigenous. They tended to celebrate an abstract notion of Indigenous people and culture located securely in the past, but also called for the modernization and assimilation of living, breathing Indigenous into the majority mestizo nation.

In the 1950s and 1960s, Mexico was considered the hemispheric leader in indigenismo, even if the outcomes of this policy were often underwhelming, contradictory, and controversial. Mexico's National Indigenist Institute (INI) opened its first coordinating center in highland Chiapas in 1951. In this region, home to the Tseltal and Tsotsil Maya, indigenistas hoped to simply "coordinate" the various federal and state ministries charged with health and sanitation, agriculture, land reform, communication and transportation, and education. But despite more than 30 years of so-called revolutionary governments, these services simply did not exist in Indigenous Chiapas. The INI would need to build these services from scratch, with woefully inadequate budgets. Meanwhile, non-Indigenous residents of the highlands' commercial entrepôt, San Cristóbal de Las Casas, remained profoundly racist. Known as ladinos, they bullied the Indigenous and forced them to cede the sidewalks to them. If they caught the Indigenous in town after dark, they rounded them up, put them in jail, and told them to clean the city streets the following morning. Tseltal and Tsotsil vendors and consumers were routinely swindled in San Cristóbal's market. Mestizaje and national integration seemed a far-off goal.

The linchpin of the INI's development program were the cultural promoters, Indigenous men (and later women) who literally promoted INI programs in their home communities. They built literacy centers and taught basic reading and writing in the mother tongue as a "bridge" to Spanish literacy. They also introduced new seeds and agricultural techniques, supported the INI's health, hygiene, and road-building campaigns, and helped introduce piped water and consumer cooperatives.

But the INI encountered fierce resistance from ladino ranchers, merchants, labor contractors, and alcohol vendors in Chiapas. Local politicians resented the intromission of a federal institute that sought to administer to and improve the lives of *their* Indians. After a series of ugly confrontations, the INI agreed to compromises that, among other things, privatized some of its operations and brought an end to its more utopian plans to restructure and industrialize the regional economy. The INI's wings were clipped at its pilot coordinating center, with profound implications for the indigenista project in the rest of Mexico.[18]

Figure 3.2 Girls at an INI school in highland Chiapas. Photographer unknown. Fototeca Nacho López, Comisión Nacional para el Desarrollo de los Pueblos Indígenas. 1968.

After the INI was forced to abandon its plans to remake the Chiapas highlands, it turned its gaze inward to the only place where it would be allowed to work—to the Indigenous themselves.[19] The indigenistas doubled down on their programs of cultural assimilation. Elsewhere in Mexico, indigenistas also struggled against local vested interests. Unable to carry out major land reform and tackle some of structural issues that made the Indigenous vulnerable to their exploiters, they too were forced to work on projects of cultural assimilation.

In 1970, five talented young Mexican anthropologists declared open season on indigenista anthropology. They published a book that carried a derisive title—*De eso que llaman antropología mexicana* (What They Call Mexican Anthropology). Contributor Guillermo Bonfil Batalla envicerated the indigenista project. "Stated brutally, it consists of disappearing Indians," he wrote. "Yes, there is talk of preserving Indigenous values, without ever explaining clearly how this is to be achieved." The indigenista's job, Bonfil concluded, was to introduce change in the communities "so that the goals of the dominant society are achieved with the least amount of conflict and tension. Stated less elegantly, the anthropologist is a specialist at manipulating Indians."[20] Fellow contributor Margarita Nolasco noted that Mexican indigenismo gave Indigenous peoples only one unattractive option. "To survive, they need to change, but the class structure of global capitalism has them immobilized," she wrote. Once they shed their indigeneity, their only hope would be to "leave their region of refuge and become proletarianized, that is, they can trade colonial exploitation for class exploitation."[21] Bonfil also believed that the INI's goal of integration on an equal plane with other Mexicans was an empty promise, since Mexican society was plagued with grave inequalities, and Indigenous groups would almost certainly enter the mainstream at the bottom.[22]

In January 1971, Bonfil joined 10 other high-profile Latin American social scientists at a symposium in Barbados to indict what they considered the colonial and classist nature of indigenista policies. They accused national states of "many crimes of genocide and ethnocide." The Barbados Declaration I called for the creation of truly multiethnic states "where each ethnicity has the right to manage its own affairs" and where all Indigenous populations have "the right to be and remain themselves."[23] For many, this emphatic statement marked the end of classic indigenismo. Years later, Bonfil would issue an eloquent call for Mexico to refound itself on its Mesoamerican roots in a book called *México profundo* (Deep Mexico).[24]

During the administration of President José López Portillo (1976–1982), the INI officially disavowed its long-standing commitment to cultural assimilation. Its director, Ignacio Ovalle Fernández, stated that native communities had an "indisputable right" to preserve their ethnic identity. He pledged to end policies "that aimed at homogenization and cultural mestizaje."[25] This decision was confirmed in 1990, when a reform to Article 4 of the Mexican Constitution read that "[t]he Mexican Nation has a multicultural composition, originally based on its Indigenous peoples" and promised to "protect and promote the development of their languages, cultures, traditions, customs, resources, and specific forms of social organization."[26]

While official Mexican indigenismo faded into irrelevance, Indigenous Mexicans began to organize themselves both inside and outside of the institutions of the PRI-government.[27] In the jungles of eastern Chiapas, four Indigenous ethnic groups joined dozens of independent peasant organizations, often with help from Indigenous catechists from the Catholic diocese of San Cristóbal de Las Casas. Radical Indigenous mobilization achieved its most dramatic expression on New Year's Day, 1994, when the Zapatistas burst onto the scene. Ironically, the state where the INI had opened its first and most celebrated coordinating center—Chiapas—was also the site of an uprising that would drive the final stake into the heart of Mexican indigenismo.

The Zapatista army was founded by a handful of mestizos who had entered the jungles of eastern Chiapas in 1983. They intended to launch a conventional leftist insurgency, similar to those being waged in Central America at the time. The Zapatista rank and file, however, was Indigenous. Ch'ols, Tseltals, Tsotsils, and Tojolabals set aside their historic differences and provided the EZLN with militants and crucial bases of support. As late as 1992, members of the EZLN pledged to "defend the revolutionary principles of Marxism-Leninism." On the eve of the insurrection, however, the Zapatista leadership began to shed its old-fashioned-sounding Marxist ideology. The Berlin Wall had come down in 1989, after all, Nicaragua's Sandinistas had been defeated at the polls in 1990, and the guerrilla insurgency in El Salvador had ended with a UN-brokered peace agreement in 1992. Taking stock of the changing times, the Zapatistas wrapped themselves in the rhetoric of Mexican nationalism.[28]

For a brief moment in January 1994, Zapatista rebels held several towns in Chiapas before retreating to the jungle. Militarily, the Zapatista uprising was a resounding failure. Some militants had actually gone into battle carrying toy rifles. But their movement resonated tremendously with national and international public opinion. What caught the media's attention, and especially the center-left Mexican daily *La Jornada*, was the movement's Indigenous character. After President Salinas declared a ceasefire, Zapatista leadership studied its national and international audience and honed its message. Led by *Subcomandante Marcos*, a mestizo from the northern state of

Tamaulipas, the Zapatistas pivoted further, recasting themselves as an ethnic insurgency fighting on behalf of Indigenous cultural rights and autonomy. As Pedro Pitarch has written, "in a little more than a year, from late 1993 to the middle of 1995, the EZLN went from being a Marxist-Leninist movement to a popular-nationalist movement to an Indianist movement."[29] The EZLN's transformation was wildly popular with an important sector of the national and international community. When new president Ernesto Zedillo temporarily broke the ceasefire in February 1995, revealed the identity of *Subcomandante Marcos* on television, and tried to have him arrested, Mexicans poured into the streets, chanting "*Todos somos Marcos*"—we are all Marcos.

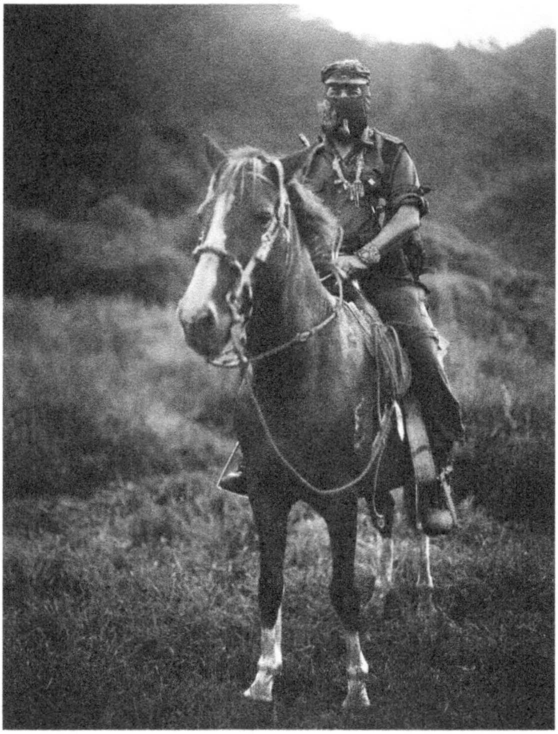

Figure 3.3 *Subcomandante Marcos* was a former university professor who hailed from the northern state of Tamaulipas. He was never photographed unmasked. Jose Villa/Wikimedia Commons/CC-BY SA 3.0

Later in 1995, the EZLN—now fully identified with the push for Indigenous autonomy—entered negotiations with a team representing the federal government. The first negotiating session began in October 1995 on the matter of Indigenous rights and culture, and it represented the final assault on the postrevolutionary Mexican state's campaign to forge a homogenous mestizo nation. "The Indigenous rebels wanted to be recognized as Mexicans, not mestizos," writes José Antonio Aguilar. "They did not demand equal treatment...but rather a different status within the national community." These demands were received favorably by a large part of Mexican society because, by 1994, the consensus surrounding Mexico's postrevolutionary ideology had been fractured.[30] A minimal accord on Indigenous rights and culture was reached by February 1996 but was not sent to the Mexican Congress until 2000. The second negotiating session, devoted to democracy and justice, began in July 1996, but no agreements were reached and talks were suspended.

The Zapatistas began to fade in the public imaginary after the 2000 presidential election, won by the PAN's Vicente Fox. Perhaps they seemed anachronistic in a country that appeared to be democratizing. Yet they tightened their grip on dozens of municipalities in Chiapas and announced the creation of autonomous pluriethnic regions. Although they no longer commanded the headlines of the country's major newspapers and had few concrete gains to show for their efforts, they continued to push Mexico to embrace the plural nature of its population.

Racism and Classism in Contemporary Mexico

Mexico today has a racialized class system. Not all dark-skinned Mexicans are poor, but almost all poor Mexicans are dark-skinned. Light-skinned people are almost never found performing manual or domestic labor. Whites in Mexico receive about twice as much schooling, on average, as dark-skinned people. They have 68.2 percent higher odds of attaining a college education (or more) than non-whites.[31]

Indigenous people are four times more likely to live in poverty. Almost 8 in 10 people who speak an Indigenous language are poor, and a third of Indigenous people live in extreme poverty. Their life expectancy is shorter, too. Afro-descendent communities on the coasts of Oaxaca, Guerrero, and Veracruz have illiteracy rates that are three times higher than the national average.[32]

Mexico's racist/classist hierarchy has been so normalized that many Mexicans accept and perpetuate it. Those who are allowed to enter Mexico City's most exclusive *antros* seem to approve of the bouncers' selection practices and enjoy being among the chosen few; those who are not often return the next weekend to try again. Some bouncers tell of women begging them for hours to let them enter so that they can take selfies inside. Others who cannot make the cut have used fake license plate holders from the Chamber of Deputies or the Senate to try to pass themselves off as advisers of politicians. Still others have used their passports as their form of identification if they are full of stamps proving foreign travel.[33]

Education is often seen as a way for individuals to transcend racism and classism, but some of Mexico's most exclusive private schools perpetuate and reproduce the country's divisive legacies. Some schools require parents to pay the entire year's tuition before the start of the academic year. Arguably, this makes it more difficult for upstarts to get in. Too many dark-skinned students might affect the prestige of the school or make it seem less exclusive. Hernán Gómez proposes, only partly in jest, that the directors of some of Mexico's most prestigious private schools have much in common with the bouncers at Mexico City's *antros*.[34]

Mexico's society pages and lifestyle magazines reproduce and perpetuate the country's deeply ingrained racial and class hierarchies. In spring 2013, Mario Arriagada sampled some of Mexico's society magazines and the weekend supplements of important daily newspapers like *Reforma*, *El Universal*, and *Excélsior* to determine, literally, who appeared in these publications and who did not. He published his stunning findings in an article titled "Quién no es quién" ("Who isn't anyone"). A March issue of *Quién* contained 348 photos of white people and just four darker people. An issue of *Caras* showed 340 whites and just four darker people, two of whom were PRI politicians. A February issue of *Reforma*'s supplement *Club* pictured 300 whites and two *morenos*, one of whom a well-known soccer star; and an issue of *Excélsor's R.S.V.P.* pictured 666 whites and 10 darker people, 7 of whom were not even identified by the magazine. They were bodyguards, caddies, and others serving in support roles. Arriagada dubbed them "*morenos-sin-nombre*," or "nameless brown people."[35]

The photographers and editors who work for these publications told Arriagada that they know their market and provide their readers with "little fairy tales meant to entertain. Entertain with glamour." They cover sailing regattas at Valle del Bravo, a rich enclave west of Mexico City; they photograph bachelorette parties at Vail, Colorado, or Lomas de Chapultepec in Mexico City. They regale their readers with photos of lavish weddings, birthday parties at the polo grounds, and graduations at private schools. In short, they photograph light-skinned people enjoying a comfortable life, where everyone seems happy and looks good. Readers are encouraged to indulge their escapist fantasies about lives that bear little resemblance to their own. While these glossy magazines might not be overtly racist, they are profoundly classist and exclusionary. "We are accustomed to think of ourselves as a nation of mestizos, but we present ourselves like a nation of whites, when we are neither one nor the other," concludes Arriagada. "We claim that our problem is classism, not racism, when the ideas that make up our definitions of class are full of race considerations." He concludes by asking, "Is it really true that another form is elegance is not possible?"[36]

Whiteness is "aspirational" in Mexico, despite the official celebration of mestizaje. Only white actors can peddle what has been called "aspirational whiteness." Mexico's advertising industry is based on the premise that purchasing certain products transmits whiteness to the consumer. "This magic, so rudimentary and banal, is the central premise of all of our advertising," writes Federico Navarrete. "If you drink a certain brandy, drive a certain car, buy a certain kind of insurance, open an account at a certain bank, use certain toilet paper or feminine hygiene products, you will have access to all those 'aspirational' qualities associated exclusively with 'whiteness.'" Buying certain products allows consumers to distance themselves "from all that might shame them or remind them of their more humble origins."[37]

Mexico's racialized class system is internalized at an early age. In 2011, Mexico's National Council to Prevent Discrimination, CONAPRED, directed a study that examined the extent to which children pick up on the country's pigmentocracy. Mexican youngsters were presented with two dolls, one white with blue eyes and the other dark brown with black eyes. They were asked which doll was pretty, which was ugly, which was good, and which was bad. Almost all the kids identified beauty and goodness with the light-skinned doll. When asked which of the dolls looked most like them, many of the children became uncomfortable and claimed that they looked like the light-skinned doll.[38]

The reality of Mexico's racialized class system means that some dark-skinned Mexicans go to great lengths to improve their life chances. Many women and a few men use hair dyes and whitening creams and resort to plastic surgery to produce sharper, more European features. Mexican racism and classism are so normalized that even dark-skinned Mexicans accept and perpetuate it. Young men and women are counselled by family members to date and marry someone who might "improve the race" and produce a light-skinned baby. When new parents are asked *¿Cómo salió?* ("How is the baby?"), they are not being queried about the sex or health status of the newborn. Rather, the question is usually about skin tone. People hope for a magical outcome, a *güerita or güerito* whose skin is lighter than that of their parents. It is easy to critique these attitudes, but family members have intimate knowledge of the society in which they live. They simply hope that the newborn can go through life without having to navigate the stigma of darker skin.

Alfonso Cuarón's "Roma"

Alfonso Cuarón's internationally acclaimed film "Roma" (2018) put Mexican racism and classism and the exploitation of Indigenous domestic workers front and center. Cuarón, a Mexican screenwriter and director, tells the story of Cleo, an Indigenous live-in nanny who works for a middle-class household in Mexico City's fashionable Colonia Roma neighborhood, circa 1970–1971. The Cleo character was inspired by Cuarón's beloved childhood nanny, Liboria Rodríguez. She is the glue that keeps the family together. Cleo is in perpetual motion, serving the family at all hours of the day and picking up after the dog. When the father leaves the family, Cleo's domestic and emotional labor enables the mother, Sofía, to take a job outside the home at an advertising firm.

For Cleo to perform her critical role in this dysfunctional family, she must hold her tongue and sacrifice her present and future. Cleo's attempt to have a life of her own, outside of the family, fails in spectacular fashion. Fermín, her love interest and father of her unborn child, is being trained as a Halcón, soon to be unleashed on student protesters in the June 1971 Corpus Christi Massacre. Cleo gives her all, but the family she works for hardly knows her. When her water breaks and she checks into a hospital, the family's grandmother does not even know her second last name or her age. When she speaks on the phone in her native Mixtec language, one of the children tells her to "stop talking like that."

Both Cleo and Sofía are abandoned by the men in their lives, but there's little sense of "sisterhood" in the film; the chasm separating a middle-class, light-skinned professional woman and an Indigenous domestic worker from Oaxaca is too great. Cuarón, who filmed in black and white, makes Mexico's pigmentocracy starkly apparent in scenes where Cleo (played by Indigenous actress Yalitza Aparicio) and Sofía (played by Marina de Tavira) are positioned side by side. At the film's climax, when Cleo rescues Sofía's kids, she breaks down and confesses that she did not want her own stillborn baby girl to live. This is the ultimate displacement of Cleo—she saves Sofía's kids but could not save her own. Shortly after her act of heroism, she returns with the family to Mexico City and resumes her domestic chores. In the film's final scene, she is once again climbing the stairs to the rooftop to hang laundry. Some critics considered Cleo's stoic silence at key moments to be a near-fatal flaw in the film,[39] but others contend that it delivered the film's most important message. It called attention to the fact that Mexico's domestic and emotional care workers, who tend to be Indigenous, female, and poor, routinely silence and erase themselves and their futures on behalf of the lighter-skinned people who usually employ them.[40]

A Netflix sensation, "Roma" was nominated for 10 Academy Awards, including Best Picture, Best Actress (Yalitza Aparicio), and Best Supporting Actress (Marina de Tavira). In February 2019, Cuarón won the Oscar for Best Director, and the film also won Oscars for Best Foreign Language Film and Best Cinematography. "Roma" won accolades at other film festivals, too. In Morelia, Michoacán, Cuarón exhorted Mexicans to support the rights of domestic workers, among those least protected by Mexican labor laws. He also condemned racism and added that "classism is as dreadful as racism, and what makes it worse is that both things are totally connected in our country."[41] At the time, only 1 in 10 domestic workers in Mexico had a formal work contract, and only one in four earned at least the federal minimum wage (about $156 USD a month).

Figure 3.4 "Roma" star Yalitza Aparicio, photographed in Los Angeles in 2018. ZUMA Press, Inc./Alamy Stock Photo

As "Roma" garnered acclaim and awards, attention focused on Yalitza Aparicio, the 25-year-old woman from Tlaxiaco, Oaxaca who played Cleo in the film. The daughter of a Triqui mother and a Mixtec father, Aparicio was a kindergarten teacher when she auditioned for the role. She had never acted professionally before. Once the film started receiving critical acclaim, she appeared on the cover of glossy magazines like *Vogue México*, *Elle*, *¡Hola!*, and *Vanity Fair*, modeling designs from exclusive brands like Gucci, Prada, and Louis Vuitton. For some Mexicans, the sight of an Indigenous woman on the silver screen and on the cover of magazines was not only unprecedented, it was highly unsettling. A range of cringe-inducing comments poured forth on social media, exposing the depths of racism and classism in Mexican society.[42] Many other Mexicans celebrated the rise and notoriety of Aparicio, however. In a country where Indigenous people have routinely been infantilized on television and in film, her renown was welcomed and long overdue.

Conclusions

Mexico has been recognized across the globe for its celebration of mestizaje, but as we have seen, many people were excluded from Mexico's "melting pot." Mexico's indigenista programs received hemispheric acclaim, but actual results fell well short of the stated goals of development and national integration. Postrevolutionary Mexico never wrote racism into law, but it's a country where, in certain stadiums, soccer fans still jeer Afro-descendent players on opposing teams with ape calls every time they touch the ball. Skin tone is still used to determine who has free access to private buildings and shopping malls, who should be watched, questioned, or excluded, who is mistreated by the police and who is suspected of criminal behavior. More than one hundred years after experiencing the world's first twentieth-century social revolution, "old colonial racial categories remain and 'passing' towards 'whiteness'...is still a goal."[43]

Figure 3.5 Mexico's fantastic National Museum of Anthropology opened in 1964. Octavio Paz called it the "womb of the *patria* (fatherland)." Photo by the author.

Mexicans have been taught to take great pride in their distant Indigenous ancestors, who left behind fabulous ceremonial architecture and colorful codices. The Indigenous past has been harnessed to promote tourism, one of Mexico's most important industries. But this past cannot get in the way of the present-day pursuit of modernity and whiteness.[44] Mexicans have learned to view the Indigenous as an essential part of their history and culture "but they do not seem to have any desire to 'look' like them."[45] Despite the quasi-indigenista lessons in the official education system and the celebration of mestizaje, "aesthetic paradigms denigrate the great majority of the population," writes Agustín Basave.[46]

Even when the Indigenous shed their indigeneity, there is no place for them in the so-called "cosmic race." Mexicans who are dark-skinned, poor, and marginalized occupy a dangerous and ambiguous position in Mexican society. They can always "regress" and revert to their Indigenous past. "It would seem that the mestizo can never do enough," writes Navarrete. "Their racial transformation is condemned to be incomplete and under suspicion."[47] The brilliant future that Vasconcelos offered the "cosmic race" was "unreachable by definition because it implied that mestizos should stop being such and should occupy the idealized space reserved for 'whiteness.'"[48]

That said, there are signs of progress. The Zapatista movement upended Mexican indigenismo and terminated the decades-long quest to forge a homogeneous mestizo nation. It also led to a surge in ethnic pride, in Chiapas and nationwide. In numerical terms, today there are more self-identifying Tseltals and Tsotsils than ever before in history. Nationally, the Indigenous population grew by more than 450,000 between 2010 and 2020. Postrevolutionary Mexico's prophets of mestizaje would be shocked by the sheer number and the cultural vitality of Indigenous people living in the country's hamlets, towns, and cities. Although most Indigenous Mexicans are still poor and marginalized, many have doctorates or law degrees or are successful merchants. And they still consider themselves to be Indigenous.

In another sign of progress, the Mexican Census Bureau in 2015 counted the Afro-Mexican population for the first time since independence. 1.4 million Mexicans—about 1.2 percent of the population—identified themselves as Afro-Mexican or Afro-descendent. More recently, when Andrés Manuel López Obrador was inaugurated as president in December 2018, an Afro-Mexican activist from Oaxaca's Costa Chica joined Indigenous elders in performing a purification ritual (*limpia*) to bless him and anoint him as leader.[49] This was a highly visible reminder to all Mexicans of the full diversity of the national population.

Mexico has also taken steps to offer higher education degree programs tailored to Indigenous and Afro-descendent students and their communities. Eleven intercultural universities in central and southern Mexico now offer Bachelor's and Master's degree programs in intercultural law, medicine, communication, language and literature, regional development, and alternative tourism. Instruction is in

Spanish and in Indigenous languages. Admission decisions are based on personal interviews, recommendations from the student's home community, and an evaluation of the student's goals and commitment to the region, not standardized test scores. Before these universities were inaugurated in 2004, only 1 percent of Indigenous youth attended university, and those who did were forced to leave home. The intercultural universities are situated in and around large Indigenous populations, making it easier for students to obtain a university degree without breaking ties with their home communities. Indigenous women are especially likely to attend an intercultural university; at some, women constitute more than 60 percent of the student body. The goal is to combine academic excellence with cultural and linguistic belonging so that the communities and regions benefit directly from the presence of the university.[50] Although they are not without their problems, intercultural universities represent a step forward in the bid to form young professionals who strongly identify with their community and region.

Although the cult of mestizaje buried and delayed a deeper discussion of racism and classism in Mexico, the conversation has recently become more open in academic research, politics, and the arts. Disrupting Mexico's pigmentocracy also involves making the dark-skinned majority visible on television, in advertising, and in the print and electronic media. Breaking with the paradigm of "aspirational whiteness" will not be easy. But perhaps the end of the "official" Mexican revolution and the collapse of two of its main ideological pillars represents an opportunity for the country to wholly embrace, respect, and make visible its full diversity.

Notes

1 Studies of the human genome show that humans share 99.9 percent of their genetic makeup. The remaining .1 percent determines a handful of visible and quite trivial differences, such as the color of our eyes, our hair, and our skin, and the shape of our noses and mouths.

2 Hernán Gómez Bruera, *El color del privilegio: el racismo cotidiano en México* (Ciudad de México: Editorial Planeta Mexicana, 2020) 21; Olivia Gall, "Identidad, exclusión y racismo: reflexiones teóricas y sobre México," *Revista Mexicana de Sociología* 66:2 (2004), 227; and Federico Navarrete, *México racista. Una denuncia* (México, D.F.: Penguin Random House Grupo Editorial, 2016), 41–46.

3 Matthew Restall and Kris Lane, *Latin America in Colonial Times* (New York: Cambridge University Press, 2011), 204–205; and Juan Pedro Viqueira, "Reflexiones contra la noción histórica de mestizaje," *Nexos* (May 1, 2010): 76–83.

4 Agustín F. Basave Benítez, *México mestizo: Análisis del nacionalismo mexicano en torno a la mestizofilia de Andrés Molina Enríquez* (México, D.F.: Fondo de Cultura Económica, 1993 [1992]), 18.

5 Tomás Pérez Vejo, "Raza y construcción nacional. México, 1810–1910," in *Raza y política en Hispanoamérica*, eds. Tomás Pérez Vejo and Pablo Yankelevich (Madrid y Ciudad de México: Iberoamericana/Bonilla Artigas Editores/El Colegio de México, 2018), 74–76, 84–85; and Rebecca Earle, *The Return of the Native: Indians and Myth-Making in Spanish America, 1810–1930* (Durham: Duke University Press, 2007).

6 Basave, 13, 121, 123.

7 López, *Crafting Mexico,* 7, 9.

8 Mónica G. Moreno Figueroa, "Distributed Intensities: Whiteness, Mestizaje and the Logics of Mexican Racism," in *Ethnicities* 10:3 (2010), 390.

9 José Vasconcelos, *La Raza Cósmica: Misión de la raza iberoamericana. Notas de viajes a la América del Sur* (Madrid: Agencia Mundial de Librería, 1925).

10 Karin Alejandra Rosemblatt, *The Science and Politics of Race in Mexico and the United States, 1910–1950* (Chapel Hill: The University of North Carolina Press, 2018), 48.

11 Olivia Gall, "Mexican Long-living Mestizophilia versus a Democracy Open to Diversity," *Latin American and Caribbean Ethnic Studies* 8:3 (2013): 286.

12 Navarrete, 106.

13 Jason Oliver Chang, *Chino: Anti-Chinese Racism in Mexico, 1880–1940* (Chicago: University of Illinois Press, 2017), 129, 130.

14 Pablo Yankelevich, "Nuestra raza y las otras. A propósito de la inmigración en el México revolucionario," in *Raza y política en Hispanoamérica*, eds. Tomás Pérez Vejo and Pablo Yankelevich (Madrid y Ciudad de México: Iberoamericana/Bonilla Artigas/El Colegio de México, 2018), 330.

15 Yankelevich, 331.

16 Gómez Bruera, 52–53.
17 Moreno Figueroa, 399.
18 Stephen E. Lewis, *Rethinking Mexican Indigenismo: The INI's Coordinating Center in Highland Chiapas and the Fate of a Utopian Project* (Albuquerque: University of New Mexico Press, 2018).
19 Jan Rus, "Rereading Tzotzil Ethnography: Recent Scholarship from Chiapas, Mexico," in *Pluralizing Ethnography: Comparison and Representation in Maya Cultures, Histories, and Identities*, eds. John M. Watanabe and Edward F. Fischer (Santa Fe: School of American Research Press, 2004), 203–204.
20 Guillermo Bonfil Batalla, "Del indigenismo de la revolución a la antropología crítica," in *De eso que llaman antropología mexicana,* eds. Arturo Warman, Margarita Nolasco Armas, Guillermo Bonfil Batalla, Merecedes Olivera de Vázquez, and Enrique Valencia (Mexico City: Editorial Nuestro Tiempo, 1970), 43, 55, 59.
21 Margarita Nolasco Armas, "La antropología aplicada y su destino final, el indigenismo," in *De eso que llaman antropología mexicana*, 81.
22 Bonfil, "Del indigenismo de la revolución," 43.
23 "Declaración de Barbados I (1971)," in *Documentos fundamentales del indigenismo en México* ed. José del Val and Carlos Zolla (Mexico City: UNAM, 2014), 611–619.
24 Guillermo Bonfil Batalla, *México profundo: una civilización negada* (México, D.F.: Grijalbo, 1987).
25 Ignacio Ovalle Fernández, "Bases programáticas de la política indigenista," in *INI, 30 años después: revisión crítica* (México, D.F.: INI, 1978), 12, 20.
26 Shannan L. Mattiace, *To See with Two Eyes: Peasant Activism and Indian Autonomy in Chiapas, Mexico* (Albuquerque: University of New Mexico Press, 2003), 94.
27 A. S. Dillingham, *Oaxaca Resurgent: Indigeneity, Development, and Inequality in Twentieth-Century Mexico* (Stanford: Stanford University Press, 2021); Neil Harvey, *The Chiapas Rebellion: The Struggle for Land and Democracy* (Durham: Duke University Press, 1998), 36–146; and María L. O. Muñoz, *Stand Up and Fight: Participatory Indigenismo, Populism, and Mobilization in Mexico, 1970–1984* (Tucson: University of Arizona Press, 2016).
28 Pedro Pitarch, "Los Zapatistas y arte de la ventriloquia," *Istor* 17 (2004), 95–99; and Juan Pedro Viqueira, *Encrucijadas chiapanecas: economía, religión e identidades* (México, D.F.: Tusquets Editores, 2002).

29 Pitarch, 119.

30 José Antonio Aguilar Rivera, *El fin de la raza cósmica. Consideraciones sobre el esplendor y decadencia del liberalismo en México* (México, D.F.: Editorial Océano de México, 2001), 29.

31 Andrés Villarreal, "Stratification by Skin Color in Contemporary Mexico," *American Sociological Review* 75:5 (2010): 666.

32 Gómez Bruera, 72–75.

33 Óscar Balderas, "'La gente es como la basura: hay que separarla': cadeneros de antros en México," *Vice News*, 2017.

34 Gómez Bruera, 66–75, 114.

35 Mario Arriagada Cuadriello, "Quién no es quién," *Nexos* (Agosto 2013).

36 Arriagada, "Quién no es quién."

37 Navarrete, 63–64, 157–158.

38 Navarrete, 56; view the video here: https://www.youtube.com/watch?v=5bYmtq2fGmY.

39 For example, Richard Brody, "There's a Voice Missing in Alfonso Cuarón's 'Roma,'" *The New Yorker*, December 18, 2018; and Gómez Bruera, 221–222.

40 Olivia Cosentino, "Feminism and Intimate/Emotional Labor," *Mediático: Special Dossier on Alfonso Cuarón's "Roma,"* Dec. 24, 2018, available at https://reframe.sussex.ac.uk/mediatico/?s=%22Roma%22&submit=Search. In the same dossier, see also Ignacio M. Sánchez Prado, "Class Trouble," and Pedro Ángel Palou, "Broken Memory, Voice, and Visual Storytelling."

41 Berenice Bautista, "Alfonso Cuarón pide legislar trabajo de empleadas domésticas," in *AP News*, Oct. 24, 2018.

42 Gómez Bruera, 216–220.

43 Moreno Figueroa, 391.

44 Navarrete, 102.

45 Moreno Figueroa, 393.

46 Basave, 142.

47 Navarrete, 149–150.

48 Navarrete, 167.

49 Theodore W. Cohen, *Finding Afro-Mexico: Race and Nation after the Revolution* (New York: Cambridge University Press, 2020), 1, 287.

50 Laura Selene Mateos Cortés and Gunther Dietz, "Universidades interculturales en México: Balance crítico de la primera década," *Revista Mexicana de Investigación Educativa* 21: 70 (2016). For more information on Mexico's intercultural universities, see https://educacionsuperior.sep.gob.mx/interculturales.html.

4

Church(es) and State in Contemporary Mexico

Nothing conveys *Mexicanidad* quite like Our Lady of Guadalupe. Legend holds that this brown-skinned image of the Virgin Mary appeared to Juan Diego Cuauhtlatoatzin four times in 1531. She commanded the Indigenous convert to tell the bishop of Mexico City to build a chapel in her honor. In time, *la morenita* became a beloved national figure, so much so that Father Miguel Hidalgo promised a crusade on her behalf when he rebelled against Spain in 1810. Even radical nineteenth-century Liberals acknowledged that devotion to the Virgin was perhaps the only bond that united Mexicans. In 2016, more Mexicans believed in Our Lady of Guadalupe than in eternal life.[1]

The overwhelming majority of Mexicans over the past five hundred years have considered themselves Catholics (and *Guadalupanos*), but not everyone has been happy with the Church's preponderant role in Mexican society. Beginning in the 1830s, Liberals pushed back against the Church's privileges, its dominant role in education, and its vast landholdings. They fought and won wars against the Church and its allies in the 1850s and 1860s. Liberals and others wrote several anticlerical articles into the Constitution of 1917. Years later, when the Mexican state attempted to enforce the anticlerical spirit of the

Mexico's Unscripted Revolutions: Political and Social Change since 1958, First Edition. Stephen E. Lewis.

Constitution, war broke out in western Mexico and claimed at least 70,000 lives. Tensions simmered elsewhere well into the middle 1930s. When Mexican bishops blessed President Lázaro Cárdenas's expropriation of U.S.- and British-held oil fields in Mexico in 1938, it was a sign that the worst of the Church-state conflict had passed. Cárdenas's successor, Manuel Ávila Camacho, declared himself a "believer" in 1940. In time, the PRI-government and the Church learned to tolerate and even benefit from one another.

Beginning in the 1970s, the PRI entered into a closer relationship with the Church hierarchy. This rapprochement eventually resulted in changes to the Constitution in 1992 that removed most of its remaining anticlerical provisions. But the Catholic Church no longer enjoys a spiritual monopoly in Mexico. Lapsed Catholics are being drawn to a kaleidoscope of religious alternatives. The Church is also being challenged from within, as many of the faithful are supplementing their devotion to the Virgin of Guadalupe with the veneration of less likely, often morally ambiguous images like the Santa Muerte (Saint Death). While the Mexican Church has improved its status in relation to the Mexican state, it has grown distant from its flock and seems unable to address the poverty, violence, and injustice that afflicts them.

Mexico's Extraordinary Religious Diversity

Mexico's religious landscape is far more diverse than one might assume. This diversity starts with the Catholic Church itself. Few could be blamed for assuming that the Mexican Church is hierarchical, monolithic, and steeped in tradition. But it would not have survived and prospered for five centuries if it were not also extraordinarily flexible and adaptable. The Spanish friars tried to impose a complicated, monotheistic religion onto polytheistic Indigenous peoples. Their attempts to impose orthodoxy notwithstanding, the result was often syncretism, the blending of religious cultures.

Today, Mexican Catholicism continues to accommodate new ideological and theological tendencies as well as new saints and regional devotions. Part of the Church's diversity and fragmentation is geographic. "There exists as many Catholic churches in Mexico as there are dioceses," writes Roderic Camp. "These dozens of autonomous units have only tenuous ties to any concept of a national, Mexican Church, and the ties are more theological than structural." Today, there are 18 large archdioceses and 72 dioceses in Mexico, each with its own bishop. The reality is that the Mexican Catholic Church is highly decentralized, as each diocese operates "with extraordinary autonomy."[2]

The Mexican Church has also become diverse in terms of ideology and theology. In 1962, Pope John XXIII convened the Second Vatican Council, commonly known as Vatican II. This was the Church's attempt to modernize certain practices and positions. It consisted of four sessions and lasted through 1965. As a direct result of Vatican II, priests could begin to say Mass in the vernacular (like Spanish) instead of Latin; music, prayers, and regalia were modernized; and relations with Protestant denominations (and other faiths) greatly improved. Bishops and priests were also encouraged to engage with the real-life, here-and-now concerns of their parishioners.

Inspired by the Vatican II document *Gaudium et spes*, Mexico's bishops issued a "Pastoral Letter about the Development and Integration of the Country" in March 1968. The letter criticized inequality in Mexico and the dire situation facing Indigenous people, peasants, and urban migrants. It also addressed the country's demographic explosion. In a searing critique of PRI corporatism and *charrismo*, the bishops condemned what they called "the lack of authentic, functional organizations."[3] Although the letter stopped short of calling for clean, truly democratic elections, it announced the reengagement of the Mexican Church with Mexican society. "For the first time since 1926," writes Soledad Loaeza, "Mexican bishops officially assumed a position of social commitment and leadership."[4]

Later in 1968, Latin American bishops met in Medellín, Colombia, to provide further guidance for implementing the spirit of Vatican II. In a nod to the region's poverty and oppression—most Latin Americans lived under dictatorship at the time—the bishops drew inspiration from the biblical Exodus. They discussed the need to meet parishioners' basic needs and overcome injustice. Part of this effort involved *concientización* or consciousness-raising. Once the faithful were aware of their plight, they were encouraged to work together and press for their rights here on Earth. Engaging with the world meant denouncing its evils—the "institutional violence" of poverty, inequality, and exploitation. The bishops called for a more just social order and noted the special place of the poor in God's eyes. They also endorsed the creation of Basic Ecclesial Communities (BECs) of 8–10 people, each one led by a catechist who held weekly meetings with priests or nuns and then returned to their community to discuss the Gospel and how it related to everyday life. This kind of lay activity ran counter to traditional Latin American Catholicism, which historically expected obedience and subordination from parishioners.

Meanwhile, what became known as "liberation theology" was gestating in the region. Liberation theology blended the most progressive elements of Vatican II and the Medellín conference. Peruvian priest Gustavo Gutiérrez first introduced the notion in 1968 and published his influential book, *A Theology of Liberation*, in 1971. Practitioners engaged in sociological analyses of poverty and worked with Marxists, agnostics, and atheists committed to radical change. The most outspoken proponent of liberation theology in Mexico was the bishop of Cuernavaca (Morelos), Sergio Méndez Arceo, who called himself a "priest and a revolutionary." "I feel fraternally linked to my Marxist brothers," he once declared. "Only socialism can give Latin America true development." While on a trip to Cuba in 1978, he suggested that Fidel Castro had been inspired by God.[5] Closer to home, Méndez Arceo supported independent unions and peasant causes and was the only bishop to participate in a group that called itself "Christians for Socialism." He denounced what he called "institutional repression" and excommunicated police officers in Morelos who applied torture in their interrogations. Méndez Arceo served as a mediator in kidnapping cases, such as when Lucio Cabañas's PDLP kidnapped Rubén Figueroa in 1974. But the "red bishop" was highly controversial, perhaps too much so to have a major impact on Mexico's other bishops.

Perhaps no Mexican embodied the transformations of the Catholic Church more than Samuel Ruiz, bishop of the diocese of San Cristóbal de Las Casas, Chiapas, from 1960 to 2000. Born into a conservative family in the state of Guanajuato, Ruiz studied in Rome in the late 1940s and early 1950s under the fiercely anticommunist Pope Pius XII. He was only 35 years of age when Pope John XXIII appointed him bishop of Chiapas in 1959. That was the same year that Fidel Castro overthrew the Batista dictatorship in Cuba. Mexican bishops and clerics shared an anti-communist, nationalist position at the time and were staunch defenders of the status quo. Ruiz was no exception. His first pastoral letter in 1961 condemned communism's "iniquities and countless crimes… and the BLACK background of its true doctrine."[6]

Ruiz would soon embark on a dramatic personal and spiritual transformation that would alter the history of modern Chiapas. He participated in all four sessions of Vatican II. When he was not in Rome, he crisscrossed his diocese and witnessed the misery and injustice in Indigenous Chiapas first-hand. To evangelize the region and counter the inroads of Protestant missionaries, he led the effort to train Indigenous lay catechists to spread the Gospel in their mother tongues. In time, he learned Tseltal (the Maya language spoken in eastern Chiapas) and endorsed an "Indianist theology" that was focused on liberation, "truly indigenous in its leadership, in its forms of worship and in its effect upon the lives of people."[7] Though often identified with liberation theology, Ruiz rejected the label. "I do not have any interest in liberation theology as a theory; I am interested in liberation," he said. Ruiz also claimed that he did not personally encourage the formation of BECs, claiming perhaps disingenuously that "if they are base communities, by definition, they emerge from the very bottom. … People will have to do that on their own."[8]

Ruiz's cagey responses stem from the fact that he—like Méndez Arceo—was often in the crosshairs of the Vatican. On at least two occasions, the apostolic delegate to Mexico, Girolamo Prigione, tried to force his resignation. Mexico's bishops supported Ruiz, however, and when the Zapatistas rose in arms on January 1, 1994, Ruiz played a pivotal role as mediator between the rebels and the federal government. Ruiz's role sparked controversy. On the one hand, he rejected violence; but on the other, he openly sympathized with the aims of the Zapatistas. He remained bishop of San Cristóbal until 2000 when he resigned at the mandatory retirement age of 75. Ruiz had dramatically transformed his diocese, which boasted more than 8000 Indigenous catechists. But he had not been able to stem the flow of Catholics into rapidly growing Protestant and Evangelical churches.

Figure 4.1 Bishop Samuel Ruiz consoles two Tsotsils during funeral ceremonies in Acteal, Chiapas, in December 1997. Forty-five people were massacred by a paramilitary group affiliated with the state-level PRI. Oriana Elicabe/AFP/Getty Images

After the Medellín conference and the emergence of liberation theology, it became impossible to speak of a unified, homogeneous Roman Catholic Church in contemporary Mexico. The Church became more plural and diverse, and regional differences began to manifest themselves as many dioceses accommodated local needs and traditions. As historian of religion Jennifer Scheper Hughes notes, "Mexican Catholicism cannot rightly be comprehended as a single, uniform, monolithic religious practice when viewed through a cultural lens of lived religion." Instead, she speaks of "diverse Catholicisms" and suggests that in Mexico, "it is possible that there is at least as much religious diversity and innovation within Roman Catholicism as there is outside of it."[9] The table below suggests the remarkable diversity within the Mexican Catholic Church today.

Tendencies Within Contemporary Mexican Catholicism[10]

Catholic expression	Theological/ideological orientation	Where found
Traditionalist	Synthesizes an Indigenous worldview with "supernatural" elements of colonial Catholicism	Indigenous communities
Mestizo or coleto	Derives from colonial Catholic ideologies and caste/class dominance over the Indigenous	Interethnic regions including highland Chiapas
Autochthonous	Fuses ethnic Catholicism with Indianist theology and Latin American liberation theology	Southeastern Mexico, especially eastern Chiapas
"Mexican" or "Popular"	Encompasses most Mexican Catholics; emphasizes the Virgin of Guadalupe	Throughout Mexico
Liberation theology	Organized as Basic Ecclesial Communities; salvation is linked with elimination of social sins like discrimination, exploitation, and oppression	Throughout, although dwindling

(*Continued*)

Catholic expression	Theological/ideological orientation	Where found
Bajío	Descendants of the Cristeros, socially conservative, critical of Vatican II. Powerful—two-thirds of Mexican bishops and priests come from this region.	Central Mexico north of Mexico City
Prosperity theology	Considers money to be a divine blessing and sees entrepreneurs as predestined leaders chosen by God. Powerful—articulated by certain bishops and clerical orders, including the Legionaries of Christ.	Throughout Mexico
Charismatic Renewal	Influenced by Pentecostals; devotees are reborn in the Holy Spirit, an emphasis on prophecy and healing.	Throughout Mexico
Vatican II/ Postconciliar	Favors a reform to the liturgy, greater participation of the laity, keeping distance from the powerful. Preferential option for the poor, but less radical than liberation theology or autochthonous Catholicism.	
Liberal Veracruz	Mixes regional culture of the Gulf of Mexico with U.S. and Caribbean influences.	Veracruz
Frontier	Can be influenced by either prosperity or liberation theology.	Northern border states and municipalities
Extra-American minorities	Catholics of Italian, German, French, or Lebanese origin with their own churches and priests that speak in the mother language. The Lebanese Catholic Church has two variants. Tends to be upper class, often linked to prosperity theology.	

The Reconciliation of the Catholic Church with the Mexican State

Taken together, Vatican II, the Medellín bishops' conference, and the emergence of liberation theology nudged the Church toward more engagement with the world. When Mexican president Luis Echeverría (1970–1976) announced a "democratic opening" early in his presidential term, the Church was well-positioned to step through that door. Echeverría—who had pondered entering the seminary as a young man—frequently consulted Mexico's bishops and invited them to participate in cabinet meetings. The president even cultivated a close friendship with the fiery bishop of Cuernavaca, Sergio Méndez Arceo, the first to visit the presidential residence since the Revolution of 1910.

Echeverría also became the first sitting Mexican president to meet a pope. In 1974, eighteen years before Mexico had reestablished formal diplomatic relations with the Vatican, he traveled to Rome in an unofficial capacity, as a tourist, to meet with Pope Paul VI. Mexican bishops did their part during this delicate rapprochement. Most had backed the regime during the 1968 student movement and held their tongues following the Tlatelolco and Corpus Christi massacres.[11]

One measure of the growing closeness between the Catholic Church and the Mexican state was the latter's support for the construction of the new modernist Basilica of Our Lady of Guadalupe in Mexico City. Although planning for the new Basilica had been underway for some time, the formal announcement of the project was made in late 1974, after Echeverría's trip to the Vatican. Seizing the opportunity to curry favor with Mexico's Catholic majority, the president enthusiastically supported the project. He even sent cabinet ministers to the abbot of the shrine to deliver suitcases full of presidential cash. In his memoirs, Monsignor Guillermo Schulenburg recalled one such delivery, made by the minister of Finance on behalf of an "anonymous donor." "I understood that it was a donation from the Government of Mexico, by order of Luis Echeverría, president of the Republic," he wrote, "but I told myself that, essentially, it was a gift from the Mexican people, which they gave with great delight. . .on behalf of their beloved Virgin."[12]

Figure 4.2 The modernist Basilica of Our Lady of Guadalupe was built next to the old Basilica of Guadalupe in Mexico City. The Marian apparition took place in 1531 on Tepeyac hill, behind the old Basilica. Photo by the author.

Schulenburg was so grateful to Echeverría that he invited him to inaugurate the new Basilica in the waning months of his presidential term. It would have made sense to formally dedicate the new shrine on December 12, the day that Mexicans commemorate the Marian apparition. But the Abbot instead proposed October 12, the Día de la Raza. Echeverría agreed with the accelerated timetable because on December 12, 1976, José López Portillo would be wearing the presidential sash.

Echeverría got to inaugurate the new Basilica, but López Portillo was the first Mexican president to receive a papal visit. Since Mexico and the Vatican still did not have formal diplomatic relations, the pretext for the visit in 1979 was the Third General Conference of Latin American Bishops, held that year in Puebla. The recently coronated Pope John Paul II flew to Mexico City, where he was received with honors and held a televised, open-air Mass. His visit violated the

Mexican constitution in multiple ways. "It was impossible to ignore the symbolic meaning of this visit," writes Loaeza, "in light of the history of Mexican liberalism and the efforts of the postrevolutionary state to make religion a private, individual phenomenon."[13] The pope also held a private Mass at the president's official residence, Los Pinos, to apparently satisfy the whims of the president's mother. When reproached for hosting the pontiff and violating the lay status of a public building, López Portillo responded that he would pay any fine out of his own pocket.

Pope John Paul II used the bishops' conference in Puebla to support the moderates who had planned the conference and had sidelined prominent liberation theologians. In his opening address to the bishops, he warned against "incorrect interpretations." "This notion of Christ as a politician and revolutionary, as the subversive of Nazareth, cannot be reconciled with Church teachings," he said.[14] While endorsing the struggle for justice and service to the poor, he advocated strict adherence to orthodox doctrine. The Polish pope, who grew up behind the Iron Curtain, had no patience for some liberation theologians' flirtations with Marxism.

The pope's widely popular visit essentially dismantled the legal framework that had governed Church-state relations since the Mexican Revolution. The anticlerical laws regulating public religious displays were unenforceable, and the ailing PRI-government needed the moral legitimacy that the Church offered. Abbot Schulenburg capitalized on the state's growing need for Church support. He wrote the López Portillo administration to ask it to forgive the debt that the Church had incurred while building the new Basilica. "Of course, my letter was not answered in writing," he wrote, "but rather orally, and from that moment forward, the debt that we contracted during the previous presidential term was cancelled by...don José López Portillo."[15]

Following the pope's widely popular visit, the Church gradually reentered the political arena. Mexico's bishop weighed in on matters as diverse as exchange rates, administrative corruption, and the transparency of elections. When the Mexican economy collapsed in fall

1982, at the end of López Portillo's administration, Mexico's bishops announced their decision to abandon the "juridical corner" to which they had been condemned by the Mexican Constitution. They would increasingly "announce and denounce...with prudence but with energy."[16]

This sometimes put the Church in the crosshairs of the PRI. During the 1986 state elections in Chihuahua, discussed in Chapter 2, bishops and priests embraced an "electoral theology" that encouraged civic participation and defended electoral transparency. Following the election, they denounced the PRI's blatant electoral fraud. Arguably, the Church was forced into this role. Sitting on the sidelines would have jeopardized its credibility in the eyes of the faithful. The Church also took a stronger stance in defense of human rights. The Dominican and Jesuit orders each opened centers in the 1980s to record and denounce human rights abuses. This typically involved direct or indirect critiques of government. In Chiapas, Bishop Samuel Ruiz's Fray Bartolomé de Las Casas Human Rights Center was created specifically to denounce the abuses to which Indigenous peoples were routinely subjected.

Mexican bishops also declared that fundamental human rights had been violated in the fraudulent 1988 presidential election. The declared winner, Carlos Salinas, responded by offering an olive branch to the Church. Breaking with precedent, he invited members of the Mexican Church hierarchy to his inauguration and announced his intention to modernize Church-state relations through reforms to the Constitution. Salinas was highly motivated to normalize relations with the Church. The PRI's legitimacy had been tarnished over the previous two decades. So too was his own election. He also wanted to shore up his popularity before attempting to implement his economic agenda, which called for more painful layoffs, more economic restructuring, more privatizations, and less social spending. He also may have been thinking of his international audience and the need to present Mexico in the best possible light ahead of debates in the U.S. Congress over his proposal for a North American Free Trade Agreement (NAFTA).

After a series of discreet negotiations with members of the Church hierarchy, the Salinas administration proposed amending Articles 3, 5, 24, 27, and 130 of the Constitution. Once the Chamber of Deputies approved the reforms in 1992, priests regained the right to vote. The Church could once again own property indispensable to its tasks and could celebrate special acts of religious worship in public. Months later, formal diplomatic relations with the Vatican were reestablished. The Church did not get everything it wanted from the reforms, but in a legal and political sense, it was in a stronger position than it had been at any point since the Mexican Revolution. After 1992, the principal challenges to the Church came not from the Mexican state but from non-Catholic denominations and—increasingly—from within.

Non-Catholic Denominations

Historically, non-Catholic Christian religious organizations have attracted only a small fraction of Mexicans. This fraction has grown considerably since the 1970s, however. In the 2020 census, 14 million Mexicans declared themselves either Protestant or Evangelical. This section will first consider the mainline, historic Protestant denominations that trace their origins to the Protestant Reformation. These include Presbyterians, Baptists, Methodists, Mennonites, and others. It then turns to Pentecostalism, a more charismatic, ecstatic form of Protestantism. Lastly, it considers the most prosperous, independent non-Catholic Mexican church, La Luz del Mundo, which has a major presence in Mexico and beyond.

North American missionaries introduced Protestantism to Mexico during the years of the Reforma (1850s and 1860s). It was closely associated with Mexican liberalism. Protestantism appealed to Mexicans who rejected the Catholic Church hierarchy and/or folk Catholicism. It seemed rational and modern, more centered on Christ and God and less focused on the Virgin of Guadalupe. In Mexico's southeast, Protestantism offered an escape from traditional folk Catholicism, known as *costumbre*, which had allowed local bosses and alcohol merchants to keep the Indigenous tied to an expensive cycle of fiestas. Beginning in the late 1930s, Protestant missionary linguists from the U.S.-based Summer Institute of Linguistic/Wycliff Bible Translators (SIL) began to teach literacy, translate the Bible into Indigenous languages, introduce antibiotics, and win converts with a clear message that emphasized sobriety. Many Indigenous converts founded Presbyterian congregations. Their conversion was often seen as an act of treason and a betrayal of local customs. Converts were sometimes attacked and expelled from their communities.[17]

Beginning in the 1950s, the SIL's missionary linguists worked alongside Mexico's National Indigenist Institute (INI) to write language primers in Indigenous languages and train Indigenous men (and later, women) to teach literacy in the mother tongue as a bridge to literacy in Spanish. This alliance of Mexico's INI, rooted in secular, revolutionary nationalism, and a U.S.-based Protestant organization was always improbable and sometimes tense, but it lasted for over 40 years. In 1978, President José López Portillo inducted the SIL's founder and director, William Cameron Townsend, into the Order of the Aztec Eagle, the highest honor that the Mexican government can bestow on a foreigner. Today, thanks largely to the spadework of the SIL's missionary linguists, various Protestant and Evangelical denominations are firmly established in the Indigenous communities of southeastern Mexico.

Elsewhere in Mexico, however, Protestants have always been vastly outnumbered. Today, roughly two million Protestants belong to dozens of often competing denominations. The biggest threat to contemporary Protestantism is not the Catholic Church but rather Pentecostal denominations that offer a more emotional religious connection to God.

Pentecostalism is a subset of Protestant Christianity that emphasizes "experiencing" God through ecstatic bodily experiences, such as speaking in tongues, prophecy, faith healing, vibrant music, and [holy] spirit possession. Pentecostals call this "baptism in the Holy Spirit." In many ways, Pentecostalism is the antithesis of historic, mainline Protestantism. "Where older forms of Protestantism had thrived among those wishing to distance themselves from the perceived 'backwardness' and superstition of folk Catholicism and local religion, Pentecostalism took the opposite tack: it offered more of the supernatural, not less," writes Todd Hartch. "Pentecostalism mended the sacred canopy and repopulated the spiritual realm, an enticing prospect for Mexicans caught in the spiritually empty confines of modernity."[18]

Pentecostalism traces its roots to the Azusa Street Revival that took place in Los Angeles, California, in the early twentieth century. Azusa Street founder William J. Seymour introduced ecstatic experiences into worship, many of them drawn from African American Christianity. Worshipers of diverse backgrounds were drawn to this more intimate, rambunctious version of religious practice.[19]

Pentecostal Christianity came to Latin America in three waves. The first wave, associated with the Azusa Street Revival, had a modest impact, and so did the second wave. Both were led by foreign missionaries. The third wave, dating to the 1980s, was led by media-savvy locals. It is often called neo-Pentecostalism, and it is focused less on the Second Coming of Christ than on the here and now. Neo-Pentecostals believe that self-improvement and material advancement are nothing to be ashamed of. Rather, they are proof of God's grace and favor.[20] This is known as prosperity theology, or the "health and wealth gospel." It appeals to the poor just as readily as it now appeals to middle-class professionals. Many Mexicans are also attracted to the strict moral code of Pentecostalism. Women experiencing abusive, womanizing, and/or alcoholic husbands are often drawn to Pentecostal denominations, and they often bring their partners with them.

Although the Pentecostal presence is not as great in Mexico as it is in other parts of Latin America, several denominations are growing rapidly. Using electric guitars and keyboards, high-quality sound systems, and relatively unlettered male and sometimes female pastors, Pentecostal denominations offer an experiential, accessible form of Christianity to parishioners. Close-knit communities give the faithful the support that they need. If imitation is the highest form of flattery, the fact that other religions have "Pentecostalized" their practices would indicate where the dynamic growth is taking place. Even the Catholic Church was forced to officially recognize its Charismatic Renewal movement—which started at the University of Notre Dame in Indiana in 1967—to prevent further defections to Pentecostalism. Some conservative Mexican bishops resisted, like Miguel García Franco of Mazatlán, who called Charismatic Renewal "the smoke of Satan that has infiltrated the Church."[21] But Charismatic Renewal is attractive to many Mexican Catholics. They can "pray in tongues, receive healing from the Holy Spirit, sway to contemporary worship tunes—and still pray to Our Lady of Guadalupe in good standing."[22] Today, it is one of the Mexican Church's fastest-growing sectors.

La Luz del Mundo/Light of the World is a homegrown independent religious association that blends aspects of Catholicism and first-wave Pentecostalism with Mexican nationalism and a cult of personality. The church's founder was a Constitutionalist soldier of Indigenous descent named Eusebio Joaquín González. In 1926, he received a divine calling to restore primitive Christianity in Mexico. He became a modern-day apostle of Jesus Christ and took the name "Aarón." In 1952, he purchased 35 acres on the gritty outskirts of eastern Guadalajara and founded a walled neighborhood called Hermosa Provincia (Beautiful Providence). His followers bought plots at reduced cost and built homes, stores, and businesses around a church.[23] Hermosa Provincia is a religious community that residents rarely have to leave. Congregants are encouraged to attend daily church services, and many marry within the congregation. La Luz del Mundo claims more than five million members in more than 50 countries, including the United States. In the greater Los Angeles area alone, its boasts dozens of churches; its massive church in Houston looks like the Greek Parthenon with a gold dome. It has 14 columns, 12 for Christ's original apostles, and one each for the church's first two apostles, "Aarón" and his son, Samuel.

Today, the founder's grandson, Naasón Joaquín García, presides over the church as the reigning apostle and "servant of God." Like most Pentecostal denominations, La Luz del Mundo offers a strict moral code, a tight-knit community, and the promise of everlasting life. But unlike most Pentecostal churches, La Luz del Mundo does not use musical instruments in its services, which they believe are an abomination to God. Instead, choirs sing *a capella*. Women are expected to wear long white dresses and head coverings; they sit apart from men during church services. Congregants can experience supernatural healing, speaking in tongues, ritualized weeping, and near fanatical devotion to the apostle. La Luz del Mundo tends to operate in poorer neighborhoods. In the United States, it appeals to recent immigrants who are in need of community and the basic tools for survival. But allegations of sexual and physical abuse have dogged all three of the denomination's apostles. Critics suggest that the allegations were never prosecuted in Mexico because the church's leadership cultivated close ties with PRI and PAN politicians.[24]

Figure 4.3 The faithful take part in the Holy Convocation of La Luz del Mundo at Hermosa Provincia in Guadalajara, August 2018. Ulises Ruiz/AFP/Getty Images

La Luz del Mundo made headlines in the United States in June 2019, when the current apostle, Naasón Joaquín García, was arrested on his private jet at Los Angeles International Airport. He initially faced 36 charges for crimes that he committed in Los Angeles County between 2015 and 2018, including rape and forcible oral copulation of a minor, human trafficking, and producing and possessing child pornography. Bail was eventually set at an astonishing $90 million, the highest ever in California. In June 2022, days before the trial was set to start, Naasón Joaquín García—the self-proclaimed apostle of God—took a plea deal to avoid a possible life sentence. He pled guilty to three counts of sexual acts with underage girls in his congregation. Days later, he was sentenced to almost 17 years in prison. But Joaquín García's many victims received no compensation, and nothing was done to dismantle the network of groomers and enablers who sent girls to the confessed sexual predator. Joaquín García's dramatic fall from grace raises the question of whether a church controlled by a self-anointed dynasty can carry on after its apostle is arrested, tried, and convicted of heinous crimes. As this book went to press, many devotees seemed unphased by Joaquín García's imprisonment and sentence. They noted that apostles have been wrongly imprisoned throughout human history.[25]

Self-inflicted Wounds in the Catholic Church Since 1992

Protestant/Evangelical inroads are taking place at a time when Mexico's Catholic Church can seem distant and even indifferent to the needs of its parishioners. Historian of religion Matthew Butler writes that the Church remains "comfortably majoritarian" but looks "complacent and declining…[and] in need of managerial, theological, and pastoral renewal."[26] To further complicate matters, Mexico's Church has suffered grave self-inflicted wounds, starting with its own sexual abuse scandal.

Mexico's story of priestly abuse bears some similarity to the scandals in other countries like the United States and Ireland. In Mexico, however, the Church was powerful enough to suppress full disclosure until the late 1990s. The principal scandal involved Marcial Maciel Degollado, the charismatic seminarian who founded the powerful

Legionaries of Christ clerical order in 1941. Maciel hailed from Michoacán; his extended family took an active role in waging war against the postrevolutionary state during the Cristero conflict (1926–1929). Under Maciel's directorship, the Legion became one of the world's wealthiest and most influential Catholic orders, with schools, universities, and seminaries in more than 20 countries. At a time when the Church was suffering from a dearth of priests, the Legion trained hundreds. The Legion had close ties with some of Mexico's richest families, who sent their children to its schools, including the Universidad Anáhuac. Maciel himself officiated at their marriages,

Figure 4.4 Pope John Paul II embraces Marcial Maciel, founder of the powerful Legionaries of Christ clerical order, in 1991. The pope's defense of Maciel delayed a thorough investigation of Maciel's crimes. MCT/Tribune News Service/Getty Images

baptisms, and funerals. Maciel was one of Pope John Paul II's escorts on his historic trip to Mexico in 1979 and again in 1990. In 1994, on another visit to Mexico, the pope described Maciel as an "efficacious guide to youth." Some openly spoke of eventual, fast-track sainthood.

Maciel was so important and well-connected that when nine former seminarians claimed in 1997 that he had abused them in the 1940s and 1950s, the Vatican refused to hear them out. Pope John Paul II valued Maciel's fierce anticommunism, his personal loyalty, and his ability to raise buckets of money. One year later, Maciel's victims filed a formal complaint in Latin and were again ignored. Maciel had literally bought the silence of the Vatican. As the pope neared death, the case was reopened. In 2006, the Vatican announced that Maciel would not be tried under canonical law, due to his advanced age. John Paul's successor, Pope Benedict XVI, ordered Maciel to leave the priesthood and dedicate himself "to a life of prayer and penance." When Maciel died two years later, in Houston, fresh evidence emerged that he had been a drug addict who had lived under a false identity with a young Mexican woman. He had fathered two children with her whom he subsequently abused.[27] He was never forced to atone for his crimes, nor did he ever issue the explicit apology sought by his accusers.

In 2009–2010, the Vatican conducted a posthumous investigation and condemned Maciel as "immoral," while the Legion issued an apology to Maciel's victims. In 2019, the Legion reported that its own investigation found that 33 of its priests and 71 of its seminarians had sexually abused minors over the past 80 years; a third of the priest abusers had themselves been abused by Maciel.[28]

It is unclear whether the Maciel scandal put a dent in the devotion of Mexican Catholics. But the negative headlines could not have helped an institution that was already reeling from revelations that priests had received drug money from narcotraffickers (*nacrolimosnas*) and that the archbishop of Mexico City from 1995–2017, Norberto Rivera Carrera, had protected pedophile priests, including one that he cycled back and forth across the border to various parishes in the United States. Rivera had been one of Maciel's fiercest defenders.

Another public relations debacle unfolded when members of the Mexican Church hierarchy feuded publicly over the canonization of

Juan Diego, the Indigenous man who received the Marian apparition. Pope John Paul II believed that venerating and canonizing local saints was one way to combat secularism and the outflow of the Catholic faithful to other religious alternatives. For Mexico, this meant placing Juan Diego on the fast track to canonization. In 1996, however, Monsignor Guillermo Schulenburg Prado, the abbot of the Basilica of Guadalupe, questioned the historical evidence for the Guadalupan miracle. Schulenburg and other prominent Catholic theologians viewed Juan Diego as a symbol used in the evangelization of natives, "not a reality." They were concerned that the Church was about to canonize someone who had never existed. Historian and priest Stafford Poole went even further, calling Juan Diego a "pious fiction." The pope's allies, including Mexico City archbishop Norberto Rivera, fought back furiously. They accused the skeptics of racism, suggested that Schulenburg was at least partly senile, and proposed that the abbot had excommunicated himself by casting doubt on Mexico's most famous Marian apparition.

In the end, Pope John Paul II got his way. Juan Diego became the 459th saint that he elevated to the altars. (Between 1903 and 1970, the pope's predecessors canonized only 98 saints.) John Paul II made it official during his fifth and final visit to Mexico in 2002. Father Poole concluded that the canonization was "a sad and tawdry spectacle that [did] little service to the Church's mission and credibility."[29] The canonization of Juan Diego was always a project of the pope and his closest allies. Ironically, now that the dust has settled, many Mexican Catholics seem indifferent to their new saint. Instead, they are embracing other devotions.

Dynamism on the Margins of the Official Catholic Church

Since the arrival of the first Spanish missionaries 500 years ago, Catholic priests in Mexico have struggled, usually unsuccessfully, to rein in traditional healers, renegade prophets, and holy persons who preached unorthodox gospels. They also combated—and sometimes accepted—saints that seemed to come out of nowhere.

Since the early 1990s, the number of folk devotions at the margins of the Mexican Catholic Church has been on the rise. Some specialists believe that the economic impact of neoliberal reforms and the failure of the state to provide for and protect its citizens might be driving Mexicans to seek new kinds of otherworldly support. The rightward drift of the Catholic Church may also be to blame. In the 1970s and 1980s, the highwater mark of liberation theology in Mexico, many parish priests were trained as community organizers not in seminaries, but in marginalized rural and urban settings. They mobilized communities around Christian-informed political activism and supported struggles for urban infrastructure and the legalization of squatter settlements. As the Church under Pope John Paul II suppressed liberation theology, however, it retreated from these communities. This may have allowed new "saints" to take root and flourish. Since the Church cannot control their proliferation, it grudgingly accepts some of them.[30]

One of the fastest-growing devotions is the Santo Niño Jesús Doctor, the infant Jesus dressed in a white doctor's jacket, usually depicted carrying a black medical bag and wearing a stethoscope. The image is gender ambiguous, even feminine; it has delicate features, pink lips, long eyelashes, and flushed cheeks. Although it is age-indeterminate—the Niño could be an infant, toddler, or small child—it is always dressed as a professional doctor or surgeon. The image was first brought to Tepeaca, Puebla, in 1942 by nuns who had arrived to serve as nurses. It was given the title "doctor" after a series of healing miracles. Today, people come to the shrine in Tepeaca to ask for favors, often health-related, or to give thanks. Devotees say rosaries and leave small gifts, usually colorful plastic toys.

Semi-authorized replicas of the Tepeaca Niño have taken up residence in other towns and cities in central Mexico. Scheper Hughes studied the devotion in Tepoztlán, Morelos, just south of Mexico City. The guardians of the cult, known as *mayordomos*, are charged with finding people to care for the Niño. This is no small matter because the image must be treated like a living child. First, the caretakers must construct a large altar. Then, they must place meals in front of the Niño twice daily. They ritually change it into pajamas at night and rock it to sleep in a bassinet. In the morning, the image must be wakened and returned to the altar. Normally, a television is turned on for entertainment. During the day, the Niño can be escorted to private homes and surrounding neighborhoods to visit the sick, the grieving, and the dying. It should return to the house of the host family by 6 pm; if not, it can be scolded.[31]

As part of her fieldwork, Scheper Hughes interviewed a Tepoztlán couple who had been chosen to care for the image after their 20-year-old son had been killed in a motorcycle accident. The mayordomos believed that caring for the image might assuage their inconsolable grief. "The Niño interrupted their loneliness by filling their lives with direction and purpose, and the small tasks and details of caring for the image became a saving grace," writes Scheper Hughes. "Don Carlos [the accident victim's father] described how the Niño seemed to speak to him all the time, a constant voice of reassurance and calm." And when Don Carlos and his wife assisted others in their pain and loss, it strengthened bonds of community and became a powerful vehicle for healing. After nearly a year of caring for the Niño, Don Carlos and his wife decided to pass along the responsibilities and blessings to someone else.[32]

Devotion to the Niño Jesús Doctor is seen as a legitimate expression of Catholic faith, and there appears to be passive ecclesial support for the image. At the time of this writing, the Niño Jesús Doctor was one of the 10 most important devotions in Catholic Mexico. Its popularity grew during the COVID-19 pandemic, which took a terrible toll on Mexicans in 2020 and 2021.

If the Catholic Church has accepted the Niño Jesús Doctor, it has openly opposed the cult of the Santa Muerte, which surged in the late 1990s and the early 2000s and has a presence today throughout Mexico. The skeletal Santa Muerte is a unique folk devotion. Instead of representing a deceased human being, it represents the personification of death itself; the saint never lived an earthy life. Instead of being a male death figure, like Argentina's San La Muerte and Guatemala's Rey Pascual, Mexico's Santa Muerte is female, dressed as a nun, a bride, the Virgin or a queen. She is often depicted holding the globe, reflecting her vast power, or shown holding the scales of justice, suggesting her ability to right wrongs in a country where impunity reigns.

Many Mexicans think that the Santa Muerte has Mexica/Aztec origins, tracing back to the female goddess of death, Mictecacíhuatl.

But she also bears a striking resemblance to the Grim Reaper, with roots in medieval Catholicism, and La Parca, the Spanish personification of death. Contemporary Mexican popular culture is rife with the iconography of death, beginning with the frivolous female skeleton La Catrina popularized by engraver José Guadalupe Posada during the early twentieth century. The Day of the Dead is the ultimate manifestation of Mexicans' creative, cherished relationship with the dead. On the night of November 1, many Mexicans construct home altars for deceased family members or visit cemeteries where they clean gravesites and decorate them with marigolds and colorful tissue-paper cutouts. They also make offerings of sugarcoated bread, sugar candies, and toys in the form of skulls. Mexican intimacy with death is part of its national identity. The iconography of the ghastly Santa Muerte certainly did not emerge out of a vacuum.[33]

The first twentieth-century references to the Santa Muerte date to midcentury. It was venerated in private homes, usually consulted to address affairs of the heart. But as the prison population grew in the 1990s, inmates turned to the Santa. They kept altars in their cells and often had her tattooed onto their bodies. As they were released back into society, they built street altars dedicated to *la flaca*, the "skinny lady," in their home neighborhoods.

The cult of the Santa Muerte went public in 2001 when Enriqueta Romero placed a life-size statue in front of her house in Tepito, a gritty neighborhood just north of Mexico City's historic district. It was a gift from one of her sons who had spent time in prison. Neighbors began to pray in front of the statue. Today, she and her family offer rosaries on the first day of every month, when thousands of the devout stream into Tepito clutching their personal Santa Muerte statues, sometimes crawling on their knees from the subway station to the shrine. The Santa Muerte rosary (and the Masses offered at other Santa Muerte shrines) is designed after familiar Catholic rites and liturgy. Santa Muerte rituals conclude with the blessing of images. Devotees hold their statues above their heads in the direction of the shrine, "creating an eerie forest of deliberately unnerving figures against a backdrop of urban decay."[34]

Figure 4.5 Devotees of the Santa Muerte pray at her shrine in Tepito, Mexico City. Shaul Schwarz/Getty Images

This author observed outdoor Santa Muerte Masses in downtown Puebla. Devotees blocked off an entire city block and erected a *lucha libre* (wrestling) ring for rambunctious kids. Street vendors hawked various treats. The makeshift altar featured a life-size statue of the Santa Muerte, another life-size statue of the Virgin of Guadalupe, and yet another life-size depiction of Christ on the cross. During the liturgy, the male officiant (dressed like a Catholic priest) recited the Lord's Prayer and asked favors of both the Virgin and the Santa. Part popular Mass and part street fair, this ceremony was well attended by families with children of all ages, many of whom cradled their own images of the Santa Muerte. Despite the grim iconography, the atmosphere was lighthearted, even warm.

Specialists disagree as to the total number of devotees in Mexico, the United States, and Central America, but they surely number in the millions. Popular media has depicted the Santa Muerte as the patron saint of organized crime, but specialists point to her broad appeal.

Devotees tend to be young, urban mestizos; one specialist claims that at least two-thirds of them are female. Most devotees are Catholics, but their Catholicism is flexible and open to new spiritual intermediaries. The Santa Muerte is believed to work quicker than more distant, official Catholic saints like San Judas Tadeo, the advocate of hopeless causes. She offers unconditional accessibility; there is no need to renounce or confess anything. The Santa also does not judge; she is willing to do the "dirty work." She can be caring and loving, but if neglected, she can be demanding and vengeful, a "high-maintenance *cabrona* [bitch]."[35]

The Santa Muerte generally attracts the victims of neoliberalism. Fittingly, the devotion took off in Tepito, the epicenter of Mexico City's informal economy. The cult appeals to the vulnerable—street vendors, the incarcerated, and others who feel unprotected (or abused) by the Mexican state and the rule of law and abandoned by the official Catholic Church. The Church hierarchy inveighs against the Santa Muerte. But if it presses too hard, it risks alienating the many self-identifying Catholics who adore her.

The Niño Jesús Doctor and the Santa Muerte are but two of a number of popular devotions in contemporary Mexico. Another one is Juan Soldado (Juan the Soldier), an unofficial saint venerated in Tijuana. Believers claim that a poor soldier named Juan Castillo Morales was framed and executed in 1938 for the rape and murder of a young girl. The cult took hold in a gritty border town where the institutional Catholic Church was weak and economic life was precarious, informal, and dominated by the vice industry. Today, this folk saint offers protection to migrants crossing the border into the United States. Another unlikely (and officially unrecognized) folk saint, Jesús Malverde, has been venerated in Culiacán, Sinaloa since the 1970s. Malverde was a Robin Hood-type bandit killed by the Porfirian army in 1909. This cult took hold when Culiacán's political leaders, drug traffickers, and drug growers split into rival, feuding groups. In the cases of both Juan Soldado and Jesús Malverde, unofficial popular devotions emerged in relatively unchurched northern cities steeped in crises.[36]

The Catholic Church has survived and thrived in Mexico for five hundred years because it is a remarkably flexible institution. It has a tremendous capacity to absorb new ideas and practices, even if it is also characterized by an intense valuing of tradition. It can accommodate the Niño Jesús Doctor. It also tolerates the repurposed San Judas Tadeo, who has become the go-to saint for the homeless, the jobless, glue-sniffers, and drug addicts.[37] But it draws the line at the Santa Muerte, whose popularity suggests that neither the Catholic Church nor the Mexican state has met the needs of many Mexicans in recent years.

Is Mexico Still an Essentially Catholic Country?

According to the 2020 census, 77.7 percent of Mexico's population is Catholic. This represents a drop of five percentage points from the 2010 census. But other surveys, including those conducted by *Latinobarómetro*, show a steeper decline and overall lower numbers for Catholics. Anthropologist Elio Masferrer Kan argues that census data overrepresents the true Catholic presence and undercounts non-Catholic religions. His research checks census data against the Church's own tallies of baptisms, First Communions, Confirmations, and marriages, and his conclusions point to a steep, possibly irreversible, decline for the Church.

Baptismal records are important because this sacrament is a rite of passage practiced by all Catholics, including those that are distanced from the Church. Those who no longer baptize their children have probably left the Church for good. Therefore, the fact that only 73.69 percent of the babies born in 2010 were baptized in the Catholic Church is an important indicator of drift. So too are the figures related to First Communion. This sacrament is typically performed when a child is between eight and 10 years of age. In 2008, the number of children who took First Communion represented only 50.61 percent of the births that year. The figures for the third rite of passage, Confirmation—which typically takes place a few years later—are even lower, representing 42.14 percent of that year's births, although many practicing Catholics are never confirmed. Catholic marriage figures have also declined. In 2008, only 52.68 percent of marriages took place through the Catholic Church. Given the rising number of unmarried people living together, Masferrer suggests that less than 50 percent of conjugal unions have been blessed by the Church. He concludes that slightly less than half of the Mexican population can truly be considered Catholic; the other half fluctuates between a host of mainline Protestant and Evangelical churches, New Age beliefs, other religions, and other options, including agnosticism and secularism.[38]

Why, then, does official census data overstate the number of Catholics in Mexico? Masferrer cites data from the National Commission to Prevent Discrimination (*Consejo Nacional para Prevenir la Discriminación*, or CONAPRED) that suggests that roughly one-third of respondents have felt discriminated against for their dissident (i.e. non-Catholic) religious beliefs. It is likely that many non-Catholics tell census-takers that they are Catholic simply to protect themselves. CONAPRED surveys indicate that religious discrimination is strongest in Aguascalientes, Guanajuato, and Querétaro. In these states, a slight majority of respondents agreed that Protestants should be expelled from their communities; only 45 percent said that they should be left alone. Respondents in the central Mexican states of Hidalgo, Morelos, Puebla, and Tlaxcala were almost as hostile toward religious dissidents. Among the more tolerant states were those along the U.S.-Mexican border and those in the largely Indigenous South with considerable Protestant and Evangelical populations: Chiapas, Guerrero, and Oaxaca.

The census itself and census-takers might also produce data that overcounts the Catholic presence. In the 2010 census, the first choice for religious preference was "Catholic." Those who did not consider themselves to be Catholic could try to find their religious expression among 266 additional options. Masferrer and others speculate that poorly paid, exhausted census takers might default to the Catholic option simply to save time.

Even if census data partially masks the true dimension of religious diversity and change in Mexico, it still shows the slow but steady drift away from the Catholic Church. In addition to the 14 million Mexicans who declared that they are either Protestant or Evangelical in the 2020 census, another 10 million Mexicans (8.1 percent) claimed to have no religion at all, a figure that includes atheists as well as those who are reluctant to disclose their true beliefs. This figure marks a 3.4 percent increase since 2010. Another three million declared themselves to be agnostic; that is, they are considered "believers" but have no religious affiliation.

The Catholic Church can take heart in the fact that in Latin America, only in Paraguay and Ecuador do Catholics represent a larger percentage of the population. The Basilica of Our Lady of Guadalupe receives over 20 million visitors a year. It is the second most visited Catholic shrine in the world, behind only St. Peter's Basilica in Rome. Our Lady of Guadalupe continues to be the most important factor uniting Mexicans. But it is also undeniably true that increasing numbers of Catholics were drifting even at a time when the Roman Catholic Church was led by a popular pope, Francis, the first ever from Latin America.

Conclusions

The proliferation of different religious beliefs and expressions must rank among the most improbable unscripted revolutions in contemporary Mexico. The diversity *within* the Catholic Church is as robust as it is unexpected; the growing diversity on the margins of the official Church and well *outside* of it is perhaps even more surprising. It is difficult to imagine a more profound transformation in a country where the Church has dominated the religious landscape and shaped people's lives for five hundred years. Ironically, the movement away from mainstream Catholicism has accelerated since the Church was freed from the political and legal shackles that regulated its activity for most of the twentieth century.

Can the Catholic Church reverse current trends? Some analysts believe that the Church is too battered, too set in its ways to stage a comeback. They suggest that the decline of the Church is part of the larger narrative of institutional weakening in Mexico (and elsewhere). But others are not so pessimistic. The Church has thrived in Mexico because it is remarkably resilient; periods of relative decline have often been followed by fresh pastoral dynamism.

The better question is whether Mexico's Catholic Church, in all its diversity, can become more relevant to the lives of its parishioners. Pope Francis used his visit to Mexico in 2016 to encourage priestly reengagement with the victims of organized crime, the urban poor, economic migrants, and the Indigenous. His itinerary was laden with rich symbolism: he visited Michoacán, one of the states ravaged and depleted by cartel violence and out-migration to the United States; Ciudad Juárez, the gritty drug-trafficking outpost on the northern border; and San Cristóbal de Las Casas, where he prayed at the tomb of Samuel Ruiz and presided over an outdoor Mass that was heard in three of the Indigenous languages spoken in the diocese. At the National Cathedral in Mexico City, Pope Francis delivered an unusually sharp rebuke to Mexico's bishops, urging them to cease their infighting and instead reengage with the Church's social mission.[39] Many believe that the target of this rebuke was the archbishop of Mexico City, Norberto Rivera, whom the pope replaced the following year with the more socially committed Carlos Aguiar Retes. Pope Francis then went on record to defend the legacy of Vatican II, calling the teachings of the Second Vatican Council "sacrosanct" and stating that they "cannot be negotiated."[40] Perhaps this popular Latin American pope and his successors can revitalize the Mexican Catholic Church and stem the tide.

Notes

1 Todd Hartch, *Understanding World Christianity: Mexico* (Minneapolis: Fortress Press, 2019), 42.

2 Roderic Ai Camp, *Crossing Swords: Politics and Religion in Mexico* (New York: Oxford, 1997), 12–13; and Roderic Ai Camp and Shannan L. Mattiace, *Politics in Mexico: The Path of a New Democracy* 7th ed. (New York: Oxford University Press, 2020 [1994]), 166.

3 Roberto Blancarte, *Historia de la Iglesia Católica en México* (México, D.F.: El Colegio Mexiquense/Fondo de Cultura Económica, 1992), 232–235.

4 Soledad Loaeza, "La iglesia católica mexicana y el reformismo autoritario," *Foro Internacional* 25:2 (Oct.–Dec. 1984): 148.

5 Carlos Fazio, *La cruz y el martillo* (México, D.F.: Editorial Joaquín Ortiz/ Planeta, 1987).

6 Carlos Fazio, *Samuel Ruiz: el caminante* (México, D.F.: Espasa Calpe Mexicana S.A., 1994), 62–63. Emphasis in the original.

7 Hartch, *Understanding World Christianity: Mexico*, 172.

8 Camp, *Crossing Swords*, 92.

9 Jennifer Scheper Hughes, "The Niño Jesús Doctor: Novelty and Innovation in Mexican Religion," *Nova Religio: The Journal of Alternative and Emergent Religions* 16:2 (2012): 7.

10 Adopted from Elio Masferrer Kan, *Pluralidad religiosa en México. Cifras y proyecciones* (Buenos Aires: Libros de la Araucaria, 2011), 22–23.

11 Camp, *Crossing Swords*, 30.

12 Monseñor Guillermo Schulenburg Prado, *Memorias del "último Abad de Guadalupe"* (México, D.F.: Miguel Ángel Porrúa, 2003), 100.

13 Soledad Loaeza, *La restauración de la Iglesia católica en la transición mexicana* (México, D.F.: El Colegio de México, 2013), 112.

14 Blancarte, *Historia de la Iglesia Católica*, 374.

15 Schulenburg, 103.

16 Loaeza, *La restauración*, 135.

17 Todd Hartch, *Missionaries of the State: The Summer Institute of Linguistics, State Formation, and Indigenous Mexico, 1935–1985* (Tuscaloosa: University of Alabama Press, 2006).

18 Hartch, *Understanding World Christianity*, 37–38.

19 Virginia Garrard and Justin M. Doran, "Pentecostalism and Neo-Pentecostalism in Latin America," in *The Oxford Handbook of Latin American Christianity* eds. David Thomas Orique, O.P., Susan Fitzpatrick-Behrens, and Virginia Garrard (New York: Oxford University Press, 2020), 304.

20 Garrard and Doran, 292.

21 Blancarte, 355.

22 Hartch, *Understanding World Christianity*, 50.

23 Jason H. Dormady, *Primitive Revolution: Restorationist Religion and the Idea of the Mexican Revolution, 1940–1968* (Albuquerque: University of

New Mexico Press, 2011), 19–62; and Patricia Fortuny Loret de Mola, “La Luz del Mundo, estado laico y gobierno panista. Análisis de una coyuntura en Guadalajara,” *Espiral,* 7:19 (Sept.–Dec. 2000) : 129–149.

24 Fortuny Loret de Mola, “La Luz del Mundo, estado laico y gobierno panista,” 129–149.

25 Elías Camhaji, “The apostle's lair,” *El País* (English), Feb. 19, 2021; Matthew Ormseth, “Judge hikes bail for La Luz del Mundo leader to $90 million,” *Los Angeles Times*, Aug. 6, 2020; and Libor Jany, Matthew Ormseth, and Leila Miller, “La Luz del Mundo church leader pleads guilty to sex abuses charges,” *Los Angeles Times*, June 3, 2022.

26 Matthew Butler, “Catholicism in Mexico, 1910 to the Present,” in *Oxford Research Encyclopedia of Latin American History* (New York: Oxford University Press, Online Publication Date Nov. 2016), 2.

27 Journalist Carmen Aristegui's 2010 interview with Maciel's wife and two sons can be seen here: https://www.youtube.com/watch?v=HtBSn0vq32c.

28 “Editorial: Finally, the Legion's terrible truth,” *National Catholic Reporter*, Dec. 23, 2019.

29 Stafford Poole, C.M., *The Guadalupan Controversies in Mexico* (Stanford: Stanford University Press, 2006), 204.

30 Scheper Hughes, 4.

31 Scheper Hughes, 17.

32 Scheper Hughes, 17–19.

33 R. Andrew Chestnut, *Devoted to Death: Santa Muerte, the Skeleton Saint* (New York: Oxford University Press, 2013), 29; and Wil Pansters, “La Santa Muerte: History, Devotion, and Societal Context,” in *La Santa Muerte in Mexico: History, Devotion, and Society* ed. Wil Pansters (Albuquerque: University of New Mexico Press, 2019), 15–19.

34 Tuckman, 130.

35 Pansters in *La Santa Muerte*, 33, citing Roush, 2014, p. 145.

36 Benjamin T. Smith, “Saints and Demons: Putting La Santa Muerte in Historical Perspective,” in *La Santa Muerte*, 76–80.

37 Marc Lacey, “Speaking God's Language, with a Gangster Dialect,” *New York Times*, July 7, 2010.

38 Masferrer Kan, *Pluralidad religiosa en México*, 75.

39 Butler, 3.

40 Joshua J. McElee, “Francis: ‘No concession’ to those who deny Vatican II teachings,” *National Catholic Reporter*, Feb. 1, 2021.

5

The Women's Revolution

Even more dramatic than contemporary Mexico's unscripted revolution in religious practice has been the revolution in women's lives. The Global Sixties were liberating for some women living in Europe and North America, but most Mexican women were still stuck with traditional gender roles. Change came to Mexico in the 1970s. Modern feminist movements emerged just as the federal government launched family planning programs. As Mexican women gained control over their reproductive lives, they entered the formal and informal economies, not that the country's economic crises in the 1980s gave them much of a choice. Their gender-based concerns became part of larger economic and political agendas. A series of electoral reforms in the early 2000s codified gender quotas; by 2018, Mexican women had achieved parity with men in the national Chamber of Deputies and Senate and in most statehouses. In the span of just two generations, the changes to women's lives at home, in the marketplace, and in politics have been nothing short of breathtaking.

These changes are all the more remarkable given that traditional Mexican culture would seem to place restraints on women. Our Lady of Guadalupe, Mexico's most evocative feminine archetype, is a

Mexico's Unscripted Revolutions: Political and Social Change since 1958,
First Edition. Stephen E. Lewis.

repository of virginal purity and selfless motherhood, a quality known as *abnegación*. Jocelyn Olcott writes that abnegación and everything it entails, including "martyrdom, self-sacrifice, an erasure of self and the negation of one's outward existence—became nearly synonymous with idealized Mexican femininity and motherhood."[1] Abnegación simultaneously exalted women and relegated them to lives of resigned domestic service. When Mexican women launched gender demands in the 1970s, transformed the workforce in the 1980s, and pushed for representation in politics in the 1990s, they challenged deeply ingrained gender expectations. Their victories are a tribute to their tenacity and their ability to take advantage of the openings offered by Mexico's democratic transition.

The Revolution in Family Size

Skeptics did not think it could be done. How could Mexico, with one of the fastest-growing populations in the world, dramatically reduce fertility rates? Wasn't the country too Catholic? Wasn't it too rural and poor? Weren't Mexican men too macho to agree with reduced fertility and smaller families?

And yet the statistics tell another story—a country that averaged 6.8 live births per woman of reproductive age in 1960 and 6.6 in 1970 had lowered that rate to 3.5 by 1990 and 2.75 by 2000. The age of mothers at first childbirth had increased, and more women were spacing their pregnancies. The remarkable decline in fertility rates in Mexico was among the fastest in the world, comparable only to the equally dramatic declines in Colombia, Indonesia, and China. It must be considered among the most significant achievements of the Mexican state. Certainly, it is among the most surprising since pronatalism—the policy and practice of encouraging reproduction—was at the heart of postrevolutionary policy as recently as 1970.

Mexico's pro-natalist policy was rooted in the country's traumatic first century of existence when it lost half of its territory to its aggressive, expansionist northern neighbor. The 1936 Population Law stated the need to increase the population for industrial and agricultural development. It led to the valuation of large, extended families and high fertility. The Mexican government designed programs to send colonists to relatively uninhabited northern states. It restricted the manufacture of contraceptives and prohibited the advertising of family planning services. Well into the 1960s, Mexico's economy grew at twice the rate of the population, and it seemed capable of absorbing an expanding workforce. The assumption that a larger population meant a stronger economy was firmly rooted in the Mexican Revolution.[2]

Large families were also a survival strategy in a country lacking strong social security programs, especially in the countryside. More children meant more hands in the fields and support during old age. Although large families are sometimes depicted as a symptom of degenerate machismo, for Mexicans in the middle decades of the twentieth century, they were sensible adaptations to precarious economic conditions.

In the 1960s, as infant mortality rates dropped worldwide and more children lived to adulthood, international attention turned to the problems associated with rapid population growth. In Mexico, the PRI-government initially resisted international pressures to limit population growth, despite the fact that a young Mexican chemist, Luis Ernesto Miramontes, is credited with co-discovering the chemical compounds that led to the global production of oral contraceptives.[3] As a presidential candidate in 1970, Luis Echeverría—the father of eight—expressed strong pronatalist views, invoking the old axiom "*gobernar es poblar*," to govern is to populate.

What caused Echeverría, as president, to later change course and embrace family planning? For one, Mexico's economic growth rate had begun to slow; its population growth rate had not. The population was growing at a rate of 3.5 percent a year, putting it on pace to double every 20 years. The problems associated with runaway population growth were most evident in Mexico City, which almost quadrupled in size between 1950 and 1975. The sprawling squatter settlement of Ciudad Nezahualcóyotl east of the capital had mushroomed from about 40,000 in 1954 to 2 million residents. The health care, education, housing, and transportation infrastructure simply could not keep pace with the ballooning population. Migrants from the increasingly crowded, impoverished countryside flooded into the cities. Typically, they entered the informal economy and tried to eke out a living on extremely disadvantageous terms. According to the Mexican government's own statistics, 25 million Mexicans—roughly half of the population—had no access to medical services, and between 30 and 40 percent of Mexican children suffered mental or physical retardation because of deficient nutrition. On a 1973 visit to Moscow, Echeverría's wife, First Lady María Esther Zuno, admitted that "the most dramatic problem in my country is the malnutrition of thousands upon thousands of children."[4] Almost half of Mexico's population was under the age of 15, meaning that a vast number of young women would soon be entering their child-bearing years.

When the Echeverría administration began to roll out its family planning programs in April 1972, it received tacit support from an unlikely source—Mexico's Catholic bishops. Just four years after Pope Paul VI's encyclical *Humanae Vitae* condemned all forms of artificial contraception, including the birth control pill and sterilization/tubal ligation, Mexico's bishops issued a pastoral letter that supported the government's early statements on population control. The first draft of the letter was released in September 1972 without authorization from the Holy See. It suggested that couples were free to choose the birth control method that suited them. As Soledad Loaeza notes, "the free interpretation of this document opened the door to the use of contraceptives that had been explicitly condemned by the pope."[5] Subsequent drafts of the letter included important nods to Church teachings but still sanctioned family planning.

The bishops' letter acknowledged that the "demographic explosion" represented a "real and anguishing emergency" for most Mexican families. The letter blamed "irresponsible fertility, aggravated by the presence of socioeconomic injustice." After placing some of the blame on illegitimate births and absentee, macho fathers, it acknowledged that many Mexicans faced unemployment and underemployment, insufficient housing and malnutrition, all of which made it difficult to sustain large families. Moreover, schools were too crowded and inadequate to offer a way out of poverty "despite the government's praiseworthy effort to increase the education budget year after year." In short, "the concrete circumstances of the majority of Mexican families are hard, even inhumane, and a radical improvement is not expected anytime soon." The letter then used Church teachings, especially the Vatican II document *Gaudiem et spes* ("Joy and Hope"), to support government policy and stress the obligations of responsible paternity. Couples planning a family should "discover, sincerely and loyally, which is God's will in the situation in which they find themselves."[6] The government, for its part, presented family planning as a way of avoiding abortions, which the Mexican Church continued to fiercely oppose. It also declared that deciding how many children to have was a basic human right.

Years later, Mexico's bishops adopted a more intransigent stance toward the government's national contraception distribution programs, in line with the Vatican's decree that men and women using "unnatural" contraception were in violation of Church teachings. But increasing numbers of Mexican women were apparently unperturbed by Church admonitions. They opted for a variety of forms of contraception anyway. Specialists agree that the Mexican Church's later intransigence was more a manifestation of the pluralism and dissidence within the Church hierarchy than it was a serious, orchestrated strategy to block government policy. The bishops were also playing a long game with the Mexican state. The Echeverría administration consulted with them frequently and gave them unprecedented, unofficial access to power. In January 1974, the same month that the government's Population Law took effect, the president announced that he would travel to the Vatican to meet with the pope. Later that year, of course, plans for a new Basilica would be announced, with state support. It is likely that the Mexican Church hierarchy realized that too much was at stake to launch organized opposition to the government's plans.

The Population Law created the National Council on Population (CONAPO), which began its work by launching a series of media campaigns aimed at shifting societal attitudes and expectations. The first, called *Vámonos Haciendo Menos* (Let's Make/Become Fewer), aggressively targeted some of the perceived social failings in Mexicans, like machismo and irresponsibility. A typical poster seen at bus stops and in media showed three men sitting at a table, having drinks and talking about the size of their families. An uncharitably drawn oaf says, "How many kids do I have? Heh! In which neighborhood? Because I'm very 'macho.'" A better-dressed drinking companion retorts, "What you are is a deadbeat who supports no-one. Let's make fewer 'machos' and more responsible men."

Another poster targeted the presumed passivity of women. One woman—thin and fashionably dressed—gestures toward the pregnant belly of a sobbing woman and says, "That's why you suffer! You look like a ranch shotgun, always loaded (pregnant) and cornered! Let's become less passive and more useful. Study, improve yourself."[7] Other publicity encouraged rural residents to remain in the countryside. The campaign was suspended after a few months over concerns that it was offending Mexican sensibilities.

The CONAPO's second population control campaign, launched in 1975, was more positive, even as it more directly tackled the issue of overpopulation. The slogan "The Smaller Family Lives Better" was disseminated in various forms of media, including radio and television. In 1976, the CONAPO introduced a third campaign titled *Señora: usted decide si se embaraza* (Ma'am, you decide if you get pregnant). It caused such a furor among men—who felt entirely left out of the decision—that another campaign was launched in 1978 called "Family Planning: It's a Couple's Choice."[8] Meanwhile, the federal government built more hospitals and clinics, especially in rural areas. Posters, pamphlets, short films, and radio dramas, along with advertising campaigns in print media and on TV, bombarded the public with messages about family planning, responsible paternity, and birth control.

The CONAPO's most successful creative venture during these early years was a collaboration with Mexican media giant Televisa. From 1977 through 1986, Televisa produced soap operas that wove family planning content into the plot lines. The first melodrama, *Acompáñame* (Accompany Me), ran from August 1977 to April 1978 and focused on three fictional sisters and the consequences of their reproductive choices. The first sister, Amanda, was a professional who planned her family with her husband. She lived happily and comfortably until her husband became sick with cancer and died, leaving her to raise three children on her own. The second sister, Raquel, married well and became rich, but was so concerned about her figure that she refused to have more than one child. The third sister, Esperanza, did not carefully plan her family. In time, her husband, Efrén, could not support their 10 children and the family became desperately poor. As Efrén turned to alcohol, Esperanza struggled to keep her family together and turned to her first sister, Amanda, for help. Apart from the obvious messaging about family planning, the melodrama stressed the pivotal role of Mexican mothers.

The success of *Acompáñame* can be measured in several ways. The CONAPO reported a dramatic increase in the number of phone calls requesting family planning information. Contraception sales increased, and more than 560,000 women enrolled in family planning clinics, an increase of 33 percent over the previous year. The CONAPO and Televisa followed up the success of *Acompáñame* with three more novellas: *Vamos Juntos* ("Let's Go Together") aired in 1979–1980 and modeled responsible parenthood; *Caminemos* ("Let's Walk") aired in 1980–1981 and promoted sex education for adolescents; and *Nosotras las Mujeres* ("We the Women") aired in 1981 and addressed machismo and highlighted women's fundamental role in family and society. Between 1977 and 1986, when these and other didactic soap operas aired, Mexico experienced a 34 percent decline in its population growth rate.[9] In 1986, Mexico's CONAPO was awarded the United Nations Population Prize for the astonishing success of its population management programs.

Since 1977, the CONAPO has required Mexican clinics and hospitals to promote birth control, with the highest priority given to intrauterine devices (I.U.D.s) and sterilization. The percentage of women using the pill as their form of contraception declined, from 36 percent in 1976 to just 15 percent in 1992, while the number of women opting for tubal ligation as their form of contraception jumped from just 9 percent in 1976 to 43 percent in 1992. I.U.D. use fell slightly, while the number of women opting for traditional methods, like rhythm, withdrawal, and abstinence, was halved. Birth control has always been free in Mexico's public health centers. Today, when a woman of reproductive age encounters a health care worker for any reason, she is offered contraception.[10]

One of the CONAPO's biggest challenges has been to extend reproductive health facilities and services to the Mexican countryside. A 1992 demographic study showed that rural fertility was twice that of urban areas. In states like Chiapas, Guerrero, and Oaxaca, characterized by rural, poor, and largely Indigenous populations, women on average were still having 4.6 children each, while in Mexico City the average was less than half that amount, at 2.2 children per woman. Women in urban areas were 60 percent more likely to practice contraception than rural women, who either lacked information about their options or did not have access to reliable supplies.[11] Throughout the 1990s and into the new millennium, federal efforts focused on extending family planning services to the historically underserved.

Statistics tell part of the story of Mexico's dramatic decline in fertility rates, but they cannot possibly capture what these changes have meant for Mexican families and women's lives. In a span of just two generations, women of childbearing age have gone from having almost seven children each to having slightly more than two. This changes how women view themselves and their roles in society. Further research will likely reveal the myriad ways that Mexican women's lives have changed as they have gained control over their own fertility. For now, however, we turn our attention to the related, parallel emergence of a new kind of Mexican feminism.

Second-Wave Feminisms

Young women did not make explicit gender demands during the tumultuous summer of 1968, as discussed in Chapter 1. But many were *protofeministas*, energized and politicized by the experience. One such woman was Marta Acevedo, who helped launch Women in Solidarity Action (*Mujeres en Acción Solidaria* or MAS) in 1971 and kick off "second-wave" Mexican feminism. On Mother's Day of that year, MAS feminists held a demonstration at Mexico City's Monument to the Mother to protest a materialist holiday that celebrated mothers once a year but expected them to work for free for the remaining 364 days. City authorities had denied permission to hold the rally; police repression was likely. Just as the rally began, however, a busload of participants in the *Señorita México* pageant arrived to leave a floral arrangement at the monument. Feminists holding placards and beauty pageant contestants in miniskirts comingled for a surreal moment. The feared police repression never materialized.[12]

According to the prolific feminist writer and philosopher Eli Bartra, second-wave feminism "is, without a doubt, the most important political and social movement in the second half of the twentieth century."[13] In the 1970s, Mexican feminists focused their movement on the body—on sexuality and abortion, principally, and in loud opposition to rape and sexual assault. They were middle-class, well-educated, and hailed from Mexico City. Those who joined the movement "had not been victims of rape or domestic violence and had not risked their lives undergoing clandestine abortions," Bartra writes. They could abort in safe, hygienic conditions, if necessary. But all had suffered sexual harassment in the streets of Mexico City.[14] The movement was cosmopolitan, influenced by U.S. feminism but also by feminist exiles who had fled authoritarian regimes in Latin America. Many leading Mexican feminists were members of the Mexican Communist Party and held a "deep suspicion of Mexican nationalism, of the PRI, and of Echeverría in particular."[15] They were leery of being coopted and neutralized by Mexico's corporatist state, which was—in fact—advancing elements of the feminist agenda.

One of the women to join Acevedo's MAS in 1971 was Marta Lamas, who would become Mexico's most prominent feminist. The daughter of Argentine immigrants, Lamas has spent more than five decades advancing feminist causes through her advocacy and academic work. She has founded, co-founded, and edited feminist journals, co-founded feminist NGOs (Non-Governmental Organizations), is active in feminist politics, teaches at two Mexican universities, and has been nominated for the Nobel Peace Prize. She traces her political awakening to the 1968 student movement. Relatively privileged, she used her car to transport activists and serve as a lookout. When her then-husband refused to shelter two members of the National Strike Committee in their apartment, she ended their marriage. Three years later, in 1971, she joined MAS and helped organize the first public feminist workshops focused on sexuality, abortion, and voluntary motherhood. She and other MAS members travelled throughout Mexico to raise feminist consciousness and support female factory workers, especially those striking in the garment industry. In 1974, a minority of women in MAS accused the

Figure 5.1 Marta Lamas at a book presentation in Mexico City, 2017. Photo by Tania Victoria/Secretaría de Cultura CDMX. Secretaría de Cultura de la Ciudad de México/Wikimedia Commons/CC-BY SA 2.0

rest of being "insufficiently Marxist."[16] This created the first of many schisms within Mexican feminism, and women like Lamas left MAS to form a new organization called the Women's Liberation Movement (*Movimiento de Liberación de la Mujer*, or MLM).

The emergence of second-wave Mexican feminism coincided with the Echeverría administration's decision to embrace population management, discussed above. In October 1974, when President Echeverría learned that Colombia might be unable to foot the bill to host the first-ever United Nations International Women's Year conference, he leapt at the opportunity to host the conference in Mexico City. Echeverría considered himself a leader of the developing world and openly jockeyed to succeed Kurt Waldheim as secretary-general of the United Nations. To further signal that Mexico's priorities aligned with those of the United Nations, he introduced a constitutional amendment to grant women equal rights to men. The proposed amendment to Article 4 not only mandated legal equality; it also guaranteed the "right to decide in a free, responsible, and informed manner the number and spacing of children."[17] Echeverría's bid worked, and in November, the United Nations chose Mexico to host the conference the following year. The amended Article 4 of the Constitution was passed in the final days of 1974.

In another context, Mexican feminists might have cheered the news that their country would host a major international conference on women's issues. Instead, they were outraged. "To feminist leaders, the idea that Echeverría would burnish his international image by holding himself up as an advocate of women's rights seemed a blatant attempt to coopt their movement," writes Olcott.[18] Adding insult to injury, the Echeverría administration planned to host the conference at the Ministry of Foreign Relations on Tlatelolco Plaza, the site where their comrades had been massacred—likely on Echeverría's orders—just seven years earlier. Mexican feminists boycotted the United Nations conference and instead staged their own.

In 1975, a group of women calling themselves *Colectivo La Revuelta* (The Revolt Collective) split from the MLM and published the first feminist newspaper, called *La Revuelta*. Members of the collective sold their papers in the streets, on university campuses, and outside of cinemas. *La Revuelta* addressed a range of issues that were important to second-wave Mexican feminists. The December 1976 issue was devoted to sexual freedom, contraception, and abortion rights. Its tone was direct and provocative. "We have specific organs, one for reproduction and the other for pleasure—THE CLITORIS," one article declared. Other articles called for the right to a free, safe, and legal abortion as a last resort in the context of an increasingly precarious economy. "The patriarchal society that PROHIBITS ABORTION REQUIRES YOU TO ABORT because if you have a child, it totally washes its hands of the situation," one article read. "Whether or not you earn a salary is your problem; whether your salary covers your expenses is your problem. . .. We demand the right to make love how and when we want and to have all the children that we want but only those that we want."[19] Eli Bartra, a founding member of the collective, later admitted that "our radical way of thinking and acting scared others easily.... We were quite ferocious."[20]

Another article in the December 1976 issue of *La Revuelta* shared *official* statistics on complications from illegal abortions in Mexico. Women typically introduced foreign objects, injected themselves, or drank medicine or something that they believed would cause them to abort. A handful resorted to blows to their bodies. Complications stemming from clandestine abortions were the fifth leading cause of feminine mortality in the country. The statistics also showed that 86 percent of the women who had experienced complications were Catholic; 70 percent were already mothers with numerous children; and 65 percent were married or were in a stable relationship.[21]

Between the late 1970s and the early 1980s, Mexican feminism entered a period of struggle and transition. There were positive signs, as feminist groups started sprouting up outside of Mexico City. Feminists created the Coalition of Feminist Women (*Coalición de Mujeres Feministas*), which attempted to unify various feminist organizations. The inaugural issue of the Coalition's newsletter, *Cihuat*, took immediate aim at the concept of abnegación: "We affirm that passive abnegation will be judged and condemned and upon its death, a human being will be born—a woman."[22] During this time, the notion of voluntary motherhood was expanded to accommodate lesbian sexuality, and the first two lesbian organizations emerged in 1978. In 1979, the National Front for Women's Rights and Liberation (*Frente Nacional por la Liberación y los Derechos de las Mujeres*, or FNALIDM) was created in a second attempt to unite feminist groups, this time with labor unions, leftist political parties, and gay rights organizations. The inclusion of lesbians caused both "happiness and irritation," writes Lamas, because some straight Mexican feminists worried that feminism could be stigmatized as a lesbian issue.[23]

Paradoxically, in the early 1980s, "formal feminist organizations withered, and women's influence expanded."[24] The two large umbrella feminist organizations, the Coalición and the FNALIDM, both disbanded after a failed attempt to introduce a law in Congress that would have legalized abortion. Looking back, Lamas writes that early second-wave feminists favored denunciation over dialogue and showed little interest in building political alliances. "By rejecting traditional political forms, these initial groups enclosed themselves in their revolutionary utopia and their discourse remained imbued in the logic of all or nothing." Lamas adds the searing observation that "women who sacralize their own identity, who feel like total victims or believe themselves to be fundamentally better, more sensitive and honest than men. . .cannot establish political relations amongst themselves and with other people."[25] Many Mexican feminists at this time devoted themselves to their academic careers and created renowned women- or gender-studies programs at major Mexican universities. Others founded and/or collaborated with feminist NGOs, often working with poor women who had been raped or were victims of domestic violence.

The collapse of the Mexican economy beginning in 1982 gave Mexican feminism a new opportunity to reinvent itself on a more popular base. By the middle 1980s, inflation was running at over 100 percent annually; interest rates had skyrocketed; and the Mexican peso, valued at 26 to the U.S. dollar in early 1982, fell to over 2280 to the dollar by 1988. Mexicans had lost their purchasing power at a time when the government was reducing its subsidies of basic food items and utilities. Between 1984 and 1987, the price of beans rose by 757 percent, eggs rose by 480 percent, and milk by 340 percent. Meanwhile, in 1987, the price of gasoline and electricity rose by about 85 percent. Many Mexican men left the country and headed north, looking for work. Increasing numbers of women had little choice but to enter the formal and informal economy. Households were forced to get creative. They cut spending, reduced fertility, and sent more family members into the workforce. "Women and daughters regularly began to contribute to the family purse," writes Victoria Rodríguez. "The old social custom whereby Mexican women worked outside the home only when they were young—that is, before marrying and having children—was no longer an option."[26]

Women who entered the workforce in the 1980s faced a series of obstacles. The postrevolutionary Mexican state had been openly biased against women workers. Organized labor conflated trade unionism with masculinity and a man's right to provide for his family. The CTM often blocked women from taking good-paying jobs; its publications generally ignored major strikes led by women. Confronted with these obstacles, most women had found work in the informal sector. But younger, single women began to make inroads in light industry, electronics assembly, food processing, the garment industry, and footwear. "Finishing-off" assembly plants (*maquiladoras*) along the U.S. border hired women in record numbers because they were seen as temporary, patient workers with nimble hands. Between 1965 and 1985, approximately 80 percent of the workers hired in the maquiladoras were women. Some scholars claim that once women began earning their own paychecks, they could assert themselves in family decision-making and use their salaries to leave abusive situations and form their own households. But others suggest that low-paid, routine factory work was hardly liberating. Women still earned only half as much as their male counterparts, and there is little evidence that men helped with domestic chores. Women, in essence, were working a double shift, a *doble jornada*.

When Mexican women found themselves unable to balance their traditional childrearing duties with their work outside the home, many entered the political arena. The Mexico City earthquake of September 1985 literally jolted feminists into action; their activism dovetailed with a women's movement more rooted in bread-and-butter issues. From this fusion would emerge a more popular feminism. Participants recall that "in 1986, the International Women's Day march was, for the first time, convened by low-income women and industrial workers."[27] At long last, urban, professional, university-educated feminists would "walk together" with working-class and working poor women.

The 1990s was a time of diverse feminisms, including a rural, Indigenous feminism that challenged the sexism and essentialism of Indigenous organizations, on the one hand, and the ethnocentricity of hegemonic feminism, on the other. Indigenous women are the poorest of Mexico's poor, with the highest rates of illiteracy and infant mortality. They have fought battles on multiple fronts, all while struggling to feed their families in a time of economic transition and scarcity. They challenged the Mexican state to recognize their right to cultural differences. But they also pushed the cultural autonomy movement to incorporate gender issues into the struggle. This meant identifying and denouncing certain traditional practices and customs (*usos y costumbres*) like early, arranged marriage and wife-beating. Meanwhile, they have challenged feminists to reject the separatist tendencies that have prevented women in other settings from joining (with men) in political alliances. The relationship between hegemonic feminism and Indigenous women has been fraught at times, to the point where many Indigenous women reject the "feminist" label. Aída Hernández suggests, however, that this tension has benefitted both feminists and the Indigenous autonomy movement. "The feminists were forced to incorporate cultural diversity in their analysis of gender relations," she writes, "and the Indigenous movement had to incorporate gender in its analysis of the ethnic and class inequalities suffered by indigenous peoples."[28]

Indigenous feminism burst onto the national and international scene with the Zapatista insurrection in 1994. Unique among Latin American insurgencies, the Zapatistas gave priority to women's issues. Women comprised about one-third of the Zapatista army, and several Indigenous women held military and political leadership positions in the EZLN. On the eve of the insurrection, the EZLN published the Women's Revolutionary Law. The Law was the result of a protracted process of consultation within Zapatista communities. A 10-point manifesto, it declared—among other things—that women have the right to an education and the right to choose their romantic partners and the number of children that they will have. It also condemned beatings and rape. The EZLN's spokesman, *Subcomandante Marcos*, called this law the "first Zapatista uprising."[29] That the Women's Revolutionary Law echoed demands that were enshrined in Article 4 of the Constitution 20 years earlier suggests a yawning gap between top-down constitutional reforms approved in the capital city and the lived experience of women in rural areas.

Figure 5.2 Zapatista *comandantas* (women commanders) at a rally in Tuxtla Gutierrez, Chiapas, on February 25, 2001. Photo by Yoray Liberman/Getty Images. Yoray Liberman/Getty Images

While scholars celebrated the apparent advance of Zapatista feminism, skepticism came from an unlikely source—*Subcomandante Marcos* himself. In a critique published in August 2004, more than ten years after the January 1 insurrection and one year after the Zapatistas had established regional governing boards known as Good Government Juntas, *Marcos* lamented that a culture of respect for women had still not taken hold.

> While the percentage of female participation in the Clandestine Revolutionary Indigenous Committees is between 33 and 40 percent, in the autonomous councils and the Good Government Juntas it is less than 1 percent on average. Women are still being ignored in the naming of *ejidal* commissioners and municipal agents. Government work is still the prerogative of the men....
>
> And not only that. Even though Zapatista women have had, and have, a fundamental role in the resistance, respect for their rights continues, in some cases, to be just words on paper. Domestic violence has decreased, it is true, but more through the limitations on alcohol consumption than through a new family and gender culture.
>
> It is a shame, but we must be honest: we still cannot give a good report regarding women, in the creation of conditions for their gender development, in a new culture that acknowledges their capacities and aptitudes that have purportedly belonged exclusively to men.[30]

Recent research on Zapatista autonomous communities suggests that women have advanced a feminist agenda through their production collectives, but overall progress remains slow.[31]

If the 1990s was a time of diverse feminisms, it was also a time when feminism could also be invisible. Lamas describes a post-feminist tendency that, she believes, was a reflection of Mexican neoliberalism. Many young women "rejected collective political activism" along with the feminist label, even if they supported key feminist issues like gender equality and reproductive choice. They associated feminism with their mothers' generation, and their participation in the movement was "almost nil."

One issue has consistently pushed young women into the streets, however—gender-based violence and its most extreme manifestation, which is feminicide, a hate crime described as the intentional killing of women or girls by males because they are female. The matter began to attract national and international attention in 1993. Young, dark-skinned, poor or working-class women with long, dark hair were being murdered (often after being raped and tortured) in and around the border metropolis of Ciudad Juárez. Their bodies were left to decompose in the desert. Most of the victims had left confining homes and poverty in remote villages across Mexico to work in Juárez's maquiladoras. In time, over 400 women had been killed. Some analysts suggested that global capitalism's use of unskilled, "cheap" women's labor made these independent, vulnerable young women seem disposable to society at large. Some maquiladora supervisors sexualized their female workers by encouraging them to dress fashionably. Industry-wide "Señorita Maquiladora" beauty contests further trivialized them.[32]

Compounding the tragedy was the bewildering incompetence of the criminal justice system in Juárez and in the state of Chihuahua. Victims' families and activists were stupefied when government authorities responded to their inquiries lethargically and often dismissed the victims as loose women or prostitutes. Did the police have something to hide? Or were they simply (and colossally) incompetent? Was there one killer, or several? What was the role of organized crime in all of this? Amid all these questions, one thing became clear—Mexican law enforcement was woefully unprepared to solve these crimes. The authorities misidentified corpses, tortured suspects, falsified evidence, threatened lawyers, and failed to file reports, conduct autopsies, or obtain semen analyses. The rise of feminicides correlated with the rise of drug trafficking in the area. The cartels threatened and corrupted already weak police institutions at the municipal and state levels. "Insufficient training, inaccurate identification of victims and suspects, the lack of DNA testing facilities, and the excessive caseloads of investigators point to pervasive problems of police training and resource capacity," write Edmonds-Poli and Shirk.[33]

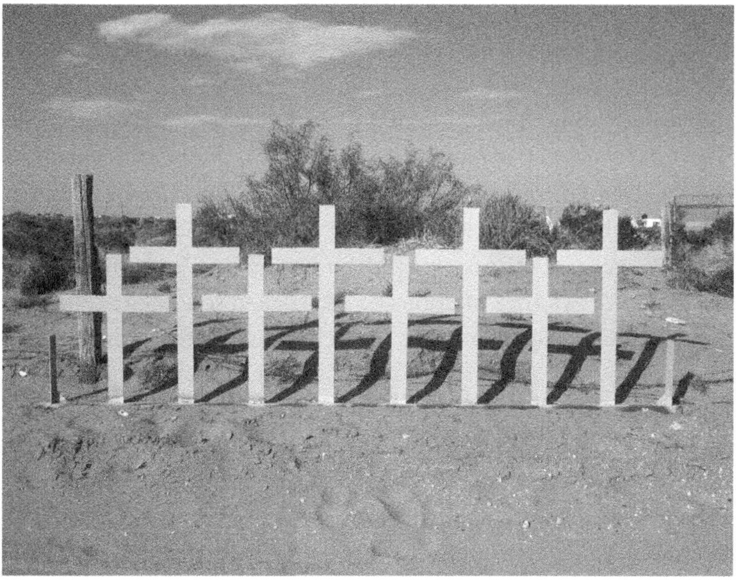

Figure 5.3 Pink crosses placed in Lomas del Poleo Planta Alta in Ciudad Juárez, Chihuahua, where the bodies of eight feminicide victims were found in 1996. iose/Wikimedia Commons/Public domain

Feminists and human rights activists worked with victims' mothers to increase awareness and expose police impunity. They placed pink and black crucifixes across the city to emphasize the gender dimension of these murders. National and international pressure, much of it led by feminist groups, forced the Chihuahua state legislature to approve a massive justice-reform package in 2006 that included training in modern forensics procedures. Unfortunately, just as the authorities began wading through the backlog of unsolved feminicides, Ciudad Juárez became the national epicenter of drug violence from 2008 to 2012, adding to the dispiriting backlog of unsolved crimes in the area.

For many women, there is no place more dangerous than their own home. Women are twice as likely as men to be killed at home by someone with whom they have a relationship. Domestic violence is widespread in contemporary Mexico, despite recent changes to the law meant to protect women's human rights. A 2016 study found that 41 percent of Mexican women 15 years of age or older had experienced some form of sexual violence; *26 percent had suffered violence at the hands of their partner during the previous 12 months.*[34] The Mexican police and local prosecutors are typically incapable of dealing with domestic violence and protecting its victims. State attorneys general offices are reluctant to issue restraining orders and often urge victims of domestic violence to seek mediation with their partner or spouse rather than press charges.[35] Local police often do not take domestic violence seriously, can be reluctant to intervene in what they consider to be a private matter, and sometimes revictimize women by suggesting that they resolve the situation of violence through sex.[36] Machista violence has been condemned by all political parties, by every government and every religious organization. But recent history shows that activists must continue to apply pressure if the scourge of gender-based violence is to be addressed effectively.

The Push for Political Representation

In the 1990s, the evolution of Mexican feminisms intersected with Mexico's slow, steady democratization process. In the 1970s and 1980s, most feminists had regarded politics as an illegitimate and exclusively masculine activity. Some leftist feminists participated in Cuauhtémoc Cárdenas's presidential campaign in 1988, however. They joined the PRD when it formed one year later. The new party became a key forum for advancing women's demands. Feminists took advantage of the democratic opening to lobby for formal political representation. Lamas describes it as a time when the feminist movement evolved from "protest" to "proposal." No longer dismissed as "man-haters" and "bra-burners" as they had been in the 1970s, female activists were taken seriously by the Mexican state and society, and gender issues were advanced through NGOs and political parties.[37]

This new strategy of coalition-building and working with mainstream political parties bore fruit quickly. Feminist legislators from across the political spectrum worked to ratchet up the penalties for rape and to protect victims. In Mexico City, they worked with the attorney general to create two new agencies focused on sex crimes. Thanks to their efforts, victims could report crimes to all-female staff that included social workers, therapists, and legal advisors.[38]

Feminists also pushed the fledgling PRD to make progress on the stubborn issue of reproductive rights. In the context of gradual democratization, women lobbied to make these rights part of the larger movement to redefine modern citizenship.[39] Feminists scored a small, gradualist victory in 2000 when Mexico City's archaic penal code was updated to allow abortion in cases of rape, serious fetal malformation, and when the woman's life was endangered. In 2007, Mexico City's PRD-dominated legislature voted to make abortion free and legal during the first trimester. After surviving a challenge in the Supreme Court brought by the PAN, abortion in Mexico City became legal, a constitutional right, in 2008. Catholic bishops and their allies in the PAN and the PRI quickly maneuvered to prevent the depenalization of abortion elsewhere in the country. They reformed the constitutions in 17 of Mexico's 32 states to assert that life begins at conception and stiffened penalties against women who aborted (and their doctors). Hundreds of women legally challenged these restrictions in national and international courts.[40]

Women also mobilized to take political power into their own hands. Mexico has been a surprisingly fertile ground for women to make political inroads. The proportional representation system—which selects 200 of the 500 seats in the Chamber of Deputies based on regional party preferences—gave politically active women a second pathway to political power. Another factor was the no-reelection clause in the Constitution of 1917. Until very recently, this clause prevented incumbency; it guaranteed that seats in the Senate and the Chamber of Deputies were turned over every six and three years, respectively. This opened the system to nonincumbents, including women.

The key to women's recent success in Mexican national politics has been gender quotas. These require that all political parties designate women to fill a certain percentage of candidate slots in any given election. Currently, 80 countries worldwide use some form of gender quota to boost women's representation in politics, including almost all of the countries in the Americas.[41] In Mexico, the quota innovator was the center-left PRD. At the PRD's Second National Congress, in 1993, women activists pushed for gender quotas for candidacies and party leadership posts. After the quota issue failed to gain traction in smaller committees, the activists had one last chance at the concluding plenary session of the Congress. Kathleen Bruhn writes that "at that point, decision-making became much more public: delegates at the plenary session had to vote by raising a ballot card in full view of national media and potential allies." This put pressure on male party members not to be seen as "'the bastard who said no'" to women's participation. The measure narrowly passed. It stipulated that no gender could have a representation greater than 70 percent on committees and candidate lists.[42]

Once the PRD agreed to gender quotas, women in the PRI successfully applied pressure on their party leaders. The PAN, meanwhile, resisted formal gender quotas. But PANista women used the *threat* of quotas to get more women included as alternates (*suplentes*) on candidate lists. Between 1991 and 1998, feminist activists from across the political spectrum met to discuss strategies to advance women candidates. Ultimately, they gained a foothold in the PRD, the newest, least institutional party. The PRD's leftist discourse of egalitarianism made it more supportive of quotas, and "women literally dared their opponents to stand up and be counted."[43]

Internal party quotas in the PRD and PRI inspired the IFE (Federal Electoral Institute) to recommend a 30 percent quota for *all* parties in the 2000 national election. But parties found workarounds that undermined the goal of gender representation. Women were often placed near the bottom of their parties' proportional representation lists, or were assigned to run in unwinnable single-member districts. The PRI and PAN also used female alternates (*suplentes*) to meet the quota meaning that, realistically, they had little chance of actually being seated in the Chamber. This is because in Mexico, voters select both the main candidate, the "owner" or *propietario*, and their alternate, the *suplente*, on the same ticket. The alternate takes over in the unlikely event that the owner must abandon the seat.

Reforms to the federal electoral code attempted to address the shortcomings that became apparent in previous electoral cycles. In 2002, for example, the IFE approved reforms that included a placement mandate so that women were not stuck at the bottom of their parties' proportional representation lists. It also specified that gender quotas could not be met with female alternates. Results from the 2003 election were positive; women won 23 percent of the seats up for election, a seven-point improvement over the 2000 election, moving Mexico up in the world ranking of women in legislative office from 55th to 29th. Most of these seats were won through proportional representation.[44]

Another round of electoral reforms in 2008 raised the gender quota from 30 percent to 40 percent. But in congressional elections held the following year, several of the victorious female candidates in the Chamber of Deputies resigned immediately so that their alternates—usually boyfriends, husbands, or male mentors—could replace them. Dubbed "Juanitas," they had agreed to add their names to proportional representation lists so that their parties could meet the new, more stringent gender quotas, with the understanding that they would later cede their seats to men. This outrageous attempt to undermine the spirit and intent of the gender quotas led to yet another round of reforms to the federal election law requiring *propietarios* and *suplentes* to be of the same sex.[45]

In 2014, Mexico's three main political parties signed a package of legislation that included a constitutional amendment mandating gender parity—a 50 percent gender quota—in all national and state legislatures. True gender parity in politics is still a work in progress, however. "Equal numbers do not mean equal influence," write Edmonds-Poli and Shirk. "Men still dominate party caucuses and congressional power centers that make committee assignments and set the legislative agenda."[46] And even parity itself is not assured, as political parties continue to find ways around gender quotas. The "Juanita" phenomenon resurfaced at the state and municipal levels, and in the 2021 midterm elections, 18 men from a minor political party in Tlaxcala registered as transexual women to get around the quota requirement.[47]

Even if we allow for the boundless creativity of Mexico's political parties, women will likely continue to close the gender gap in politics. Women are more likely to participate in elections than men. In the 2015 midterm elections, for example, 50.89 percent of registered women voted, compared to 42.95 percent of men, a difference of almost 8 percentage points. This margin was roughly duplicated three years later, in the 2018 election, when 66.2 percent of registered women voted, compared to 58.1 percent of men. Mexican women are also more likely than men to join political parties and view democracy in positive terms. Whether gender parity at the national and state levels will help women make progress on several issues that disproportionately affect them, like gender discrimination and unequal pay, domestic violence, and reproductive choice, remains to be seen.

Conclusions

The lives of Mexican women have changed dramatically since the early 1970s. The federal government's interest in population control and poverty reduction coincided with second-wave feminism and ongoing economic crises that exerted a downward pressure on fertility rates. Women increasingly draw their own salaries, have a higher status within their families, and make decisions about family size. Since 80 percent of Mexico's population now resides in cities, where children have less economic value, part of the rationale for large families no longer applies to the bulk of the population.

In 2020, Mexico's fertility rate was 2.1 live births for every woman of reproductive age, which is considered the fertility replacement rate. Important regional differences in fertility persist. The lowest fertility rate, not surprisingly, is in Mexico's largest city, the capital, at just 1.47 per woman of childbearing age; the highest rate is in largely rural Chiapas, at 2.69 per woman. Demographers estimate that by 2050, Mexican women of childbearing age will average about 1.7 children each, well below the fertility replacement rate. At that point, Mexico will enter a new kind of demographic crisis, as a smaller population of workers will be asked to support a larger population of retirees.

The evolution of Mexican feminism during this period, from "protest" to "proposal," coincided with the agony of Mexico's statist economic model and its transition to democracy. Concerns that used to be the domain of a few dozen educated middle-class women in the 1970s went mainstream when they fused with the popular feminist movement of the 1980s. Women crossed party lines in the 1990s to push for gender quotas in politics. We should know soon whether today's gender parity in state and national politics produces a better democracy.

Despite women's undeniable recent gains, there is still much work to do. Mexico is still a dangerous place for women. *Machista* violence and feminicides have drawn national and international attention, but they show little sign of abating. On Mexican television, young female models "with impossible cleavage" present the daily weather forecast. "Stunning curves, long legs, and miniskirts—the shorter the better—reduce women to objects of consumption."[48] And Mexico City, the epicenter of Mexican feminism for decades, is still a place where the public transit system sets aside seats for women because otherwise the levels of sexual harassment are insufferable. In the subway (Metro), entire cars at the front of trains are reserved exclusively for women; on the Metrobus, the first half of the long, articulated buses are likewise reserved. This, is in a city that is home to some of Latin America's leading feminists and the country's best institutions of higher learning, where abortion on demand has been available since 2007, where half of the city's 16 mayors are women and where equal numbers of women and men sit on the city's legislative assembly and worked alongside a female governor, Claudia Sheinbaum (2018–2023).

Notes

1 Olcott, *Revolutionary Women*, 15–16; see also Rosario Castellanos, "La abnegación: una virtud loca," *Excélsior*, Feb. 21, 1971.

2 Ann Blum, *Domestic Economies* (Lincoln: University of Nebraska Press, 2010), 131–132; and Carlos Brambila, "Mexico's Population Policy and Demographic Dynamics: The Record of Three Decades," in *Do Population Policies Matter? Fertility and Politics in Egypt, India, Kenya, and Mexico* (New York: Population Council, 1998), 161.

3 Gabriela Soto Laveaga, *Jungle Laboratories: Mexican Peasants, National Projects, and the Making of the Pill* (Durham: Duke University Press, 2009), 66–70.

4 "Mexico Offers Family-Planning Help," *New York Times*, May 27, 1974.

5 Soledad Loaeza, "La iglesia católica mexicana y el reformismo autoritario," *Foro Internacional* 25:2 (Oct.–Dec. 1984), 154.

6 "Mensaje del episcopado al pueblo de México sobre la paternidad responsable," *Demografía y economía* 7:01 (1973): 124–134.

7 https://www.dememoria.mx/inedita/vamonos-haciendo-menos/

8 Gabriela Soto Laveaga, "'Let's Become Fewer': Soap Operas, Contraception, and Nationalizing the Mexican Family in an Overpopulated World," *Sexuality Research & Social Policy* 4:3 (September 2007): 25.

9 William N. Ryerson, "The Effectiveness of Entertainment Mass Media in Changing Behavior." Retrieved April 14, 2021 from the Population Media Center website: http://www.populationmedia.org/wp-content/uploads/2008/02/effectiveness-of-entertainment-education-112706.pdf; see also Alan Riding, "Soap Opera in Mexico Dramatizing Birth Control," *New York Times*, Jan. 5, 1982.

10 Matthew Gutmann, *Fixing Men: Sex, Birth Control, and AIDS in Mexico* (Berkeley: University of California Press, 2007), 55.

11 Brambila, 181–183.

12 One month later, however, students were murdered just blocks away in what is remembered as the Corpus Christi massacre. Lamas, "Del 68 a hoy," 275.

13 Eli Bartra, "¿Y siguen las brujas conspirando? En torno a las luchas feministas en México," in *Las políticas del subjeto en Nuestra América* coords. Francesca Gargallo and Rosario Galo Moya (México, D.F.: UACM, 2013), 180.

14 Eli Bartra, "Tres décadas de neofeminismo en México," in Eli Bartra, Anna M. Fernández Poncela and Ana Lau, *Feminismo en México, ayer y hoy* (México, D.F.: Colección Molinos de Viento, 2002), 47.

15 Jocelyn Olcott, *International Women's Year: The Greatest Consciousness-Raising Event in History* (New York: Oxford, 2017), 57.

16 Adriana Ortiz-Ortega and Mercedes Barquet, "Gendering Transition to Democracy in Mexico," *Latin American Research Review* Special Issue 45 (2010): 113; and Marta Lamas, "Mis diez primeros años: el MAS y el MLM," *fem* (October 1996): 9.

17 Quoted in Olcott, *International Women's Year*, 55.

18 Olcott, *International Women's Year*, 56–57.

19 *La Revuelta* 3 (December 1976). Emphasis in the original.

20 Eli Bartra, "El Colectivo La Revuelta o de cuando las brujas conspiraron," *fem* 20: 163 (Oct. 1996), 20–21; the collective published a selection of its writings in Eli Bartra, María Brumm, Chela Cervantes, Bea Faith, Lucero González, Dominque Guillemet, Berta Hiriart, and Ángeles Necoechea, *La Revuelta: Reflexiones, testimonios y reportajes de mujeres en México, 1975–1983* (México, D.F.: Martín Casillas Editores, 1983).

21 "Algunos datos sobre el aborto," *La Revuelta* 3 (December 1976).

22 "Trayectoria," *Cihuat: Voz de la Coalición de Mujeres* 1:1 (May 1977).

23 Lamas, "Mis diez primeros años," 13–14.

24 Marta Lamas, Alicia I. Martínez, María Luisa Tarrés, and Esperanza Tuñón, "Building Bridges: The Growth of Popular Feminism in Mexico," in *The Challenge of Local Feminisms: Women's Movements in Global Perspective* (Boulder: Westview Press, 1995), 334.

25 Marta Lamas, "De la protesta a la propuesta: el feminismo en México a finales del siglo XX," in *Historia de las mujeres en España y América Latina Vol. IV: Del siglo XX a los umbrales del XXI* coords. Guadalupe Gómez-Ferrer, Gabriela Cano, Dora Barrancos, and Asunción Lavrin (Madrid: Cátedra, 2006), 906, 912.

26 Victoria Elizabeth Rodríguez, *Women in Contemporary Mexican Politics* (Austin: University of Texas Press, 2003), 50–51.

27 Lamas, et al.,"Building Bridges," 334.

28 Rosalva Aída Hernández Castillo, "Toward a Culturally Situated Women's Rights Agenda: Reflections from Mexico," *Women's Movements in the Global Era: The Power of Local Feminisms* ed. Amrita Basu (Boulder: Westview Press, 2010), 325–326, 328, 339–340; see also Sonia Toledo Tello and Anna María Garza Caligaris, "Gender and Stereotypes

in the Social Movements of Chiapas," in *Dissident Women: Gender and Cultural Politics in Chiapas* eds. Shannon Speed, R. Aída Hernández Castillo, and Lynn M. Stephen (Austin: University of Texas Press, 2006), 97–114.

29 *La Jornada*, January 30, 1994.

30 Subcomandante Insurgente Marcos, "Leer un video. Segunda parte: Dos fallas," *La Jornada*, México, D.F., Aug. 21, 2004.

31 Mariana Mora, *Kuxlejal Politics. Indigenous Autonomy, Race, and Decolonizing Research in Zapatista Communities* (Austin: University of Texas Press, 2017), 149–171, 214.

32 Jessica Livingston, "Murder in Juárez: Gender, Sexual Violence, and the Global Assembly Line," *Frontiers: A Journal of Women Studies* 25:1 (2004): 67; see also Norma Iglesias Prieto, *Beautiful Flowers of the Maquiladora: Life Histories of Women Workers in Tijuana* (Austin: University of Texas Press, 2001 [1997]).

33 Edmonds-Poli and Shirk, *Contemporary Mexican Politics*, 4th ed., 272; see also Kathleen Staudt and Gabriela Montoya, "Violence and Activism at the Mexico-United States Border," in *Feminist Agendas and Democracy in Latin America* ed. Jane S. Jaquette (Durham: Duke University Press, 2009), 187, 192.

34 INEGI, "Encuesta Nacional sobre la Dinámica de las Relaciones en los Hogares (EDIREH), 2016," Aug. 18, 2017.

35 Amnesty International, *Women's Struggle for Justice and Safety: Violence in the Family in Mexico*, 2008.

36 Sonia M. Frías, "Resisting Patriarchy within the State," *Women's Studies International Forum* 33:6 (2010): 546.

37 Rodríguez, 110.

38 Rodríguez, 93.

39 Marta Lamas, "The Feminist Movement and the Development of Political Discourse on Voluntary Motherhood in Mexico," *Reproductive Health Matters* 5:10 (November 1997), 58, 60, 61.

40 Marta Lamas, "Cuerpo y política: la batalla por despenalizar al aborto," in *Un fantasma recorre el siglo: luchas feministas en México, 1910–2010* coords. Gisela Espinosa Damián and Ana Lau Jaiven (México, D.F.: UAM-Xochimilco/Conacyt/Ecosur/Editorial Itaca, 2011), 196–204.

41 See the International Institute for Democracy and Electoral Assistance website at https://www.idea.int/data-tools/data/gender-quotas.

42 Kathleen Bruhn, "Whores and Lesbians: Political Activism, Party Strategies, and Gender Quotas in Mexico," *Electoral Studies* 23 (2003), 110.

43 Bruhn, 117.

44 Lisa Baldez, "Primaries vs. Quotas: Gender and Candidate Nominations in Mexico, 2003," *Latin American Politics and Society*, 49:3 (Fall 2007), 71, 77–78, 88.

45 Caroline C. Beer and Roderic Ai Camp, "Democracy, Gender Quotas, and Political Recruitment in Mexico," *Politics, Groups, and Identities* 4:2 (2016), 186.

46 Edmonds-Poli and Shirk, 189; see also https://cnnespanol.cnn.com/2018/08/31/igualdad-de-mujeres-y-hombres-en-el-congreso-de-mexico-si-pero-no-todo-es-como-lo-pintan/

47 Carmen Morán Breña, "Paridad electoral con falsas trans en México," *El País*, May 15, 2021.

48 Almudena Barragán, "Dos muestras de violencia contra la mujer cada hora: el machismo que impregna la televisión mexicana," *El País*, June 27, 2021.

6

Finally, a Democracy Without Adjectives?[1]

In 2000, Mexico completed an improbable democratic transition, ending more than seven decades of one-party rule. But essential elements of the old regime remained, including its corporatist structure, its authoritarian criminal justice system, and a legacy of clientelism, corruption, and impunity. Could Mexico's electoral democracy pull the rest of the country onto a sounder, more democratic footing? This chapter explores whether Mexico is becoming a consolidated democracy, that is, a political system characterized by the rule of law, increased transparency and accountability, increased respect for human rights, the subordination of the armed forces to civilian control, and a citizenry that embraces democratic beliefs and practices.[2]

The PAN in the Driver's Seat: 2000–2012

Getting elected proved to be the easy part for President Vicente Fox. Although the PRI had lost its absolute majority in both chambers of Congress, it still held more seats than any other party and it could work with smaller, satellite parties to block Fox's legislative initiatives. Twenty-one of Mexico's 32 governors were PRIístas. Thanks to efforts

Mexico's Unscripted Revolutions: Political and Social Change since 1958, First Edition. Stephen E. Lewis.

to decentralize political control, governors had become powerful and they had money to burn. They had become the "new viceroys," benefitting from unprecedented money transfers from Mexico City.[3] Mexico's erstwhile hegemonic party also controlled virtually every state legislature, most municipalities, and the main unions and peasant corporations. But hadn't the PAN been negotiating with the PRI since 1989? Didn't it share the PRI's neoliberal vision? And didn't Fox enjoy a *bono democrático*, a sense of democratic legitimacy and widespread goodwill that might facilitate real change?

Most analysts today feel that the Fox administration failed to put Mexican democracy on a more solid footing. Instead of dismantling Mexico's corrupt corporatist system, it tried to harness it. Instead of pushing hard to investigate the past crimes of the PRI-government, as candidate Fox had promised, President Fox pulled back because he needed PRI votes if he had any hope of getting his legislative agenda through Congress. Shortly after taking office, Fox called for the drafting of a new constitution. But the PRI, anxious to retain its privileges, held veto power over constitutional amendments and effectively blocked that initiative. The Fox administration had a mixed record on democratic institution building. On the one hand, it created the National Commission to Prevent Discrimination (CONAPRED) and the National Freedom of Information Institute (*Instituto Nacional de Transparencia, Acceso a la Información y Protección de Datos Personales,* or INAI), which was designed to promote transparency in government spending. But his administration negotiated with the PRI to politicize the crown jewel of Mexican democratization, the IFE, and undermine its autonomy.[4] Lastly, Fox intervened in the 2006 presidential election in a blatant attempt to eliminate the strongest center-left candidate from the contest.

The Fox administration also failed to transform Mexico's security and judicial institutions into something more appropriate to a democracy. Multiparty electoral competition does not necessarily translate into essential military, policing, and judicial reforms. New democracies need to dismantle the networks of state repression and criminality that were built during authoritarianism. Otherwise, "thin" electoral democracy can lead to destabilization.[5] Although this was not apparent during the Fox years, which were relatively peaceful, Fox's successors would find themselves embroiled in ongoing struggles with deadly drug trafficking organizations.

In the run-up to the 2006 presidential election, President Fox—the beneficiary of strengthened democratic institutions—tried to wield his power in a profoundly undemocratic way to shape the outcome. The 2000 presidential election had pitted two candidates and parties (PRI and PAN) that largely agreed on political and economic policy. But the frontrunners in the 2006 election offered starkly different proposals for the country. Felipe Calderón was a lifelong PANista, son of one of the party's founders. He promised to continue the neoliberal project, now entering its third decade. The PRD's Andrés Manuel López Obrador (known as AMLO) pledged a return to nationalist, state-led development and swore to halt the gradual privatization of the national petroleum industry, PEMEX. Their bitter clash—and Calderón's razor-thin margin of victory—produced a post-electoral conflict that truly tested the strength of Mexico's electoral institutions.

AMLO, the dominant figure in the Mexican left since 2000, had been victimized—twice—by PRIísta fraud. In 1988, the National Democratic Front recruited him to run for governor of Tabasco. He lost that rigged election.[6] Six years later, he lost another gubernatorial contest in Tabasco, this time to Roberto Madrazo. Madrazo spent $50 million on his campaign, about $135 USD for every vote won.[7] The PRI also resorted to the kind of fraud that it used in the 1988 presidential election—the vote-tallying computer mysteriously blacked out, then turned back on again with 4% fewer votes cast.[8] After Madrazo's "victory" was announced, AMLO led two months of oil field takeovers and street protests in Tabasco, followed by a protest march to Mexico City. When President Zedillo tried to force Madrazo's resignation, Tabasco's PRIístas threatened widespread violence. Zedillo backed down. For the first time since the 1930s, a governor had defied the president and gotten away with it. Many saw it as a sign that the federal PRI had lost its ability to discipline local political machines. Madrazo took office, and AMLO took his struggle to Mexico City, where he was elected mayor in 2000.

López Obrador was a broadly popular mayor with his eye on the presidency. To prevent AMLO from running in the 2006 election, President Fox and the PAN—with support from the PRI—tried to disqualify him. Fox's attorney general attempted to prosecute AMLO in 2004 for bypassing a Supreme Court order and allowing the construction of a hospital access road on expropriated land. This initiated legal proceedings that would have barred AMLO from running for office until the case was resolved. No Mexican politician had ever been charged for such a minor offense. AMLO vehemently denounced the PRI-PAN pact and began referring to the two parties as the "PRIAN." By combining both party names, AMLO suggested that they were one and the same. AMLO organized mass mobilizations and forced Fox to back down. (The president saved face by firing his attorney general.) Years of struggle against the PRI had taught AMLO that when the political system failed him, he could mobilize his supporters and hope for a moral (and sometimes tangible) victory.[9]

When the 2006 presidential campaign began, López Obrador was the clear frontrunner. But his lead began to shrink as PAN candidate Calderón ran a fiercely negative campaign that labeled AMLO "a danger to Mexico," a leftist extremist, a clone of Venezuela's Hugo Chávez. AMLO and the PRD complained that the IFE was biased against him. AMLO's rhetoric hardened and his appeal narrowed. He ended up losing the election by about one-half of a percentage point (233,831 votes out of a total of over 41,700,000 cast), the kind of close election that in the 1990s might have prompted a *concertacesión*.

AMLO and his followers refused to recognize Calderón's victory and demanded a full recount of every ballot cast. But Mexican electoral regulations at that time did not allow for full recounts; instead, legal challenges could be filed in districts where alleged violations of electoral law had occurred. AMLO's supporters persisted. They blocked Mexico City's Paseo de La Reforma, the capital's most important thoroughfare, for six weeks. They rightly alleged that President Fox had interfered in the campaign and claimed that the PAN had tied the provision of social services to partisan support. They also argued that the IFE had committed several procedural errors in the vote tabulation. The prominent nongovernmental organization Alianza Cívica cited party finance violations and vote-buying in the electoral process (all three major parties were guilty) but otherwise claimed that Mexico had made progress in the 2006 election. The electoral court performed a recount of 9% of the ballot boxes that revealed no widespread pattern of determinant and deliberate fraud.[10] López Obrador still refused to concede. On September 16, Mexican Independence Day, he pronounced himself Mexico's *presidente legítimo*. On November 20, Mexico's Day of the Revolution, ten days before president-elect Calderón could be sworn in, AMLO went through a preemptive ceremony of installation as Mexico's "legitimate" president and announced the creation of a parallel government.

The 2006 post-electoral conflict took a serious toll on all the protagonists—president-elect Calderón, the IFE, the PRD, and AMLO himself. AMLO's popularity began to wane during the blockade of Reforma and fell further when his supporters forcibly took control of the Chamber of Deputies to prevent the swearing-in of president-elect Calderón.[11] Calderón had to contend with the fact that about one-third of Mexican voters felt the election had been fraudulent. Immediately following his inauguration ceremony, he launched his war on Mexico's drug trafficking organizations. He thought it would be an easy fix to an acute political crisis. "Security issues were largely absent during the campaign," write Guillermo Trejo and Sandra Ley, "but the incoming president declared that the fight against the drug cartels, crime, and insecurity was his administration's top priority."[12] Days later, Calderón deployed the first of 16 military operations to quell growing inter-cartel violence. The man who had campaigned as the "president of employment" ended up using tens of thousands of soldiers and federal police to fight a poorly planned war, with tragic consequences.

Early in the Calderón sexenio, Mexico's main parties in the Congress agreed to rewrite most of the federal electoral code to avoid a repeat of the 2006 post-electoral conflict. They introduced sweeping reforms that shortened the legal general campaign season to just ninety days and prohibited the sale and purchase of campaign advertising in electronic media. Henceforth, the IFE would allocate access to the mass media for election purposes.[13] In response to AMLO's strident complaints about Fox's interference in the election, the electoral code now strictly prohibited presidential intromission in the process. Equally noteworthy was the prohibition of negative advertising. The IFE was authorized to order the suspension of advertisements deemed unlawful, especially those that "denigrated" a candidate, a political party, or institutions. "Censorship was thus adopted to prevent campaigning that many believed pushed Mexico dangerously to the brink of violence in 2006," wrote one political scientist.[14]

Calderón and the Mexican state survived AMLO's postelectoral challenge, but an estimated 70,000 Mexicans—more than the number of U.S. soldiers killed during the Vietnam war—perished in drug-related violence between 2006 and 2012. Another 26,000 Mexicans were forcibly disappeared. More than 300 local officials, political candidates and party activists were targeted for assassination. Worst of all, Calderón's war on the cartels had not worked. At the end of his sexenio, 95% of the cocaine consumed in the U.S. still passed through Mexico. Meanwhile, Mexico's criminal underworld had morphed and mutated and multiplied like a Hydra head and became harder to fight. The five major cartels fragmented into more than sixty, and the street gangs working for them multiplied from dozens to hundreds.[15] These groups expanded their range of activities to include extortion and kidnapping for ransom. They plundered mines, illegally logged forests, and stole gasoline and oil from pipelines.

The Calderón sexenio was marked by several especially appalling incidents—the 2010 massacre of 15 people at a teenager's birthday party in Ciudad Juárez in a case of apparent mistaken identity; the 2011 discovery of mass graves in Tamaulipas containing 196 bodies of Central and South American migrants; the discovery that same year of mass graves in Durango containing another 250 bodies; and the murder and incineration of as many as 300 people in Allende,

Coahuila by the Zetas drug cartel and local police.[16] Mutilated corpses were hung from highway overpasses with nauseating frequency. This appalling toll was made even worse by the fact that so few of these deaths and disappearances were investigated. It was as if the victims had never existed.

The December 2019 arrest of Calderón's top security chief, Genaro García Luna, in the United States lent credence to the rumor that the Calderón administration had fought a partial, partisan war against drug-trafficking organizations. García Luna headed Mexico's Ministry of Public Security from 2006 to 2012, a cabinet-level position, and was the architect of the "decapitation" strategy that targeted drug kingpins. A Brooklyn jury in February 2023 convicted him of receiving millions of dollars from the Sinaloa drug cartel in exchange for letting the cartel operate with impunity and traffic drugs into the U.S.[17] If Mexico's top cop was taking bribes from Joaquín "El Chapo" Guzmán's criminal organization, what could be expected of the outgunned state and municipal police?

In a tragic turn, federalism and democratization dismantled the mechanisms that had kept drug violence in check during the years of PRI hegemony, when top officials linked to the Federal Security Directorate (DFS) managed Mexico's criminal underworld. Drug traffickers did not need to build up private militias or fight turf wars because the DFS protected them and managed drug trafficking routes. When the DFS was dissolved in 1985, its functions devolved to state attorneys general and state police. They took over the task of managing drug-trafficking organizations. When opposition parties began winning gubernatorial elections in northern states, they appointed new personnel in state attorneys' offices and the state judicial police. This injected uncertainty into the criminal underworld. Drug lords responded by creating their own armies. Once they had the capacity to protect themselves and their trafficking routes, they were also poised to take advantage of subsequent democratization experiences in other states and send militias to conquer rivals' territories.[18] "When new democratic elites fail to reform authoritarian sources of state coercive power and leave a long history of state impunity for gross human rights violations intact,—as Mexican political elites did in 2000—democratic institutions are likely to become intimately intertwined with organized crime," write Trejo and Ley. Their sober conclusion is that democratization can trigger large-scale criminal violence.[19]

Additional factors help explain the surge of violence in democratic Mexico. The collapse of Mexico's protectionist economic model and cuts in agrarian subsidies pushed tens of thousands of unemployed, impoverished Mexicans into the drug trade. The passage of NAFTA and the dramatic increase in the flow of goods across the U.S.-Mexican border made it easier to smuggle drugs into the world's largest drugs market.[20] Finally, although Mexico itself has strict gun laws, organized crime syndicates took advantage of lax gun laws in the United States to build their lethal arsenals. Between 2009 and 2014, 74,000 firearms recovered at crime scenes by Mexican authorities were traced back the United States. Mexican law enforcement estimated in 2020 that 2.5 million guns had been smuggled from the United States into Mexico during the previous decade. For this reason, in August 2021, the Mexican government sued U.S. firearms manufacturers. Once known as the "arsenal for democracy" during World War II, the United States had become the arsenal for Mexico's organized crime syndicates. The inability and unwillingness to pass meaningful national gun legislation in the United States—combined with that country's appetite for illicit drugs—makes it directly complicit in the breakdown of order south of the border. Mexico is left to fight an American war on its own soil, a war it cannot possibly win.[21]

2012: The Return of the PRI

Compared with the drama that accompanied the 2006 presidential election, the 2012 election showed every indication of being predictable, even dull. Twelve years of PAN control of the presidency had brought disappointing economic returns and a ferociously bloody war among and against drug trafficking organizations. The 2012 election was largely a referendum on a violent sexenio that left most Mexicans feeling like they were worse off than in prior years. Many doubted whether Mexican democracy could address the country's most pressing needs.

The PRI's candidate was the 45-year-old Enrique Peña Nieto, the former governor of Mexico State and member of the Grupo de Atlacomulco, Mexico's most powerful political clan. Before the election, the handsome Peña Nieto married a popular soap opera actress, Angélica Rivera, after the pliant Mexico City archdiocese agreed to annul her prior marriage on a technicality. Peña began advertising nationally on Televisa as early as 2009, talking up his achievements as governor. He was clearly Televisa's candidate, which led one of Mexico's most venerable politicians, Porfirio Muñoz Ledo, to quip that "Televisa began as an annex of Los Pinos [the presidential residence] and, with the passing of time, Los Pinos became an annex of Televisa."[22]

On the campaign trail, Peña Nieto promised a new, renovated PRI that could be trusted with democracy. He pointed to a generation of young PRI governors as evidence of his party's revival and mentioned three by name—Veracruz's Javier Duarte de Ochoa, Quintana Roo's Roberto Borge Angulo, and Chihuahua's César Duarte Jáquez.

Peña led his closest rival, the PAN's Josefina Vázquez Mota, by double digits for most of the campaign. Vázquez Mota was Mexico's first female presidential candidate from a major political party. During the campaign, she struggled to separate herself from the unpopular Calderón presidency and from Calderón himself, who had actually backed another candidate in the PAN's primary. The PRD's AMLO polled a distant third. Given his rocky relationship with many PRD leaders, AMLO ran his campaign mainly through a new civil society organization called the Movement of National Regeneration (*Movimiento de Regeneración Nacional*, or Morena).[23]

The 2012 presidential election was Peña's to lose. On May 11, however, he was challenged by students at the private (Jesuit) Universidad Iberoamericana just outside of Mexico City. They booed him lustily, calling him out for human rights abuses committed when he was governor. Peña was literally chased off campus. His campaign angrily claimed that the protesters were provocateurs sent by AMLO and the PRD. After most of the Mexican media faithfully repeated the accusation, 131 students responded in a way that sparked a political movement. They recorded a video in which they identified themselves as protestors and read off their student ID numbers to refute the accusation that they were outside agitators. Using YouTube, Facebook, and Twitter, they circumvented Peña-friendly media outlets. Their video quickly went viral as others denounced Peña, the PRI, and Televisa and pledged to be the 132nd protestor (hence the Twitter hashtag #YoSoy132).[24] For the next several weeks, the #YoSoy132 movement staged marches in Mexico City and organized a successful presidential debate in which the major candidates, minus Peña, participated.

Peña Nieto still won the election, but he fell short of winning 40% of the vote. The PRI won pluralities in both houses of the Mexican Congress but fell short of absolute majorities. AMLO came in second place, trailing Peña by about seven points; the PAN's Vázquez Mota ran a disorganized campaign and came in third. Although the #YoSoy132 movement faded shortly after the election, the involvement of media-savvy youth offered a glimpse of what politics in Mexico might look like going forward.

Early in his presidency, Peña Nieto announced what would be his administration's biggest achievement—the Pact for Mexico. Mexico's three major parties—PRI, PAN, and PRD—signed historical and controversial legislation to reform the administration of public education, increase competition in the telecommunications sector, and change the constitutional provisions that had prohibited foreign investment in the oil sector. Other elements of the Pact for Mexico had direct implications for Mexico's democratic consolidation. The IFE was restructured and given a new name—the National Electoral Institute (INE)—and given the task of overseeing all national, state, and local elections. As noted in the previous chapter, the signatories to the Pact also agreed to a constitutional amendment calling for gender parity in all state and national legislatures. Finally, the three main parties agreed to reform the Constitution to allow federal senators elected in 2018 to run for reelection in two consecutive six-year terms. Federal and state representatives (*diputados*) would be allowed to run for up to four consecutive three-year terms. (The president and state governors are still limited to a single six-year term.)

Anti-reelectionism, as it turns out, may have been a cure worse than the disease. Francisco Madero's anti-reelectionist crusade against Porfirio Díaz was intended to promote electoral democracy and prevent people like Díaz from having themselves reelected in perpetuity. But anti-reelectionism meant that politicians could not be held accountable. Because they could not be reelected, they could safely ignore their constituents. They owed their jobs to their parties, and to party leaders. Anti-reelectionism also meant that politicians lacked expertise, especially in the Chamber of Deputies, where they were turned out after just three short years. Inexperienced deputies were less likely to challenge the president. In practice, what seemed like a measure to protect democracy actually corrupted and weakened it. Anti-reelectionism strengthened political parties and the president at the expense of the voting public. Time will tell whether the gradual lifting of anti-reelectionism yields a political system that is more responsive to constituent needs.[25]

During his campaign, Peña Nieto made vague promises to change his country's approach to the drug war, but his administration ended up using the same "decapitation" strategy embraced by his predecessors, with tragically similar results. Violence in Mexico began to surge once again in 2014, and 2017 was even worse than the bloodiest year of the Calderón presidency. The number of cartels and organized criminal groups proliferated further during Peña's sexenio, which saw 80,000 homicides associated with criminal wars.

The most haunting single act of violence during the Peña Nieto sexenio was the September 2014 "disappearance" of 43 students from the Ayotzinapa rural normal school in Guerrero. The students had commandeered five buses in Iguala to use as transportation to Mexico City, where they planned to attend the annual commemoration of the 1968 massacre at Tlatelolco. But municipal police blocked their exit from the city, while gunmen—some of them uniformed—shot at the buses. Army troops stationed nearby did nothing. Three students were killed in the hail of bullets. The 43 who survived the initial assault simply "disappeared." The federal government conducted a hasty investigation. Its version of the events, which pinned the blame on local police and drug gangs, fell apart almost as soon as it was presented to the public. International forensics experts found several major oversights and inconsistencies. They also found evidence of the widespread use of torture during interrogations. Drone footage later emerged showing that the Navy had planted evidence to support the official, fabricated version. Subsequent investigations pointed to a murky, lethal partnership between drug traffickers, municipal and state police, local politicians, and the federal army.[26] Grieving family members took matters into their own hands and combed the countryside for unmarked graves. They found several containing not the

Figure 6.1 Friends and relatives of the 43 students missing from the Ayotzinapa teacher training school march in Mexico City on September 26, 2020, the sixth anniversary of their disappearance. Rodrigo Arangua/AFP/Getty Images

bodies of their sons but rather the remains of others who had been dead ("missing") for two or three years.

The Ayotzinapa tragedy in fall 2014 served as an inflection point for Peña Nieto's presidency. His promise of a new, renovated PRI sounded increasingly hollow. Late in his sexenio, several former governors, all PRIístas, were arrested on charges brought by Mexico or the United States (or both). First, the former governor of Coahuila and ex-president of the PRI, Humberto Moeira (2005–2011), was arrested in Spain and charged with money laundering and embezzlement. He is believed to have worked closely with the Zetas. In April 2017, the former PRI governor of Tamaulipas, Tomás Yarrington, was captured by Italian police, ending five years on the run. Both Mexico and the United States charged that he took bribes from the Gulf Cartel and allowed drugs to flow unimpeded through his border state. The United States also accused him of racketeering, money laundering, bank fraud, and tax evasion.[27] A week after Yarrington's arrest, Guatemalan authorities took the former PRI governor of Veracruz, Javier Duarte de Ochoa (2010–2016), into custody. Duarte, one of three governors mentioned by Peña Nieto as emblematic of the PRI's renovation, was wanted in Mexico for money laundering and his links to organized crime. Duarte and his inner circle looted Veracruz's state pension fund and its university, took tens of millions of dollars earmarked for social programs and sent them to phantom companies, and dispensed fake medicine to cancer patients. In 2015 alone, Duarte's financial scams totaled more than $850 million. Meanwhile, violence exploded in Veracruz and seventeen journalists were killed during his term of office. Shortly before his arrest in 2017, mothers searching for their missing children were led to a mass grave containing more than 250 skulls.[28]

Two months after Duarte's capture, Panamanian authorities caught up with the former governor of Quintana Roo, Roberto Borge Angulo (2011–2016), as he tried to board a plane to Paris. Borge, another one of Peña's "renovated" PRIístas, was sought for money laundering and for seizing state property in Cancún and Cozumel and selling it to family members and associates. Rounding out Peña Nieto's triumvirate of renovated PRIístas, former Chihuahua governor César Duarte Jáquez (2010–2016) was charged with embezzlement and is believed to have directed an elaborate scheme involving the illegal use of public money to finance political campaigns in states where PRI candidates faced strong opposition. Other former PRI governors were either in hiding, under investigation, or were fighting prosecution on corruption charges. PRI politics had simply become another form of organized crime.[29]

Heading into the 2018 presidential election, the PRI brand had been battered by violence and corruption, impunity, and incompetence. With so much at stake, Peña Nieto could not allow an unpredictable party primary to select the PRI's candidate. Instead, he reverted to a scaled-back version of the *dedazo*, a practice that many analysts believed had been swept into the dustbin of history. His chosen successor, Finance minister José Antonio Meade, had worked in the Fox, Calderón, and Peña administrations and was not even a PRI party member. The choice of an apolitical technocrat was designed to appeal to disaffected PRI voters as well as to PANistas who were discouraged by the persistent infighting within their own party.

If the PRI was in crisis ahead of the 2018 election, so too was the PAN. Internal divisions burst out into the open. The party's president and presidential hopeful, Ricardo Anaya, locked horns with Margarita Zavala, the wife of former president Calderón who had presidential ambitions of her own. After months of bitter infighting, Zavala left the PAN and ran a short-lived presidential campaign as an independent. Anaya and his inner circle then negotiated an electoral alliance with the pragmatic PRD. In December, the 38-year-old Anaya presented himself as the candidate of a highly improbable coalition that allied Mexico's weakened center-right party with the weakened center-left PRD. For both parties, opportunism papered over seemingly irreconcilable ideological differences.

The PRD, for its part, suffered major blows during the Peña presidency, many of them self-inflicted. Its two-time presidential candidate, AMLO, left the party shortly after the 2012 election and in 2014 registered Morena as a political party. He took many PRDistas with him. In November of that same year, Cuauhtémoc Cárdenas renounced the party that he helped found after a series of disagreements with its leadership. Left without the two charismatic men who had dominated the party since its inception, the PRD could do no better in 2018 than back Ricardo Anaya and hope for the best.

Institutionalized corruption, the surge in violence, and weak, opportunistic political parties led several analysts to argue that Mexico's democratic consolidation was unravelling, that the transition had failed, and an opportunity had been lost. Lorenzo Meyer questioned whether the transition had happened at all, noting that the PRI and PAN were so similar ideologically that the 2000 presidential election "was a dispute between parties that had been cooperating systematically since 1989. . .with projects so similar that they did not offer a true alternative."[30] Alberto Olvera noted that both the PRD and the PAN had used the PRI's time-worn practices to compete successfully in elections. This meant "the reproduction of clientelism, electoral manipulation, and pacts with the local de facto powers…the generalization of the old regime's electoral practices and political culture." For these reasons, "the new political elite could not be a bearer of democratic innovation."[31] Ordinary Mexicans feared that their democracy had devolved into a kleptocracy. When asked in a 2017 poll whether their country was governed by powerful groups for their own benefit, 90 percent of Mexican respondents agreed. Only Brazilians took a dimmer view of their political class.[32]

That year, INE president Lorenzo Córdova Vianello admitted publicly that Mexico's democracy was "going through a rough patch (*en un bache*)." He blamed erroneous public policies, corruption, and impunity, and said that the rule of law in Mexico was "weak, precarious, and in many ways nonexistent." "This is a very delicate moment in the life of the country," he added. "There is a lot of justifiable anger, but we cannot allow ourselves to lose the country and lose the still precarious democracy that we have."[33] With all eyes fixed on the July 2018 presidential election, Mexico's democratic consolidation looked precarious indeed.

Landslide: the 2018 Elections

In spring 2018, as Mexico's official campaign season got underway, there were ominous signs that the July election would be compromised. In April, the federal electoral court ruled that the governor of Nuevo León, Jaime Rodríguez Calderón (a former PRIísta known as "El Bronco"), should be included on the presidential ballot despite overwhelming evidence that he had falsified more than one million signatures in his bid to qualify as an independent candidate.[34] Meanwhile, an unprecedented rash of political killings swept the country, targeting at least 145 men and women from all parties. Many of them were mayoral candidates. Many others who were not killed were threatened, beaten, assaulted, or kidnapped. Most of the attacks were attributed to organized crime syndicates who sought to eliminate candidates who threatened their ability to cultivate or transport drugs, control the municipal police, steal from PEMEX pipelines, and/or tax and extort civilian populations.[35]

Given that somber backdrop, when Mexico's democratic consolidation seemed to hang in the balance, its citizens overwhelmingly voted for AMLO, his fledgling party (Morena), and his coalition (*Juntos Haremos Historia*), which also included the socialist Labor Party (*Partido del Trabajo*, or PT) and, improbably, an evangelical party called Encuentro Social. AMLO defeated his closest rival, Ricardo Anaya, by thirty-one points, not the twenty points that most polls had predicted. Outgoing president Peña Nieto facilitated this outcome. In the months ahead of the election, his attorney general opened a politically motivated investigation into Anaya's business practices. The young PANista was soon accused of money laundering. Perhaps Peña sought to weaken Anaya to ingratiate himself with the likely winner of the election, AMLO, and avoid prosecution for acts of corruption after he left office. In any case, few were surprised when Anaya was exonerated shortly after the election. Meanwhile, the PRI's candidate, José Antonio Meade, took only 16 percent of the vote, a historic, worst-ever drubbing for Mexico's erstwhile hegemonic party. Given the magnitude of López Obrador's victory, both

Anaya and Meade conceded less than forty-five minutes after the polls closed.

Equally surprising were Morena's victories in other federal, state, and municipal races. Morena won 59 seats (out of 128) in the Senate and its coalition partners picked up an additional 11 seats. In the Chamber of Deputies, Morena won 259 seats out of 500. In Mexico City, the Morena candidate for governor, engineer Claudia Sheinbaum, defeated the PRD's candidate (and party president) Alejandra Barrales and thereby wrested control of the nation's capital from the party that had controlled it ever since Mexico culminated its democratic transition.

Morena's victories extended into areas where its organizational strength was still weak. It scored important victories in the border state of Sonora and won the battered city of Ciudad Juárez in neighboring Chihuahua. In Baja California Sur, it swept the local and federal congressional elections and took the state capital, La Paz. Its victories in federal, state, and local elections from northwestern Mexico to the southeast were extraordinary for a party that had only been in existence since 2014.[36]

These breathtaking results represented a clear repudiation of the PRI. Its presidential candidate had been walloped, it did not win a single one of the nine contested gubernatorial races, and its representation in the Senate fell from 55 seats to just 14. In the state of Hidalgo, the PRI lost control of the legislature for the first time in 80 years.

If the PRI got shellacked, the PRD fared even worse. Its representation in the presidential election fell to just 2.3 percent of the vote, a stunning collapse for a party that took 35.3 percent of the vote in 2006, when AMLO was its presidential candidate. In 2012, the PRD had 99 seats in the Chamber of Deputies; in 2015 it still retained 58; but in the new Congress, that number fell to just 11. The PRD had suddenly become a minor party in danger of losing its registry with the INE.[37]

The PAN's situation may not be so dire. It retains its social base and its stronghold in central and northern Mexico. But it was clearly punished in the 2018 election cycle for being too much like the PRI, too much a part of the system that had failed too many Mexicans for too long.

Current Threats to Mexico's Democratic Consolidation

As Mexican democratization moves through its fifth decade, it is still too soon to declare that the country has a "democracy without adjectives." Today, analysts use descriptors like "partial," "beleaguered," "fragile," and "thin" to qualify Mexico's democracy. Some believe that the term "electoralism" best describes Mexico's political system. Most agree that the quality of Mexico's democracy cannot be judged simply on the grounds of a vastly improved electoral process. A truly healthy democracy flourishes where the state can guarantee the rule of law, where the media is plural and free to do its work, where citizens are represented politically and can put their faith in the judicial system, and where they can provide for themselves and their families.[38]

Yet the Mexican state cannot even provide its citizens with basic security. Between 2006 and 2022, according to official figures, more than 350,000 Mexicans were murdered and 100,000 were reported missing. Experts estimate that as many as two-thirds of these murders and disappearances can be directly attributed to organized crime. Between 2006 and 2012, Mexico's homicide rate went from 9 to 22 per 100,000 inhabitants. By 2018, the rate had jumped to 29 per 100,000 inhabitants, where it remained in 2023. "Paradoxically and tragically, [Mexicans] in a democracy are demanding what citizens demanded of the military leaders during the twilight of authoritarianism in the Southern Cone," wrote one analyst, "[including] respect for human rights, the location of the disappeared, and accurate information about the deaths of the victims."[39] Official obstruction and cover-up in the Ayotzinapa investigation and the emergence of self-defense militias in Guerrero, Michoacán and elsewhere during the Peña sexenio suggested that where the Mexican state was not incompetent and/or complicit, it was entirely absent. It also became clear that organized crime controlled municipal and even some state governments. Analysts openly debated whether Mexico had become a failed state.

Mexicans were reminded daily, in myriad ways, that the rule of law had only a tenuous hold on the country. State-level prosecutors failed to conduct effective investigations into most crimes, and most suspects were never brought before a judge. According to several reports, 98% of homicides went unsolved.[40] The Peña administration's most embarrassing fiasco was the 2015 escape of Joaquín "El Chapo" Guzmán from a federal maximum-security prison by means of a lighted, ventilated, mile-long tunnel that connected to the shower of his prison cell. Not only were the authorities unable to defeat organized crime in various states and municipalities but they apparently could not even control criminals *inside* Mexico's prisons. (El Chapo was later recaptured and extradited to the United States.)

Journalists, especially those who investigated drug-trafficking organizations, were among those most directly affected by Mexico's chilling spike in violence. During the Peña administration, Mexico became the most dangerous country in the Western Hemisphere for journalists to exercise their profession, and the third most dangerous in the world, after war-torn Syria and Libya. According to Mexico's National Commission on Human Rights, 162 journalists were murdered between 2000 and 2020. An additional twenty-two journalists had disappeared since 2006 and fifty-four attacks had been carried out against media outlets. According to the London-based media watchdog group Article 19, nearly half of the attacks against Mexican journalists during the Peña sexenio could be traced to political authorities.[41] As one historian notes, "Soft authoritarianism Mexico was a much safer place for journalists than contemporary democratic Mexico."[42] Mexico is also one of the world's most dangerous countries for environmental activists; 153 were murdered between 2008 and 2020.

Not surprisingly, organized crime, often in league with state politicians, succeeded in silencing the press, especially in northern Mexico. In 2012, the daily *El Mañana* of Tamaulipas announced that it would stop reporting on local disputes between drug gangs after its offices were attacked three times with grenades and gunfire. *El Mañana* had also been attacked for *refusing* to publish information as requested by organized crime.[43] In Chihuahua, the 2017 murder of reporter Miroslava Breach convinced one of the papers that printed her work, *Norte de*

Ciudad Juárez, to stop publishing. Breach had written stories linking organized crime to PRI and PAN politicians.[44] The result of this extraordinary assault on the press was self-censorship, similar to that which existed in the days of the hegemonic, authoritarian PRI.

Peña Nieto's administration also had little patience for journalists. In 2017, the *New York Times* revealed that it had hired an Israeli firm to infect the cellphones of reporters, human rights activists, lawyers, opposition politicians, academics, and others with Pegasus malware that turned their phones into tracking devices. Among the targets were the widely respected journalist Carmen Aristegui and her teenage son. Aristegui's crime? Her news team had broken the news that Peña's favorite construction firm had essentially gifted a mansion (the "Casa Blanca," or White House) worth seven million dollars to First Lady Angélica Rivera. Aristegui paid a steep price for her journalistic excellence. Not only was her phone infected, but she was also fired by her employer, MVS Radio. Driven off the air, she created her own internet portal.[45]

Mexico's democratic transition and consolidation have also coincided with pervasive poverty and growing inequalities. For the last three decades, per capita income has grown at an anemic rate of less than 1% annually. Meanwhile, a handful of politically connected men have grown incredibly rich; since 2002, Mexico's sixteen billionaires have seen their wealth triple. Mexico's neoliberal economic reforms have brought depressed real wages, very modest job creation, and reduced social welfare programs. Some observers worry that the discontent *in* democracy becomes discontent *with* democracy.[46]

Persistent poverty leaves marginalized populations vulnerable to clientelism. The PRI perfected this kind of machine politics, but the PAN, PRD, the Green Party (Partido Verde Ecologista Mexicano, or PVEM), and now Morena have been quick learners. After the 2012 election, Morena presented the national electoral tribunal with evidence that the PRI had distributed gift and debit cards in marginal communities that could be redeemed at the Soriana national supermarket chain after the election. Analysts note that the Soriana scandal became notorious when many card recipients complained that their cards turned out to be worth less than promised, or nothing at all.[47] All parties—Morena included—distributed gift cards during the 2021 midterm elections.

This leads to a final, dispiriting observation about Mexico's political parties. The country is currently saddled with lots of well-financed parties that few Mexicans actually like.[48] The parties of Mexico's democratic transition—the PRI, the PAN, and the PRD—are in deep crisis. The smaller, satellite parties, often referred to as "remoras," are opportunistic and ideologically untethered, motivated solely by their desire for public financing and the spoils of office. The most cynical party is the Mexican Green Party (PVEM), a family business with no connection to the global environmental movement. According to *Latinobarómetro*'s 2018 survey, only 11 percent of Mexicans trusted political parties. Most Mexicans identify themselves as independents. No wonder, then, that Morenistas claim that theirs is a *movement*, not a party.

As this book went to press, Morena had become Mexico's new dominant, possibly hegemonic, political party, as it cannibalized the PRI from within and destroyed what remained of it in state and local elections. The PAN remained hobbled by internal rivalries and had a weak presence in the south of the country. The most debilitated political party, though, was the PRD. During Mexico's democratic transition, the PRD represented the most important attempt to unify the chronically divided Mexican left, and it did more to further women's issues than any other party. That said, it has never been more than a conglomeration of often rancorous factions commonly referred to as "tribes" (*tribus*). Elections for internal party leadership positions were occasionally marred by fraud, which raises the question of whether the PRD could ever carry out the democratic revolution that its name promised.[49]

Mexico's democratic consolidation is therefore threatened by violence, corruption and impunity, persistent poverty and clientelism, and unpopular political parties. Support for democracy in Mexico may be waning among the general population. During the presidency of Vicente Fox (2000–2006), roughly 60 percent of those surveyed by

Latinobarómetro felt that democracy was the best form of government. This number began to slide during the Calderón and Peña Nieto presidencies. By 2018, the percentage of Mexicans who believed democracy to be the best form of government fell to 38 percent. When asked whether they were satisfied with *their* democracy, only 16% reported that they were.[50] These numbers rebounded somewhat after AMLO's 2018 victory. Still, these survey results are disappointing given that Mexico's current democratic political system is one of the most expensive in the world.

Conclusions

There is a lot to celebrate about Mexico's democratic consolidation. Women have used the party system to achieve gender parity in the national and state legislatures for the first time in Mexican history. The INE, while imperfect, attempted to level the playing field for all parties and modified the electoral code to address problems as they emerged. On election day, Mexican women and men still turn out to vote in large numbers and still volunteer to work at polling places, while others serve as party representatives and poll watchers. Voting takes place from 8 am to 6 pm on Sundays. On election night, tens of thousands of Mexicans spend hours hand-counting ballots into the wee hours of Monday morning before heading to work. A palpable civic culture around elections has emerged, and most elections can produce *alternancia*, or a change from one party to another.

But democratic consolidation has also coincided with a horrific spike in violence related to the drug trade, and Mexico's criminal justice system seems incapable of solving crimes and sentencing criminals. Persistent poverty and clientelism have raised concerns about the *quality* of democracy. Mexican democracy also remains hobbled by the inability to hold true primary elections. None of the major parties in the 2018 elections held legitimate primaries to select candidates for the highest office in the land. Party insiders, not ordinary Mexican citizens, made these decisions. For all the undeniable progress made in strengthening electoral institutions and practices, a combination of old vices and new challenges threatens to undermine Mexico's precarious electoral democracy.

Notes

1 This chapter title was inspired by Enrique Krause's timely essay "Una democracia sin adjetivos," published in 1984 in *Nexos*.

2 Camp and Mattiace, 11.

3 Leo Zuckermann, "Los nuevos virreyes", *Proceso*, April 28, 2004.

4 Denise Dresser, *Manifiesto mexicano: Cómo perdimos el rumbo y cómo recuperarlo* (Ciudad de México: Penguin Random House, 2018); 158, 162–163; and Alberto J. Olvera, "The Elusive Democracy: Political Parties, Democratic Institutions, and Civil Society in Mexico," *Latin American Research Review*, Special Issue: Living in Actually Existing Democracies (2010): 86–89.

5 Guillermo Trejo and Sandra Ley, *Votes, Drugs, and Violence: The Political Logic of Criminal Wars in Mexico* (New York: Cambridge University Press, 2020), 12–13.

6 George W. Grayson, *Mexican Messiah: Andrés Manuel López Obrador* (University Park, PA: The University of Pennsylvania Press, 2007), 62–69.

7 Citing PRD sources, Grayson claims that Madrazo spent more than sixty times the legal limit in his 1994 campaign; p. 99.

8 Eisenstadt, *Courting Democracy*, 111–113.

9 Todd Eisenstadt, "The Origins and Rationality of the 'Legal versus Legitimate' Dichotomy Invoked in Mexico's 2006 Post-Electoral Conflict," *PS: Political Science & Politics* 40:1 (January 2007), 41.

10 Eisenstadt, "The Origins," 42; and Eisenstadt and Jennifer Yelle, "Ulysses, the Sirens, and Mexico's Judiciary: Increasing Precommitments to Strengthen the Rule of Law," in Camp, ed., 215–217.

11 See https://www.youtube.com/watch?v=cFTzIoqFeiQ.

12 Trejo and Ley, 159.

13 Eric Magar, "The Electoral Institutions: Party Subsidies, Campaign Decency, and Entry Barriers," in *Mexico's Evolving Democracy: A Comparative Study of the 2012 Elections* eds. Jorge I. Domínguez,

Kenneth F. Greene, and Alejandro Moreno (Baltimore: Johns Hopkins University Press, 2015), 64–66, 70.

14 Ibid., 78.

15 Trejo and Ley, *Votes, Drugs, and Violence*, 2.

16 The National Security Archive at George Washington University contains useful dossiers of the massacres in Tamaulipas and Allende, Coahuila; see https://nsarchive2.gwu.edu/NSAEBB/NSAEBB445/ and https://nsarchive.gwu.edu/briefing-book/mexico/2021-03-18/allende-massacre-decade-impunity.

17 Alan Feuer and Nate Schweber, "Mexico's Ex-Top Security Official is Convicted of Cartel Bribery," *New York Times*, Feb. 21, 2023.

18 Guillermo Trejo and Sandra Ley, "Why Did Drug Cartels Go to War in Mexico? Subnational Party Alternation, the Breakdown of Criminal Protection, and the Onset of Large-Scale Violence," *Comparative Political Studies* 51:7 (2017), 4, 12, 16.

19 Trejo and Ley, *Votes, Drugs, and Violence*, 293–294.

20 John Bailey, "Drug Traffickers as Political Actors in Mexico's Nascent Democracy," in *The Oxford Handbook of Mexican Politics*, ed. Roderic Ai Camp (New York: Oxford University Press, 2012), 471–472.

21 Ioan Grillo, *Blood Gun Money: How America Arms Gangs and Cartels* (New York: Bloomsbury Publishing Inc., 2021), 11, 15; and Christopher Ingraham, "Why Mexico's drug cartels love America's gun laws," *The Washington Post*, Jan. 14, 2016.

22 Porfirio Muñoz Ledo, *La vía radical: para refundar la república* (México, D.F.: Grijalbo, 2010).

23 Kathleen Bruhn, "Chronicle of a Victory Foretold," in *Mexico's Evolving Democracy: A Comparative Study of the 2012 Elections* eds. Jorge I. Domínguez, Kenneth F. Greene, and Alejandro Moreno (Baltimore: Johns Hopkins University Press, 2015), 49–50.

24 The students' original video can be found here: https://www.youtube.com/watch?v=hca6lzoE2z8.

25 Edmonds-Poli and Shirk, 118–119.

26 "Ayotzinapa, una investigación opaca," *Proceso*, April 21, 2017; Dresser, 195–218; and Anabel Hernández, *La verdadera noche de Iguala: La historia que el gobierno trató de ocultar* (Ciudad de México: Penguin Random House Grupo Editorial, S.A. de C.V., 2016).

27 In October 2017, Mexican authorities arrested Yarrington's successor, fellow PRIísta Eugenio Hernández Flores (2005–2010), on charges of embezzlement, money laundering, and links to organized crime.

28 Ioan Grillo, "The Paradox of Mexico's Mass Graves," *The New York Times*, July 19, 2017.

29 Elisabeth Malkin, "Corruption at a Level of Audacity 'Never Seen in Mexico,'" *The New York Times* April 19, 2017; and Azam Ahmed and J. Jesús Esquivel, "Mexico's Graft Inquiry Deepens with Arrest of a Presidential Ally," *The New York Times*, Dec. 20, 2017.

30 Bizberg, 122-139; and Meyer, *Nuestra tragedia persistente: La democracia autoritaria en México* (México, D.F.: Debate, 2013), 278.

31 Olvera, 88–89.

32 *Latinobarómetro Informe* 2018, 38.

33 José Antonio Román, "De cara a las elecciones, la democracia en un 'bache': INE," *La Jornada*, June 22, 2017.

34 Carlos Acosta y Luciano Campos, "El caso 'Bronco': Las pruebas del INE que el TEPJF ignoró," *Proceso*, April 16, 2018.

35 Ioan Grillo, "A Victory for Mexican Democracy," *The New York Times*, July 10, 2018; and Marcela Turati, "Cuando las balas votan," *Proceso*, June 24, 2018, 30–32.

36 Jenaro Villamil, "Para la coalición de Morena, carro semicompleto en el Senado y en los estados," *Proceso*, July 8, 2018.

37 Álvaro Delgado, "El PRD se derrumbó: no recibió votos de todos sus militantes," *Proceso*, July 4, 2018

38 Cadena-Roa y López Leyva, "La consolidación," 420.

39 Ilán Bizberg, "México: una transición fallida," *Desacatos* 48 (mayo-agosto 2015), 129, 132.

40 See, for example, Héctor Aguilar Camín, "Nocturno de la democracia mexicana," *Nexos* (mayo 2016), 24; and Middlebrook, "Mexico's Democratic Transitions," 27.

41 Elisabeth Malkin, "In Mexico, Firing of Carmen Aristegui Highlights Rising Pressures on News Media," *The New York Times*, March 27, 2015.

42 Smith, *The Mexican Press*, 281.

43 Zorayda Gallegos, "El periodismo en México nada a contracorriente," *El País*, April 20, 2017.

44 "Miroslava Breach muere acribillada," *La Jornada*, March 24, 2017.

45 Aristegui's internet portal can be found here: https://aristeguinoticias.com.

46 Bizberg, 124; Dresser, 82–83; and Ciro Murayama, "México 2018: la democracia a prueba," *El País* July 2, 2017.

47 Simeon Nichter and Brian Palmer-Rubin, "Clientelism, Declared Support, and Mexico's 2012 Campaign," in *Mexico's Evolving Democracy: A Comparative Study of the 2012 Elections* eds. Jorge I. Domínguez, Kenneth F. Greene, and Alejandro Moreno (Baltimore: Johns Hopkins University Press, 2015), 205–206.

48 *Latinobarómetro Informe 2018*, 53; and Camp and Mattiace, 75.

49 Kathleen Bruhn, "The PRD and the Mexican Left," in *The Oxford Handbook of Mexican Politics*, 195–201.

50 *Latinobarómetro Informe* 2018, 35.

7

Mexico's Unscripted Revolutions and the "Fourth Transformation"

This book has argued that the lives of ordinary Mexicans have undergone significant changes over the last several decades, changes possibly more consequential than those wrought by the famous Revolution of 1910. By 1958, this officially appropriated and carefully curated revolution was, literally, "history" for many Mexicans. The Long Sixties ushered in a new era, when Mexicans in the mountains of Guerrero and the railyards of Mexico City, in rural normal schools and on university campuses challenged the PRI to live up to the promises enshrined in the Constitution of 1917. When it did not, they went on strike, took to the streets, and sometimes took up arms. Unofficial, unheralded, unscripted, and relatively unstudied mini-revolutions remade the lives of ordinary Mexicans.

The lives of Mexican women changed most dramatically, beginning in the 1970s. Second-wave feminism, initially led by middle-class, university-educated women, took on a more popular character in the 1980s as poor and working-class women struggled to balance their domestic duties with their work outside of the home. Increasingly, women had greater control over their reproductive futures, as the Mexican government supported family planning programs.

Mexico's Unscripted Revolutions: Political and Social Change since 1958,
First Edition. Stephen E. Lewis.

In the 1990s, ordinary Mexicans pushed against the PRI-government and its legacy on multiple fronts. The Zapatistas in Chiapas simultaneously snuffed out the government's fading indigenista programs and drew attention to the plight of contemporary Indigenous people. The PRI-government finally abandoned the decades-long drive to forge a homogenous mestizo nation. Paradoxically, after the government made important concessions to the Catholic Church and strengthened its legal and constitutional standing, many Mexicans left the church of their birth and instead embraced diverse forms of religious expression. Elections in the twilight of the twentieth century suggested that two decades of political reforms—initiated from above but also pushed from below—were bearing fruit. By 2000, Mexico was politically plural, largely democratic, mostly urban, and fully integrated into the world economy. And the size of Mexican families had shrunk by half.

Mexico's unscripted revolutions continued into the new millennium. Mexicans continued to explore religious alternatives, including secularism. Women successfully pushed the federal electoral system to mandate gender quotas in politics. In the 2018 elections, women achieved gender parity in the national congress and in most statehouses, and a populist who promised to destroy the old regime and initiate Mexico's "Fourth Transformation" became president.

The "Fourth Transformation" at a glance

Historians will eventually judge whether Andrés Manuel López Obrador's presidency rose to the level of its presumptuous billing. Surely the "Fourth Transformation" was different from the Fox, Calderón, and Peña Nieto presidencies. It was a watershed moment in Mexican history, albeit in surprising ways. Although the "Fourth Transformation" sounded radical, in practice, AMLO's presidency was actually quite conservative. The life-long leftist pivoted to the political center; in some of his political, economic, and social policies, he aligned with the Right. Mexican intellectual Roger Bartra labeled

AMLO a "retropopulist," citing his attacks on Mexico's electoral institutions, its feminists, journalists, and intellectuals (most of whom voted for him), his conservative fiscal policies, his moralizing discourse, his promotion of fossil fuels and his willingness to militarize public life. Confusingly, however, AMLO considered himself a liberal and labeled his adversaries "*conservadores*."[1]

AMLO showcased his populist style at his daily press conferences, known as *mañaneras*. From seven to nine in the morning, from Monday to Friday, he riffed about the news of the day, expounded on Mexican history, and fielded questions from an audience of mostly docile reporters. His supporters claimed that the mañaneras brought unprecedented transparency to government; never had a Mexican president been so visible and available to his constituents. But critics noted that these "civic Masses" disseminated propaganda and were used by AMLO and his communication team to distract attention away from some of Mexico's intractable problems. His improvisation was often at odds with his own government's policies and with the factual record. Stated bluntly, half-truths and lies were the order of the day.[2]

Figure 7.1 AMLO at one of his morning briefings, known as "mañaneras." Hector Vivas/Getty Images

AMLO employed polarizing rhetoric at his mañaneras and divided the Mexican people into two camps. His supporters were *el pueblo* or the *pueblo bueno*, the good people. Other Mexicans were "adversaries," "sellouts," "pimps," "racists," "traitors," and "defenders of foreign interests."[3] "In spite of having all the power, [AMLO] behaved as if his were a minority government, cornered by forces that prevented him from launching his programs," wrote Leonardo Curzio and Aníbal Gutiérrez. "The past and his predecessors chased him like ghosts in the presidential palace. . . His real and imagined enemies soured his mood every morning."[4] His favorite targets were neoliberalism, former president Felipe Calderón, and what he called the "fraud" of 2006, which he used to nurture the notion of a permanent confrontation between good and evil, between those who are honest and those who are corrupt.

AMLO also used the bully pulpit to target public intellectuals and critical journalists by name. Reporters who dared to ask probing questions at the mañaneras were tarred and feathered in social media in what were clearly coordinated attacks.

Beginning in June 2021, the mañaneras included a weekly segment known as "Who's who in the week's lies." Every Wednesday, a member of AMLO's inner circle spent several minutes attacking what she claimed was "fake news" and the purveyors of that news—journalists. It was a serious provocation. In May 2022, after the eighth journalist had been murdered that year, the Inter-American Commission on Human Rights, the European Parliament, and the journalism advocacy organization Article 19 asked AMLO to suspend the segment out of concern that its messaging put reporters' lives at risk. But AMLO, who spoke of regeneration and transformation but stoked confrontation and resentment, insisted that the feature continue. In November 2022, he threatened that the segment would become a daily feature of the mañaneras "due to the increase in the number of lies and the desperation of our adversaries."[5]

AMLO's populist style was also on display during the COVID-19 pandemic, which hit Mexico about fifteen months into his administration. Like Donald Trump, Jair Bolsonaro, and other right-wing populists, AMLO tried to brush away the pandemic, minimized its seriousness, and expressed disdain for scientific expertise. When health officials introduced a stay-at-home order, he continued to tour the country and was filmed going out of his way to shake the hand of the mother of Joaquín "El Chapo" Guzmán in Sinaloa. A jury in Brooklyn was about to give her son a life sentence.[6] At his mañaneras, AMLO displayed religious pendants and holy cards that he said protected him from the virus. Honesty and a clear conscience were the best protection, he claimed, since corruption was the true plague. Then AMLO contracted COVID himself in January 2021. After he recovered, he still refused to wear a face covering. By April 2021, Mexico had the third-highest number of deaths from COVID in the world, surpassed only by the United States and Brazil. Even AMLO's undersecretary of health admitted that the true count of Mexico's COVID-19 deaths was probably much higher simply because so many Mexicans died before they could be tested for the virus.

During the pandemic, governments around the world injected money into their economies to keep businesses afloat and support the most vulnerable. AMLO's administration resisted this impulse. Like the neoliberal economists that he so despised, AMLO prioritized a balanced budget over taking on more debt. The Mexican economy, the world's fifteenth largest, shrunk by 8.4 percent in 2020, and an estimated 3.8 million Mexicans fell into poverty. Although the economy grew at a modest rate of almost 5 percent the following year, it struggled to recover its pre-pandemic vitality.[7]

AMLO's reluctance to meet the economic challenges of the COVID pandemic was part of an overall *laissez-faire* (or "hands-off") approach to the economy, which was surprising, given his legendary commitment to the poor and downtrodden. As a young man, he directed an INI coordinating center in his home state of Tabasco. The experience of working with the Chontal people left a deep impression on him, "a quasi-religious commitment with poor." He carefully cultivated an image of personal austerity. As president, AMLO loved travelling to the farthest corners of the country, flying almost exclusively in coach on commercial airlines and reaching out to the *pueblo bueno* in a manner that he himself described as apostolic.

On the campaign trail, AMLO promised to grow the economy at a rate of four percent a year, reduce poverty, end corruption, end the war on drugs, and send the military back to their barracks. One might expect a lifelong leftist to change the tax code to make the rich pay more taxes, but AMLO left it untouched. He claimed that ending corruption would provide enough money to support his social programs. But this was wishful thinking. To pay for his legacy infrastructure projects, which included a new international airport north of Mexico City, a new oil refinery in his home state of Tabasco, and a 965-mile train loop in the Yucatán Peninsula called the Tren Maya, AMLO imposed a policy of "republican austerity" on public administration. Believing that civil servants were likely to be disloyal and corrupt, he reduced their salaries and cut their benefits. Public universities, scientific research, and hospitals suffered draconian cuts. Not even the Ministry of Public Education (SEP) was spared.

AMLO's administration also gutted existing welfare programs and sent direct cash transfers to millions of Mexicans, with no strings attached. The elderly and disabled received more generous pensions, small- and medium-scale farmers received support to cultivate corn, wheat, rice, beans, coffee, and sugar and to plant trees, and university students received scholarships that allowed them to finish their degree programs. In Mexico's impoverished south and southeast, nearly every household benefited from at least one of the entitlement programs. But economists feared that less money went to the people who truly needed it because AMLO had cut other, more targeted programs.[8]

AMLO's commitment to the poor inspired a new approach to Mexico's drug-related violence that he dubbed *Abrazos, no balazos* (hugs, not gunshots). Scholarship programs were designed to help youngsters stay in school or learn a trade, and the army, the navy, and the fledging National Guard were discouraged from directly engaging the drug cartels. Mexico's homicide rate did not decline, however, despite the military's less confrontational approach and the investment in social programs meant to help young Mexicans avoid a life of crime.

Mexico's most important foreign policy relationship is with the government of the United States. Here, too, AMLO's behavior was perplexing. As a presidential candidate, AMLO authored a book with the title *Listen, Trump!* that defended Mexicans residing in the United States from the U.S. president's racist attacks. He claimed repeatedly that Trump and his advisors spoke of Mexicans in the way that Hitler and the Nazis spoke of Jews. As president, however, AMLO underwent a remarkable transformation. First, he agreed to use his National Guard to carry out Trump's orders to crack down on Central American immigrants passing through Mexico. Then, in summer 2020, he agreed to visit Washington, DC to boost Trump's reelection chances with Latinos. AMLO delivered a speech in which he called Trump his "amigo," compared him to George Washington, and declared against all evidence that Trump "has behaved toward us with courtesy and respect."[9] The Trump campaign used those words in campaign ads that ran in Latino-heavy districts. After Trump lost the 2020 presidential election, AMLO did his mercurial friend the favor of waiting forty days before congratulating Democratic candidate Joe Biden on his victory. This was a delicate time when Trump and his allies stopped at nothing to overturn the results of the election.

The "Fourth Transformation" brought an additional surprise to Mexicans who thought they had elected a progressive leftist. AMLO, who grew up in the oil-rich state of Tabasco, seemed nostalgic for the days when PEMEX fueled Mexican growth and development and propped up the hegemonic PRI. Determined to reverse what he believed was the corrupt privatization of the oil industry, he spared no expense to bail out PEMEX, the world's most indebted oil company and historically one of the most corrupt. AMLO also committed to restoring the near-monopoly position of Mexico's Federal Electricity Commission (*Comisión Federal de Electricidad*, or CFE). The Peña Nieto administration had opened Mexico's energy market to foreign companies, including wind and solar firms. They were about to begin operating within the national power grid when

AMLO's government cancelled their startup permits. The FCE favored instead coal, gas, and fuel oil-burning plants owned or run by the state, and planned to invest billions to build fifteen additional fossil fuel-powered plants by 2024. The spike in oil prices following Vladimir Putin's invasion of Ukraine in 2022 gave short-term vindication to AMLO's investments in fossil fuels. But as the global

Figure 7.2 Mexican president López Obrador standing with his *amigo* Donald Trump on July 8, 2020. Trump White House Archived/Wikimedia Commons/Public Domain

economy shifts to renewable energy, Mexico will find itself playing catch-up. And it will almost certainly fail to meet its international commitments to reduce its carbon output.[10]

It has been said that populists campaign but they do not govern; that they blame others rather than take responsibility; that they offer simplistic solutions for complicated problems.[11] Despite all of this, populists can be quite popular. As this book went to press, AMLO's government claimed an overall reduction in poverty thanks to the policy of direct cash transfers and the increase in the minimum wage. But more Mexicans were in extreme poverty than when he was elected. AMLO's anti-corruption crusade had yet to yield one big-name conviction, and the violence raged on. If the number of Mexicans apprehended at the United States border was any indication—over 800,000 in 2022—people were beginning to vote with their feet.

Remarkably, though, AMLO's approval ratings hovered in the 60% range, even when polling showed that many Mexicans were critical of his handling of the pandemic, the economy, and the security situation in the country. Most Mexicans found AMLO likeable, genuine, and austere. They agreed with his diagnosis of Mexico's problems even if his programs failed to adequately address them. AMLO was a masterful politician who spent decades traveling the country and getting to know *el pueblo*. His utterances were well-calibrated to appeal to these people, not the urban, educated, often female middle-class Mexicans who were more likely to be his critics.

What did the Fourth Transformation mean for some of the unscripted revolutions that we have considered in this book? Preliminary analysis points to several surprising, if tentative, conclusions.

The Fate of Mexico's Dark-Skinned Majority

The name of AMLO's party, Morena, is an acronym for Movement of National Regeneration (*Movimiento de Regeneración Nacional*). It also spells out "brown," a clever nod to the skin tone of most of the

Mexican population and to Our Lady of Guadalupe, the beloved *morenita* of Tepeyac. Morena promised to be a new type of movement/party, one that at last represented the interests of Mexico's majority. It's debatable whether the "Fourth Transformation" made headway in combatting racism and its inescapable partner, classism. But Mexican society began tackling the matter on its own. *Poder Prieto* (Brown Power), a group of darker-skinned actors and actresses, called attention to the institutional racism in Mexican television and film; the nongovernmental organization *Racismo MX* flagged racism and classism in all its dimensions.[12] Nightly televised talk shows like "Es la hora de opinar" dedicated episodes to the matter, and scholars increasingly published on racism and spoke about it on university campuses.

Rhetorically and symbolically, AMLO portrayed himself as a defender of Mexico's Indigenous people. Four months into his administration, in March 2019, he made the surprising announcement that he had written Pope Francis and the King of Spain, Felipe VI, asking them to admit historic responsibility and apologize for the abuses committed against Indigenous people during the conquest and the colonial period. The Spanish government reacted sharply after the letter was made public; Spain is Mexico's second most important source of direct foreign investment, after the United States.[13] The Church, for its part, tersely replied that it had already apologized for the excesses of the conquest—multiple times, in fact—starting with Pope John Paul II in Santo Domingo in 1992 and again in 2000. Most recently, Pope Francis asked for *perdón* in Bolivia in 2015 and again in San Cristóbal de Las Casas, Chiapas in 2016.[14] Asking for these apologies served a larger political purpose for AMLO. They allowed him to take up the cause of *el pueblo bueno* and put Mexico's former colonial masters on the defensive. The maneuver backfired with some of Mexico's Indigenous population, however. The Zapatistas condemned his "stale nationalism" that not only revindicated the predatory Aztec empire but also confirmed the narrative "that with the fall of this empire, the original people of these lands were defeated."[15]

When it came time to commemorate the quincentenary of the conquest in August 2021, AMLO again chose to score political points with his base. Most professional historians today view the conquest of México-Tenochtitlán as a civil war between powerful Indigenous city-states. The Spaniards were certainly important protagonists and antagonists, but most research suggests that Indigenous combatants outnumbered them by at least 99 to 1. It was a gruesome war between and among the Indigenous. The August 2021 commemorations made it clear, however, that AMLO preferred the time-worn, dated narrative that pitted heroic but doomed Aztec warriors against rapacious Spaniards. Professional historians lamented that a teachable moment had been lost.[16] Instead of embracing and disseminating a complicated historical truth, AMLO chose the simplistic "us-versus-them" telling of the conquest that fit squarely with his polarizing populism.

AMLO claimed profound respect for Indigenous and Afro-descendent Mexicans, but they dared not get in the way of his signature infrastructure projects. When the Zapatistas and other Indigenous groups opposed construction of the Tren Maya, in Mexico's southeast, AMLO's government conducted a regional referendum to gauge residents' support for the project. These polls were often criticized for their lack of transparency and their questionable methodology. Moreover, they invariably confirmed policy decisions that had already been made by AMLO and his inner circle. At a December 2019 press conference, the director of the National Institute of Indigenous Peoples,[17] Adelfo Regino, announced the result of the consultation: 92.3 percent of the more than 100,000 people who participated indicated their support for the project. The United Nations later noted that the consultation did not meet international human rights standards, as it only noted the possible benefits of the project and not the possible negative impacts. Few Indigenous women participated in the process, the consultation was rushed, and translations into Indigenous languages were few and inadequate. Only 2.36 percent of eligible voters participated.[18]

AMLO's government, however, was undeterred. It had consulted *el pueblo* and got the result that it wanted. When Indigenous organizations and grassroots environmental groups challenged the project legally, the government charged ahead and approved contracts to build the train. More legal challenges were raised. AMLO's Tren Maya will run through the greatest expanse of rainforest in the Americas outside of Brazil, home to jaguars and other endangered species. Although AMLO pledged that "not a single tree" would be cut, millions of trees were sacrificed as bulldozers cut a broad swath through the jungle.[19] Environmentalists, hydrologists, and archeologists noted that the Yucatán Peninsula is a karstic zone replete with cenotes, the world's largest underground river, and hundreds of unexplored underground caves. Geologists feared that the ground might give way under the weight and vibrations of the trains. Mexican archeologists worked feverishly to recover artefacts, sometimes within earshot of bulldozers. On one stretch of the project, archeologists were given just 18 days to assess and excavate 37 miles of jungle. By late 2022, they had documented dozens of previously unknown ancient settlements and uncovered 25,000 monuments, 600,000 fragments of ceramics, and 450 human remains. They also discovered more than 900 caves and cenotes. But only in exceptional cases was the train rerouted around archeological sites. AMLO claimed that the train would spur development and bring opportunity to some of the country's poorest communities. But a project meant to draw tourists to the cradle of Maya civilization ended up demolishing or burying some of the physical evidence of that very culture.[20]

When legal challenges temporarily halted construction of the Tren Maya in 2022, AMLO excoriated his domestic adversaries and "pseudo-environmentalists financed by the United States government."[21] He was careful not to malign the Indigenous communities that were among the first and most steadfast opponents of the project. AMLO then ruled that the Tren Maya—essentially, a tourist train—was a matter of national security and therefore could not be challenged in court. Contractors were under great pressure to finish the project before AMLO left office in 2024.

Religion, Civic Virtues, and the Fourth Transformation

Some of the most intriguing aspects of the Fourth Transformation concerned religion and civic virtue. AMLO was deliberately ambiguous about his own personal beliefs. He affirmed that he was Catholic and was personally close to progressive, liberationist Catholic priests like Father Alejandro Solalinde and the retired bishop Raúl Vera. But he also liked to define himself as a "Cristiano," perhaps in a bid to get Evangelicals to think that he was one of them. In his home state of Tabasco, Protestants and Evangelicals have made tremendous inroads. Growing up and attending school among them, AMLO learned to speak their language. This partly explains his 2018 electoral alliance with the Evangelical/Pentecostal Social Encounter Party, whose founder promised two million votes. Progressive Morenistas were surprised that AMLO would ally with a party that opposed key elements of the Left's social agenda, like feminism, reproductive choice, marriage equality, and gay adoption rights.

Supporters and detractors alike agreed that AMLO saw himself as a redeemer, a "tropical messiah" who believed that God had chosen him to carry out the transformation of Mexico.[22] After AMLO's inauguration ceremonies, which included a ritual "cleansing" (*limpia*) by Indigenous leaders, Porfirio Muñoz Ledo tweeted that the president had experienced a "transfiguration." He was "an authentic, lay son of God and servant of the fatherland" who "revealed himself to be a mystical character, a crusader," tweeted the then-president of the Chamber of Deputies.[23] Perhaps AMLO *had* transcended the cult of personality, which is common in political leadership, and had attained a quasi-religious status among his followers. Roberto Blancarte called him "a president who at times turns into a preacher. . .not only for his biblical invocations, but because he thinks he is responding to a divine calling to save the country." He admonished his flock to "behave themselves" so that they could go to the temples and churches with a clean conscience. "His anti-corruption proposals and his promises to moralize political life make him seem like a healer of history, a purifier of twisted political souls."[24]

AMLO's first concrete attempt to heal Mexican civic life came in 2019 when the Ministry of Public Education printed millions of copies of Alfonso Reyes's *Cartilla Moral* (Moral Primer).[25] Written in 1944 for use in adult literacy campaigns, it contained simple lessons on the need to respect oneself, one's family, society, Mexico, and nature. The SEP made slight modifications and updates to Reyes's original draft, but the nostalgia in his prescriptions (and the Judeo-Christian messaging) was unmistakable. Some specialists argued the *Cartilla* violated Article 130 of the Constitution, which separates Church and state; others were more concerned that AMLO's administration had handed over its distribution to some Pentecostal churches.

AMLO's administration made a second bid to cleanse Mexican civic life a year later, when it published its "Ethical Guide for the Transformation of Mexico" (*Guía Ética para la Transformación de México*).[26] Six of AMLO's intellectual friends organized more than 50 meetings, discussion groups, and debates and sought input from churches, institutions of higher learning and civil society. The Ethical Guide promoted twenty universal principles for societal and spiritual renewal, such as dignity, honesty, gratitude, love, respect for others, forgiveness, and the importance of hard work. Ten million copies were printed and distributed to elderly pension recipients with the suggestion that they discuss and analyze its contents with their children and grandchildren.

When AMLO presented the *Guía Ética* at a *mañanera*, he declared that "Mexico's crisis is not just economic; it's also a loss of cultural, moral, and spiritual values."[27] In his diagnosis, decades of neoliberal economic policies and political corruption produced grave inequalities, damaged the social fabric, and produced a crisis in values that manifested itself in violence. AMLO was "convinced that *el pueblo* is good, a great repository of moral and spiritual values," wrote Blancarte. But he also knew that *el pueblo* was violent. "Due to the lack of social justice and out of necessity, it can be led to rob, participate in corruption and, on occasion, commit more serious crimes."[28]

Critics reacted swiftly. How dare the government promote respect for difference, when AMLO used polarizing rhetoric in his mañaneras to shame rival politicians, undermine institutions, and bully members of the independent media? How could it promote respect for the environment when it doubled down on extractivism? When its Tren Maya project dismissed environmental reviews and clearcut a 40-meter (131-foot) swath of devastation through the jungle? How dare it lecture the public on the evils of corruption, when the corruption of members of AMLO's inner circle—like director of the Federal Electricity Commission Manuel Bartlett—was a matter of public record?[29] When two of his brothers were filmed taking illegal cash contributions from a Green Party operative?[30] If the country needed ethical guidance and civic lessons, why not turn to the 1.5 million public school teachers?[31]

On the other hand, given growing inequalities in Mexico, the surge in violence since 2006, and the indisputable corruption of many of its institutions, perhaps AMLO was right to call for a public discussion about societal values. As the Catholic Church ceded its spiritual dominance over the country, AMLO's moralizing lessons were politically astute. Maybe he filled an ethical, even religious void. Political analysts fretted that AMLO undermined the state's lay tradition, but most Mexicans seemed unbothered by his foray into moral, ethical, and spiritual matters and even welcomed it.

Women and the Fourth Transformation

The Fourth Transformation coincided perfectly with the culmination of a hard-fought battle for gender parity in Mexican politics. After the 2018 elections, women held 49 percent of the seats in the national Chamber of Deputies and 51 percent in the Senate. The extension of the gender quota to the state level also produced the desired result: women won 48.8 percent of the seats in state legislatures, including exactly 50 percent of the seats in Mexico City. Change came more slowly at the local (municipal) level, where the gender quota laws still did not universally apply.[32] By way of comparison, after the 2018 elections in the United States, women held just 20 percent of the seats in the House of Representatives and 23 percent in the U.S. Senate. In 2019, Mexico ranked fourth in the world in terms of women's formal political representation in the lower or single house of Congress (the Chamber of Deputies); by comparison, the United States was tied for 76th place with Afghanistan (before the August 2021 return of the Taliban) and Cabo Verde.[33]

AMLO's presidency started off on a promising note for women. His campaign had been coordinated by a woman, Tatiana Cloutier, and his close political ally, Claudia Sheinbaum, was elected to lead Mexico City. Sheinbaum was immediately vaulted into speculative discussions about whether she would be Morena's candidate for the presidency in 2024. AMLO appointed Mexico's first-ever cabinet with gender parity and named top feminists to prominent posts.

Figure 7.3 Mayor of Mexico City, Claudia Sheinbaum, at a news conference on January 15, 2023. AMLO revived the traditional *destape* by indicating repeatedly that Sheinbaum was his favorite to succeed him as president. Luis Barron/Eyepix Group/Future Publishing/Getty Images

His problems with women began shortly after taking office with his decision to cancel funding for many civil society organizations. One group targeted was the National Network of Shelters (*Red Nacional de Refugios*) and its 41 domestic violence shelters that assist abused women. After human rights groups protested loudly, he backed down. But he went ahead and cut the budget for daycare centers.

The president's relationship with Mexican feminists worsened in early 2020. In the lead-up to International Women's Day (March 8), AMLO made a series of comments in his morning press conferences that revealed a blind spot on women's issues. He minimized the issue of feminicide and tried to blame it on the neoliberal economic model of previous governments. Then, he claimed that the feminist movement had been infiltrated by his conservative "enemies." This suggested little respect for Mexican feminists, who for decades had marched to demand reproductive rights and condemn misogynistic violence.

During the COVID-19 pandemic stay-at-home order, AMLO's government reported that domestic violence shelters saw a 77 percent increase in calls. But AMLO dismissed his own cabinet's figures, blithely claiming that 90 percent of the calls to domestic violence hotlines were "fake." He then insisted that the lockdown had not made life more dangerous for women because, unlike in other countries, Mexicans "were accustomed to living together." Wendy Figueroa, head of Mexico's network of domestic violence shelters, told the *New York Times* that AMLO was "the first president to outright deny that the violence is happening." Adding insult to injury, AMLO's Interior Ministry and CONAPO produced videos and posters during the lockdown urging would-be abusers "to not lose patience" and "breathe and count to ten" before striking anyone in their household. Critics ridiculed the campaign, claiming that it trivialized domestic violence and shifted responsibility for the crime onto its victims.[34]

Tensions rose again in spring 2021 when one of AMLO's longstanding allies, Félix Salgado Macedonio, positioned himself to run for governor of the embattled state of Guerrero. Salgado, known locally as "The Bull" (*El Toro*) for his rough machismo, faced at least five allegations of sexual assault, including two rapes. AMLO seemed unperturbed by these allegations, especially since Salgado seemed poised to win the election. Five hundred Morena party militants, including women senators, called on party leaders to replace Salgado.[35] Eventually, the INE suspended Salgado's candidacy for failing to file spending reports during the pre-campaign period. AMLO's defense of Salgado seemed like a provocation ahead of another International Women's Day demonstration in March 2021. Anticipating violence and the destruction of property, Mexico City authorities erected steel barriers around the national palace, where the president lived with his wife. The wall symbolized the divide between AMLO and today's women's movement. Activists covered the wall with the names of feminicide victims. The photo on this book's cover shows an activist attempting to scale the wall.

Against this somber backdrop, women and feminists won a hard-fought victory midway through AMLO's presidential term when the Supreme Court decriminalized abortion. Before September 2021, abortion on demand was legal only in Mexico City and in the state of Oaxaca. That month, however, Mexico's Supreme Court struck down Coahuila's restrictive law that had criminalized abortion for women and their doctors, even in cases of rape.[36] The vote was unanimous on the eleven-member court. (Four of the justices were women.) Decriminalizing the practice was not the same as legalizing it nationwide, however. Over the next few months, the states of Veracruz, Hidalgo, Baja California and Baja California Sur, Colima, Sinaloa, and Guerrero legalized abortion on demand, usually within the first twelve weeks of pregnancy. The chief justice of Mexico's Supreme Court, Arturo Zaldívar Lelo de Larrea, acknowledged that Mexico's feminists had won this victory for themselves.[37] For his part, AMLO was uncharacteristically silent on the matter. In his mañaneras before and immediately after the Supreme Court ruling, he sidestepped the issue.

In his morning news conferences, AMLO rarely missed an opportunity to remind the press that the principal opposition parties (PRI, PAN, and PRD) were "morally defeated." But Mexico's young feminists were not. They emerged as his most legitimate and implacable adversaries. They marched, did live theatre, spray-painted graffiti on iconic monuments, occupied university buildings to demand more security and the dismissal of sexual predators, placed homemade bombs in church buildings to protest pedophile priests, and burned vehicles owned by newspapers to protest the publication of gruesome feminicides.[38] AMLO incorporated an older generation of feminists into his party and cabinet. The feminists in the streets today are younger, hail from areas outside Mexico City, and have more experience with violence than the feminists of the 1970s and 1980s.[39] AMLO distrusted social movements that he could not control, and either misunderstood or dismissed the demands of Mexico's young feminists. On the other hand, his cabinet appointments provided Mexican women and feminists with more political power than they had ever had. "I don't like what López Obrador says about women, but he is giving feminists total freedom to enact feminist policies," concluded Marta Lamas.[40]

Democracy and the Fourth Transformation

Shortly before the 2021 midterm elections in Mexico, *The Economist* published an article noting that, to his credit, AMLO "lacks some of the vices of his populist peers" who were eroding their country's democratic institutions. Unlike Hungary's Viktor Orbán, India's Narendra Modi, and Brazil's Jair Bolsonaro, AMLO "does not deride gay people, bash Muslims or spur his supporters to torch the Amazon…[H]e speaks out loudly and often for Mexico's have-nots, and he is not personally corrupt. Nonetheless," concluded the article, "he is a danger to Mexican democracy."[41]

Many observers expected AMLO to support the growth and maturation of civil society and lead Mexico further down the path of democratic consolidation. AMLO's critics questioned his commitment to democracy, however, noting that he never once personally accepted an electoral defeat. As president, he attacked institutions that might have provided checks and balances to his growing presidential authority, including the crown jewel of Mexico's democratic transition, the INE (formerly IFE). In the lead-up to the June 2021 midterm election, AMLO savaged the INE repeatedly, calling it biased and expensive. He argued that elections should be run by the Interior Ministry, as they were during the days of the hegemonic PRI.

Still haunted by the results of the 2006 election, and angry that the INE had disqualified Morena candidates, AMLO resumed his attacks on Mexico's elections watchdog in the run-up to the 2024 elections. Morena and its satellite parties approved legislation in February 2023 that reduced the number of INE career civil servants by 85 percent, cut their salaries and benefits, and limited the INE's ability to regulate campaign spending, fine parties, and disqualify candidates. Most analysts agreed that the legislation severely weakened an autonomous institution that organized elections at the local level, guaranteed an objective vote count, and attempted to enforce Mexico's complicated electoral laws.[42] After Mexico's Supreme Court ruled that the legislation was unconstitutional, AMLO accused it of staging a coup against his government. He and his allies viciously attacked the court's new president, Norma Piña, the first woman to hold the post.

Two additional Mexican institutions were targets of the president's ire: the National Commission on Human Rights (*Comisión Nacional de Derechos Humanos*, or CNDH), and the National Freedom of Information Institute (INAI). The CNDH was created by President Carlos Salinas in 1990 to bolster his image as a democratic leader. It is one of the largest and best-funded organisms of its type in the world. Critics claim that the CNDH is deliberately weak; it documents abuses but cannot ensure that its recommendations are implemented.[43] Given the opportunity to strengthen the CNDH, however, AMLO decided to place it in the hands of political loyalists and marginalize it at a time of escalating attacks on women, the Indigenous, environmentalists, and journalists.[44] The INAI, created during the Fox presidency, had a better track record. Citizens used it to uncover several corruption cases during the Peña Nieto presidency. But AMLO was not committed to this kind of transparency.

He called the INAI a "sham," cut its budget, and pressed his allies in the Senate to refuse to replace three outgoing commissioners. Denied a legal quorum, the INAI was frozen in its tracks.[45] Critics claimed that crony capitalism flourished during the Fourth Transformation just as it had under Peña Nieto.

While AMLO attacked public institutions, he also took clear steps to militarize the country. The candidate who promised to return soldiers to their barracks greatly increased the military's role, profile, and budget as president. Indeed, only the military was spared AMLO's "republican austerity." Believing that the federal police force was irredeemably corrupt, he disbanded it and created a 100,000-person National Guard. After first promising to keep the National Guard under civilian control, as mandated by the Constitution, AMLO immediately maneuvered to place it under military control. In September 2022, his administration used threats, bribes, and espionage to get PRI members in Congress to support a constitutional amendment to use the army as a civil police force until at least 2028.

AMLO also turned over his administration's legacy projects to the army, to the tune of 45 billion dollars. Soldiers also built thousands of new banks, operated ports and customhouses, and helped with social programs and vaccine distribution. Some worried that this degree of militarization represented a grave risk to Mexican democracy. "Inviting the men with guns to handle huge sums of public money with scant supervision has proved catastrophic, as any Egyptian or Pakistani could warn," noted *The Economist*.[46] The militarization of public life during the Fourth Transformation unraveled one of the great achievements of the postrevolutionary Mexican state, which had generally kept soldiers on the sidelines. One analyst suggested an additional reason AMLO turned his megaprojects over to soldiers—future governments will not be able to touch them, because it would mean violating the economic interests of an armed bureaucracy.[47]

As AMLO concluded his fourth year in office, in October 2022, Mexico's Defense Ministry (*Secretaría de la Defensa Nacional*, or SEDENA) was hacked by a Latin American transparency group that calls itself Guacamaya (macaw, or "loudmouth"). It was the most damaging and extensive hack in Mexican history. Six terabytes of information containing more than four million emails shed light on the military's inner workings and confirmed the fears of many pro-democracy advocates. Despite AMLO's assurances to the contrary, Mexico's military had continued spying on journalists, environmentalists, feminists, and politicians.[48] Ironically, it spent more money on Israeli-made Pegasus spyware than it did on cybersecurity software that might have prevented the hack. "Guacamaya Leaks" linked dozens of prominent senators, deputies, and municipal authorities to organized crime syndicates. Military intelligence believed that Adán Augusto López, AMLO's Minister of the Interior, turned over security duties to members of the Jalisco Nueva Generación cartel when he was governor of Tabasco. The state of Morelos, just south of Mexico City, had become a narco-state, according to military intelligence that linked the governor (former soccer star Cuauhtémoc Blanco), 17 municipal presidents, seven state deputies from all parties, nine judges, and one senator to organized crime.[49] The military also believed that governors and municipal presidents in Mexico's southeast—mostly Morenistas—were in league with drug-trafficking organizations.

The hack also revealed ugly truths about the Mexican military itself, which had just been given new constitutional authority to patrol Mexico's streets. Top-level officers were flagged for being on the payroll of drug-trafficking organizations; former military pilots flew planes for drug traffickers; and officers sold technical equipment, weapons, and key information about rival gangs to drug cartels. The hack also revealed how the army obstructed the Ayotzinapa investigations and protected its members from prosecution for their roles in the tragedy.

The militarization of the country was, perhaps, complete. Future administrations will have to contend with a powerful military that enjoys its enhanced profile, aspires to a greater economic role, and began operating its own airline in December 2023. Meanwhile, it still resists civilian oversight. When called to testify in front of Congress about Guacamaya Leaks and plans to prevent future hacks, the Secretary of Defense, General Luis Cresencio Sandoval, refused.

As this book went to press, there were ominous signs that the Fourth Transformation represented a threat to Mexico's democratic transition and consolidation. Paradoxically, AMLO debilitated the INE even as his party performed well in state and local elections. In another paradox, Morena had become the country's dominant, even hegemonic party, but its internal structure was weak, its militants badly divided, and its internal elections marred by violence, clientelism, and other practices long perfected by the PRI. To choose its candidates for elected office, Morena conducted internal polls whose methodologies and results were questioned by everyone except the winner. In summer 2021, AMLO revived the PRIísta tradition of the *destape* (unveiling) and made it clear that his loyal acolyte, Mexico City mayor Claudia Sheinbaum, was his preferred candidate for the presidential election that would take place in three years. In summer 2023, he selected five loyalists to compete with her for the opportunity to be Morena's candidate to become not the president of the republic, but "Coordinator in Defense of the Transformation." This semantic slight-of-hand allowed Morena to begin the candidate selection process months before it was permitted by Mexico's electoral law. After a tightly controlled process that was clearly biased in Sheinbaum's favor, few were surprised when she won the nomination. Meanwhile, the opposition coalition (PAN, PRI, PRD) scrambled to select a common candidate. It settled on Xóchitl Gálvez, a pugnacious senator from the state of Hidalgo. For the first time in history, the two frontrunners heading into a presidential election were women. Backed by AMLO and seemingly limitless campaign funds, the election was Sheinbaum's to lose.

For many analysts, AMLO's Fourth Transformation was like an upside-down world. The lifelong leftist governed from the center-right. The candidate who promised to return soldiers to their barracks invited them to co-govern with him. The candidate who claimed he would never allow Trump to treat Mexico "like a piñata" showed a servile deference to the U.S. president unprecedented in the history of Mexican diplomacy. Instead of strengthening the democratic institutions that made his victory possible, he attacked them.

Instead of supporting a contemporary leftist agenda, which would include support for women's rights and the environment, AMLO disdained contemporary feminism and doubled down on extractivism. Despite his rhetoric on behalf of the poor, relatively little was done to reduce inequality, apart from raising the minimum wage and sending out direct cash transfers. This, arguably, turned the poor and the elderly into reliable political clients. Despite his policy of "Hugs, not gunshots," tens of thousands continued to perish each year in the drug wars. Meanwhile, Mexico's pre-transition, authoritarian criminal justice system continued to incarcerate poor Mexicans, sometimes for years at a time, without bringing formal charges against them.[50] AMLO promised an anti-corruption crusade, but his attorney general failed to try and convict a single member of Enrique Peña Nieto's famously corrupt inner circle, while Peña himself lived a carefree life of luxury in Madrid with his new girlfriend, Mexican model Tania Ruiz.

The Mexican president seemed nostalgic for the 1970s when he joined the PRI and cut his political teeth. His leftism seemed rooted in the past, before feminism, environmentalism, and democratic rights were priorities. For all his attacks on his predecessors, AMLO was strangely mute about the Echeverría and López Portillo administrations (1970–1976 and 1976–1982, respectively), a time of hyperpresidentialism and authoritarianism, when oil revenues supported PRI hegemony, economic nationalism, and populism—for a time. For all the talk of transformation during AMLO's presidency, some observers saw a great degree of revolutionary nationalist continuity as Morena absorbed the PRI's militants, its values, and its vices. The Fourth Transformation promised peaceful revolution, but in practice, it seemed to embody the *other* meaning of "revolution"—a full rotation, a complete cycle, a return to origin.[51]

Meanwhile, most Mexicans cannot help but look forward, to the future. We will know soon whether women can consolidate their political gains and their new reproductive freedoms; whether Mexicans continue to leave the Catholic Church in search of other religious experiences; and whether dark-skinned Mexicans can overcome the country's pigmentocracy and claim their rightful place in society and on the silver screen. Time will tell if the military ever returns to the barracks now that soldiers will patrol the streets until at least 2028. Upcoming election cycles will tell us whether the Fourth Transformation derailed Mexico's fragile democratic consolidation. As this book went to press, there were ominous signs that it had.

Notes

1 Constanza Lambertucci, "Roger Bartra: López Obrador es un populista de derechas de manual," *El País*, March 28, 2021.

2 Luis Estrada, *El imperio de los otros datos: tres años de falsedades y engaños desde Palacio* (Ciudad de México: Grijalbo, 2022).

3 Gabriel Zaid called AMLO a "poet of insults;" see Zaid, "AMLO poeta," *Letras Libres*, June 25, 2018.

4 Leonardo Curzio and Aníbal Gutiérrez, *El presidente: las filias y fobias que definirán el futuro del país* (Ciudad de México: Grijalbo, 2020), 12.

5 Daniel Alonso Viña, "López Obrador redobla su ofensiva contra la prensa: 'Quién es quién en las mentiras' se convierte en un programa diario," *El País*, November 9, 2022; and Carlos Loret de Mola A., "Para AMLO, el periodismo es enemigo número uno," *The Washington Post*, February 6, 2022.

6 Néstor Jiménez and Alonso Urrutia, "Confirma López Obrador saludo a la madre de 'El Chapo,'" *La Jornada*, March 30, 2020. AMLO made a total of four trips to Badiraguato, Sinaloa, to supervise the construction of a highway. Critics questioned why the president took such interest in this municipality, home to about 30,000 residents, as well as the birthplace of some of Mexico's most notorious drug kingpins, like Rafael Caro Quintero, co-founder of the Guadalajara cartel; the Beltrán Leyva family of drug traffickers; and 'El Chapo' Guzmán. AMLO defended his repeated visits to the so-called "Golden Triangle," infamous for its cultivation of marijuana and poppies, and proposed that it should be renamed the "Triangle of good, hardworking people" ("Triángulo de la gente buena y trabajadora").

7 Maria Abi-Habib and Óscar López, "Mexico's leader says poverty is his priority. But his policies hurt the poor," *New York Times*, July 18, 2022.

8 Curzio and Gutiérrez; and Kate Linthicum, "Why is AMLO one of the world's most popular politicians? We took a road trip through Mexico to find out," *Los Angeles Times*, December 19, 2022.

9 Roger Bartra, *Regreso a la jaula. El fracaso de López Obrador* (Ciudad de México: Penguin Random House Grupo Editorial, 2021), 115–116; see also Curzio and Gutiérrez, 441–443, 470–479.

10 Enrique Krauze, "Mexico's Ruinous Messiah;" and Óscar López, "Mexico sees its energy future in fossil fuels, not renewables," *New York Times*, August 17, 2022.

11 Curzio and Gutiérrez, 15.

12 See www.poderprieto.mx and www.racismo.mx.

13 One of AMLO's grandfathers was born in Cantabria, Spain.

14 Bernardo Barranco Villafán and Roberto Blancarte, *AMLO y la religión: El Estado laico bajo amenaza* (Ciudad de México: Grijalbo, 2019), 69, 163

15 Bartra, 112–114.

16 Federico Navarrete, "Cuatro falsas lecciones y cuatro legados problemáticos," *Proceso* Edición especial 60 (2021); and Matthew Restall, *Seven Myths of the Conquest* (New York: Oxford, 2003)

17 The Instituto Nacional de los Pueblos Indígenas, or INPI, is the successor institution to the INI.

18 Curzio and Gutiérrez, 240–242.

19 "AMLO aseguró no tirar ningún árbol para el Tren Maya," *Expansión Política*, April 21, 2022.

20 Kevin Sieff and Whitney Leaming, "Destroying Maya treasures to build a tourist train," *The Washington Post*, December 9, 2022.

21 Maria Abi-Habib, "Over caves and over budget, Mexico's train barrels toward disaster," *New York Times,* August 28, 2022.

22 Barranco and Blancarte, 62; and Enrique Krause, "Mexico's Ruinous Messiah," *The New York Review of Books,* July 2, 2020.

23 "AMLO, un iluminado: Muñoz Ledo," *El Universal*, December 3, 2018; Bartra called the limpia "one of the most ridiculous and artificial acts that I had ever seen, and it reminded me of the cheesy indigenismo of Echeverría and López Portillo. . .It was a fake and absurd production, truly shameful, a joke played on the Indigenous." Bartra, 93–94.

24 Barranco and Blancarte, 9, 25, 27, 120.

25 Alfonso Reyes, *Cartilla Moral* 2nd ed. (Ciudad de México: Secretaría de Educación Pública, 2018 [1992]).

26 *Guía Ética para la Transformación de México* (Ciudad de México: Gobierno de México, 2020).

27 Bernardo Barranco V., "*Guía ética* y el catecismo político de AMLO," *Proceso* December 8, 2020.

28 Barranco and Blancarte, 39.

29 Another notorious case of inner-circle corruption involved one of AMLO's Supreme Court picks, Yasmín Esquivel, who was found to have plagiarized both her bachelor's thesis and her doctoral dissertation but refused to step down. Esquivel was married to one of AMLO's favorite contractors, José María Riobóo; see Zedryk Raziel and Beatriz Guillén, "La ministra Yasmín Esquivel plagió en su tesis de doctorado," *El País*, February 24, 2023.

30 Elena Chávez alleges that AMLO's political rise was financed by close allies who skimmed cash from municipal governments and major construction projects, like the accident-prone Line 12 of the Mexico City subway; see *El rey del cash: el saqueo oculto del presidente y su equipo cercano* (Ciudad de México: Penguin Random House, 2022).

31 For a critical discussion of the *Guía Ética* on Leo Zuckermann's program "Es la hora de opinar" with Mario Arriagada, Denise Dresser, and Pablo Majluf, click here: https://laicismo.org/la-guia-etica-de-amlo-es-un-avance-para-un-gobierno-laico/227470.

32 INEGI, *Mujeres y hombres en México, 2019* (Aguascalientes: Instituto Nacional de Geografía y Estadística, 2019); and INEGI, *Censo nacional de gobiernos municipales y demarcaciones territoriales de la Ciudad de México, 2019*, 8–9.

33 Inter-parliamentary Union data available at http://archive.ipu.org/wmn-e/classif.Htm

34 Natalie Kitroeff, "Mexico's President Says Most Domestic Violence Calls Are 'Fake,'" *New York Times*, May 31, 2020.

35 Elisabeth Malkin, "'AMLO Made us Public Enemy No.1': Why Feminists are Mexico's Voice of Opposition," *The Guardian*, March 8, 2021.

36 Coahuila's law had also assigned a lesser penalty for marital rape.

37 Arturo Rodríguez García, "'El mérito' es de las mujeres que lucharon por despenalizar el aborto: Zaldívar," *Proceso*, September 8, 2021; and Natalie Kitroeff, "How Mexico's Top Justice, Raised Catholic, Became an Abortion Rights Champion," *New York Times*, July 9, 2022.

38 Laura Castellanos, "La rabia de las jóvenes feministas cimbra al gobierno de AMLO," *The Washington Post* March 6, 2020.

39 Lidia Arista, "El movimiento feminista, el único que hace trastabillar a AMLO," *Expansión política*, March 9, 2020.

40 Natalie Kitroeff, "Mexico's president says most domestic violence calls are 'fake,'" *New York Times*, May 31, 2020.

41 "The false messiah," *The Economist*, May 29, 2021.

42 Alberto J. Olvera, "El Plan B y el futuro de la democracia," *El País*, Dec. 15, 2022; and Natalie Kitroeff, "Mexico Hobbles Election Agency that Helped End One-Party Rule," *New York Times*, Feb. 22, 2023.

43 Meyer, *Nuestra tragedia persistente*, 106–108.

44 Gloria Leticia Díaz, "El cuestionado viraje de la CNDH: alejarse de las víctimas y acercarse al poder," *Proceso* 2402, November 13, 2022.

45 Isabella González, "El organismo para la transparencia en México queda paralizado por tiempo indefinido," *El País*, April 1, 2023.

46 "The false messiah," *The Economist*, May 29, 2021.

47 Leo Zuckermann, "La deriva autoritaria de López Obrador," *Excélsior*, August 11, 2022.

48 Natalie Kitroeff and Ronen Bergman, "How Mexico Became the Biggest User of the World's Most Notorious Spy Tool," *New York Times*, April 18, 2023.

49 Diana Lastiri, "La SEDENA documenta los nexos de Cuauhtémoc Blanco con el crimen organizado," *Proceso* 2402, November 13, 2022.

50 In 2021, *Animal político* documented how Mexico's prison system victimizes innocent poor people; see "Prisión preventiva: el arma que encarcela pobres e inocentes," "Pobres, las víctimas de la prisión preventiva," and "Hay más mujeres inocentes que condenadas en la cárcel," at https://www.animalpolitico.com/prision-preventiva-delitos-encarcela-pobres-inocentes/.

51 Javier Sicilia, "La transformación traicionada," *Proceso* 2402, November 13, 2022.

Bibliography

Periodicals

AP News, New York City.
Cihuat: Voz de la Coalición de Mujeres, Mexico City.
The Economist, London.
Excélsior, Mexico City.
Expansión Política, Mexico City.
fem, Mexico City.
The Guardian, London.
La Jornada, Mexico City.
La Revuelta, Mexico City.
Letras Libres, Mexico City.
Los Angeles Times, Los Angeles.
National Catholic Reporter, Kansas City, MO.
The New York Times, New York City.
The New York Review of Books, New York City.
The New Yorker, New York City.
Nexos, Mexico City.
El País, Madrid.
Proceso, Mexico City.
El Universal, Mexico City.
Vice News, New York City.

Mexico's Unscripted Revolutions: Political and Social Change since 1958,
First Edition. Stephen E. Lewis.

Published Sources

Aguilar Rivera, José Antonio. *El fin de la raza cósmica. Consideraciones sobre el esplendor y decadencia del liberalismo en México*. México, D.F.: Editorial Océano de México, 2001.

Alegre, Robert F. *Railroad Radicals in Cold War Mexico: Gender, Class, and Memory*. Lincoln: University of Nebraska Press, 2013.

Amnesty International. *Women's Struggle for Justice and Safety: Violence in the Family in Mexico*. 2008.

Aviña, Alexander. *Specters of Revolution: Peasant Guerrillas in the Cold War Mexican Countryside*. New York: Oxford University Press, 2014.

Aviña, Alexander. "A War against Poor People." In *México Beyond 1968: Revolutionaries, Radicals, and Repression during the Global Sixties and the Subversive Seventies*, eds. Jaime M. Pensado and Enrique Ochoa. Tucson: University of Arizona Press, 2018, 134–152.

Bailey, John. "Drug Traffickers as Political Actors in Mexico's Nascent Democracy." In *The Oxford Handbook of Mexican Politics*, ed. Roderic Ai Camp. New York: Oxford University Press, 2012, 466–494.

Baldez, Lisa. "Primaries vs. Quotas: Gender and Candidate Nominations in Mexico, 2003." *Latin American Politics and Society*, 49:3 (Fall 2007): 69–96.

Bantjes, Adrian. *As If Jesus Walked on Earth: Cardenismo, Sonora, and the Mexican Revolution*. Wilmington, DE: Scholarly Resources, Inc., 1998.

Barranco Villafán, Bernardo and Roberto Blancarte. *AMLO y la religión: El Estado laico bajo amenaza*. Ciudad de México: Grijalbo, 2019.

Bartra, Eli. "¿Y siguen las brujas conspirando? En torno a las luchas feministas en México." In *Las políticas del subjeto en Nuestra América*, coords. Francesca Gargallo and Rosario Galo Moya. México, D.F.: UACM, 2013, 179–197.

Bartra, Eli. "Tres décadas de neofeminismo en México." In Eli Bartra, Anna M. Fernández Poncela and Ana Lau, *Feminismo en México, ayer y hoy*. México, D.F.: Colección Molinos de Viento, 2002, 45–81.

Bartra, Eli, María Brumm, Chela Cervantes, Bea Faith, Lucero González, Dominque Guillemet, Berta Hiriart, and Ángeles Necoechea. *La Revuelta: Reflexiones, testimonios y reportajes de mujeres en México, 1975*-1983. México, D.F.: Martín Casillas Editores, 1983.

Bartra, Roger. *Regreso a la jaula. El fracaso de López Obrador*. Ciudad de México: Penguin Random House Grupo Editorial, 2021.

Basave Benítez, Agustín F. *México mestizo: Análisis del nacionalismo mexicano en torno a la mestizofilia de Andrés Molina Enríquez*. México, DF: Fondo de Cultura Económica, 1993 (1992).

Beer, Caroline C. and Roderic Ai Camp. "Democracy, Gender Quotas, and Political Recruitment in Mexico." *Politics, Groups, and Identities* 4:2 (2016): 179–195.

Benjamin, Thomas. *La Revolución: Mexico's Great Revolution as Memory, Myth, and History*. Austin: University of Texas Press, 2000.

Bizberg, Ilán. "México: una transición fallida." *Desacatos* 48 (May–Aug. 2015): 122–139.

Blancarte, Roberto. *Historia de la Iglesia Católica en México*. México, D.F.: El Colegio Mexiquense/Fondo de Cultura Económica, 1992.

Blum, Ann. *Domestic Economies*. Lincoln: University of Nebraska Press, 2010.

Bonfil Batalla, Guillermo. "Del indigenismo de la revolución a la antropología crítica." In *De eso que llaman antropología mexicana*, eds. Arturo Warman, Margarita Nolasco Armas, Guillermo Bonfil Batalla, Mercedes Olivera de Vázquez, and Enrique Valencia. México, DF: Editorial Nuestro Tiempo, 1970, 39–65.

Bonfil Batalla, Guillermo. *México profundo: una civilización negada*. México, D.F.: Grijalbo, 1987.

Boyer, Christopher. *Becoming Campesinos: Politics, Identity, and Agrarian Struggle in Postrevolutionary Michoacán*. Palo Alto: Stanford University Press, 2003.

Brambila, Carlos. "Mexico's Population Policy and Demographic Dynamics: The Record of Three Decades." In *Do Population Policies Matter? Fertility and Politics in Egypt, India, Kenya, and Mexico*. New York: Population Council, 1998, 157–191.

Bruhn, Kathleen. "Chronicle of a Victory Foretold." In *Mexico's Evolving Democracy: A Comparative Study of the 2012 Elections*, eds. Jorge I. Domínguez, Kenneth F. Greene, and Alejandro Moreno. Baltimore: Johns Hopkins University Press, 2015, 32–62.

Bruhn, Kathleen. "The PRD and the Mexican Left." In *The Oxford Handbook of Mexican Politics*, ed. Roderic Ai Camp. New York: Oxford University Press, 2012, 187–209.

Bruhn, Kathleen. "Whores and Lesbians: Political Activism, Party Strategies, and Gender Quotas in Mexico." *Electoral Studies* 23 (2003), 101–119.

Buchenau, Jürgen. *The Last Caudillo: Álvaro Obregón and the Mexican Revolution*. Malden, MA: Wiley-Blackwell, 2011.

Buchenau, Jürgen. *Plutarco Elías Calles and the Mexican Revolution*. Lanham, MD: Rowman and Littlefield Publishers, 2007.

Butler, Matthew. "Catholicism in Mexico, 1910 to the Present." In *Oxford Research Encyclopedia of Latin American History*. New York: Oxford University Press, Nov. 2016.

Cadena-Roa, Jorge y Miguel Armando López Leyva. "La consolidación de la democracia en México: avances y desafíos (2000-2006)." *Estudios sociológicos de El Colegio de México* 29:86 (May–Aug. 2011): 415–462.

Camp, Roderic Ai. *Crossing Swords: Politics and Religion in Mexico*. New York: Oxford University Press, 1997.

Camp, Roderic Ai and Shannan L. Mattiace. *Politics in Mexico: The Path of a New Democracy*. 7th ed. New York: Oxford University Press, 2020 (1994).

Castañeda, Jorge. *Perpetuating Power: How Mexican Presidents were Chosen*. Trans. Padraic Arthur Smithies. New York: The New Press, 2000 (1999).

Chang, Jason Oliver. *Chino: Anti-Chinese Racism in Mexico, 1880–1940*. Chicago: University of Illinois Press, 2017.

Chávez, Elena. *El rey del cash: el saqueo oculto del presidente y su equipo cercano*. Ciudad de México: Penguin Random House, 2022.

Chesnut, R. Andrew. *Devoted to Death: Santa Muerte, the Skeleton Saint*. New York: Oxford University Press, 2013.

Cohen, Theodore W. *Finding Afro-Mexico: Race and Nation after the Revolution*. New York: Cambridge University Press, 2020.

Crespo, José Antonio. "Party Competition in Mexico: Evolution and Prospects." In *Dilemmas of Political Change in Mexico*, ed. Kevin Middlebrook. London: Institute of Latin American Studies, 2004, 57–81.

Curzio, Leonardo and Aníbal Gutiérrez. *El presidente: las filias y fobias que definirán el futuro del país*. Ciudad de México: Grijalbo, 2020.

Dawson, Alexander. *First World Dreams: Mexico since 1989*. New York: Zed Books, 2006.

Dawson, Alexander S. *Indian and Nation in Revolutionary Mexico*. Tucson: University of Arizona Press, 2004.

"Declaración de Barbados I (1971)." In *Documentos fundamentales del indigenismo en México*, eds. José del Val and Carlos Zolla. México, D.F.: UNAM, 2014, 611–19.

Dillingham, A. S. *Oaxaca Resurgent: Indigeneity, Development, and Inequality in Twentieth-Century Mexico*. Stanford: Stanford University Press, 2021.

Domínguez, Jorge. "Mexico's Campaigns and the Benchmark Elections of 2000 and 2006." In *The Oxford Handbook of Mexican Politics*, ed. Roderic Ai Camp. New York: Oxford University Press, 2012, 523–544.

Domínguez, Jorge. "Mexico's 2012 Presidential Election: Conclusions." In *Mexico's Evolving Democracy: A Comparative Study of the 2012 Elections*, eds. Jorge I. Domínguez, Kenneth F. Greene, and Alejandro Moreno. Baltimore: Johns Hopkins University Press, 2015, 252–270.

Dormady, Jason H. *Primitive Revolution: Restorationist Religion and the Idea of the Mexican Revolution, 1940-1968*. Albuquerque: University of New Mexico Press, 2011.

Dresser, Denise. *Manifiesto mexicano: Cómo perdimos el rumbo y cómo recuperarlo*. Ciudad de México: Penguin Random House, 2018.

Earle, Rebecca. *The Return of the Native: Indians and Myth-Making in Spanish America, 1810-1930*. Durham: Duke University Press, 2007.

Edmonds-Poli, Emily, and David A. Shirk. *Contemporary Mexican Politics*. 4th ed. Boulder: Rowman and Littlefield, 2020 (2009).

Eisenstadt, Todd. *Courting Democracy: Party Strategies and Electoral Institutions*. New York: Cambridge University Press, 2004.

Eisenstadt, Todd. "The Origins and Rationality of the 'Legal versus Legitimate' Dichotomy Invoked in Mexico's 2006 Post-Electoral Conflict." *PS: Political Science & Politics* 40:1 (January 2007): 39–43.

Eisenstadt, Todd and Jennifer Yelle. "Ulysses, the Sirens, and Mexico's Judiciary: Increasing Precommitments to Strengthen the Rule of Law." In *The Oxford Handbook of Mexican Politics*, ed. Roderic Ai Camp. New York: Oxford University Press, 2012, 210–233.

Estrada, Luis. *El imperio de los otros datos: tres años de falsedades y engaños desde Palacio*. Ciudad de México: Grijalbo, 2022.

Fallaw, Ben. *Cárdenas Compromised: The Failure of Reform in Postrevolutionary Yucatán*. Durham: Duke University Press, 2001.

Fazio, Carlos. *La cruz y el martillo*. México, D.F.: Editorial Joaquín Ortiz/ Planeta, 1987.

Fazio, Carlos. *Samuel Ruiz: el caminante*. México, D.F.: Espasa Calpe Mexicana S.A., 1994.

Fortuny Loret de Mola, Patricia. "La Luz del Mundo, estado laico y gobierno panista. Análisis de una coyuntura en Guadalajara." *Espiral,* 7:19 (Sept.–Dec. 2000): 129–149.

Frazier, Lessie Jo and Deborah Cohen. "Mexico '68: Defining the Space of the Movement, Heroic Masculinity in the Prison, and 'Women' in the Streets." *Hispanic American Historical Review* 83:4 (Nov. 2003): 617–660.

Frías, Sonia M. "Resisting Patriarchy within the State." *Women's Studies International Forum* 33:6 (2010): 542–551.

Gall, Olivia. "Identidad, exclusión y racismo: reflexiones teóricas y sobre México." *Revista Mexicana de Sociología* 66:2 (2004), 221–259.

Gall, Olivia. "Mexican Long-living Mestizophilia versus a Democracy Open to Diversity." *Latin American and Caribbean Ethnic Studies* 8:3 (2013): 280–303.

Garrard, Virginia, and Justin M. Doran. "Pentecostalism and Neo-Pentecostalism in Latin America." In *The Oxford Handbook of Latin American Christianity*, eds. David Thomas Orique, O.P., Susan Fitzpatrick-Behrens, and Virginia Garrard. New York: Oxford University Press, 2020, 290–307.

Gillingham, Paul. "Mexican Elections, 1910-1994: Voters, Violence, and Veto Power." In *The Oxford Handbook of Mexican Politics*, ed. Roderic Ai Camp. New York: Oxford University Press, 2012, 53–76.

Gillingham, Paul. *Unrevolutionary Mexico: The Birth of a Strange Dictatorship.* New Haven: Yale University Press, 2021.

Gillingham, Paul and Benjamin T. Smith. "Introduction: The Paradoxes of Revolution." In *Dictablanda: Politics, Work, and Culture in Mexico, 1938-1968*, eds. Paul Gillingham and Benjamin T. Smith. Durham: Duke University Press, 2014, 1–43.

Gilly, Adolfo, with Rhina Roux, Gerardo Ávalos Tenorio, Felipe Arturo Ávila Espinosa, and Dagoberto Vargas Méndez. *Cartas a Cuauhtémoc Cárdenas.* México, D.F.: Ediciones Era, 1989.

Gómez Bruera, Hernán. *El color del privilegio: el racismo cotidiano en México.* Ciudad de México: Editorial Planeta Mexicana, 2020.

Gómez Tagle, Silvia. "Public Institutions and Electoral Transparency in Mexico." *Dilemmas of Political Change in Mexico*, ed. Kevin J. Middlebrook. London: Institute of Latin American Studies, 2004, 82–107.

Grayson, George W. *Mexican Messiah: Andrés Manuel López Obrador.* University Park, PA: University of Pennsylvania Press, 2007.

Grillo, Ioan. *Blood Gun Money: How America Arms Gangs and Cartels.* New York: Bloomsbury Publishing Inc., 2021.

Guía Ética para la Transformación de México. Ciudad de México: Gobierno de México, 2020.

Gutmann, Matthew. *Fixing Men: Sex, Birth Control, and AIDS in Mexico*. Berkeley: University of California Press, 2007.

Hart, John M. *Revolutionary Mexico: The Coming and Process of the Mexican Revolution*. Berkeley: University of California Press, 1987.

Hartch, Todd. *Missionaries of the State: The Summer Institute of Linguistics, State Formation, and Indigenous Mexico, 1935-1985*. Tuscaloosa: University of Alabama Press, 2006.

Hartch, Todd. *Understanding World Christianity: Mexico*. Minneapolis: Fortress Press, 2019.

Harvey, Neil. *The Chiapas Rebellion: The Struggle for Land and Democracy*. Durham: Duke University Press, 1998.

Heredia, Blanca, and Hernán Gómez Bruera. *4T. Claves para descrifrar el rompecabezas*. Ciudad de México: Penguin Random House Grupo Editorial, 2021.

Hernández, Anabel. *La verdadera noche de Iguala: La historia que el gobierno trató de ocultar*. Ciudad de México: Penguin Random House Grupo Editorial, S.A. de C.V., 2016.

Hernández Castillo, Rosalva Aída. "Toward a Culturally Situated Women's Rights Agenda: Reflections from Mexico." In *Women's Movements in the Global Era: The Power of Local Feminisms*, ed. Amrita Basu. Boulder: Westview Press, 2010, 315–342.

Hughes, Sallie. "Democracy in the Newsroom: The Evolution of Journalism and the News Media." In *The Oxford Handbook of Mexican Politics*, ed. Roderic I. Camp. New York: Oxford University Press, 2012, 367–397.

Iglesias Prieto, Norma. *Beautiful Flowers of the Maquiladora: Life Histories of Women Workers in Tijuana*. Austin: University of Texas Press, 2001 (1997).

Knight, Alan. *The Mexican Revolution*. 2 vols. New York: Cambridge University Press, 1986.

Lamas, Marta. "Cuerpo y política: la batalla por despenalizar al aborto." In *Un fantasma recorre el siglo: luchas feministas en México, 1910-2010*, coords. Gisela Espinosa Damián and Ana Lau Jaiven. México, D.F.: UAM-Xochimilco/Conacyt/Ecosur/Editorial Itaca, 2011, 196–204.

Lamas, Marta. "Del 68 a hoy: la movilización política de las mujeres." *Revista Mexicana de Ciencias Políticas y Sociales* 63:234 (Sept.-Dec. 2018): 265–285.

Lamas, Marta. "The Feminist Movement and the Development of Political Discourse on Voluntary Motherhood in Mexico." *Reproductive Health Matters* 5:10 (Nov. 1997): 58–67.

Lamas, Marta, Alicia I. Martínez, María Luisa Tarrés, and Esperanza Tuñón. "Building Bridges: The Growth of Popular Feminism in Mexico." In *The Challenge of Local Feminisms: Women's Movements in Global Perspective*. Boulder: Westview Press, 1995, 324–347.

Lamas, Marta. "De la protesta a la propuesta: el feminismo en México a finales del siglo XX." In *Historia de las mujeres en España y América Latina. Vol. IV: Del siglo XX a los umbrales del* XXI, coords. Guadalupe Gómez-Ferrer, Gabriela Cano, Dora Barrancos, y Asunción Lavrin. Madrid: Cátedra, 2006, 903–921.

Lawson, Chappell H. "Building the Fourth Estate: Media Opening and Democratization in Mexico." In *Dilemmas of Political Change in Mexico*, ed. Kevin J. Middlebrook. London: Institute of Latin American Studies, 2004, 373–400.

Lawson, Chappelle H. "The 2012 Election in Context." In *Mexico's Evolving Democracy: A Comparative Study of the 2012 Elections*, eds. Jorge I. Domínguez, Kenneth F. Greene, and Alejandro Moreno. Baltimore: Johns Hopkins University Press, 2015, 1–31.

Lenti, Joseph U. *Redeeming the Revolution: The State and Organized Labor in Post-Tlatelolco Mexico*. Lincoln: University of Nebraska Press, 2017.

Lewis, Stephen E. *The Ambivalent Revolution: Forging State and Nation in Chiapas, 1910-1945*. Albuquerque: University of New Mexico Press, 2005.

Lewis, Stephen E. *Rethinking Mexican Indigenismo: The INI's Coordinating Center in Highland Chiapas and the Fate of a Utopian Project*. Albuquerque: University of New Mexico Press, 2018.

Livingston, Jessica. "Murder in Juárez: Gender, Sexual Violence, and the Global Assembly Line." *Frontiers: A Journal of Women Studies* 25:1 (2004): 59–76.

Loaeza, Soledad. "La iglesia católica mexicana y el reformismo autoritario." *Foro Internacional* 25:2 (Oct.–Dec. 1984): 138–165.

Loaeza, Soledad. *La restauración de la Iglesia católica en la transición mexicana*. México, D.F.: El Colegio de México, 2013.

López, Rick A. *Crafting Mexico: Intellectuals, Artisans, and the State after the Revolution*. Durham: Duke University Press, 2010.

Magar, Eric. "The Electoral Institutions: Party Subsidies, Campaign Decency, and Entry Barriers." In *Mexico's Evolving Democracy: A Comparative Study of the 2012 Elections*, eds. Jorge I. Domínguez, Kenneth F. Greene, and Alejandro Moreno. Baltimore: Johns Hopkins University Press, 2015, 63–85.

Mora, Mariana. *Kuxlejal Politics. Indigenous Autonomy, Race, and Decolonizing Research in Zapatista Communities*. Austin: University of Texas Press, 2017.

Masferrer Kan, Elio. *Pluralidad religiosa en México. Cifras y proyecciones*. Buenos Aires: Libros de la Araucaria, 2011.

Mateos Cortés, Laura Selene and Gunther Dietz. "Universidades interculturales en México: Balance crítico de la primera década." *Revista Mexicana de Investigación Educativa* 21: 70 (2016): 683–690.

Mattiace, Shannan L. *To See with Two Eyes: Peasant Activism and Indian Autonomy in Chiapas, Mexico*. Albuquerque: University of New Mexico Press, 2003.

Mattiace, Shannan. "Social and Indigenous Movements in Mexico's Transition to Democracy." In *The Oxford Handbook of Mexican Politics*, ed. Roderic Ai Camp. New York: Oxford University Press, 2012, 398–422.

McCormick, Gladys. "The Forgotten Jaramillo: Building a Social Base of Support for Authoritarianism in Rural Mexico." In *Dictablanda: Politics, Work, and Culture in Mexico 1938-1968*, eds. Paul Gillingham and Benjamin T. Smith. Durham: Duke University Press, 2014, 196–215.

Meyer, Lorenzo. *Nuestra tragedia persistente: La democracia autoritaria en México*. México, D.F.: Debate, 2013.

Mitchell, Stephanie. "Revolutionary Feminism, Revolutionary Politics: Suffrage under Cardenismo." *The Americas* 72:3 (July 2015): 439–468.

Moreno Figueroa, Mónica G. "Distributed Intensities: Whiteness, Mestizaje and the Logics of Mexican Racism." *Ethnicities* 10:3 (2010): 387–401.

Muñoz, María L. O. *Stand Up and Fight: Participatory Indigenismo, Populism, and Mobilization in Mexico, 1970-1984*. Tucson: University of Arizona Press, 2016.

Muñoz Ledo, Porfirio. *La vía radical: para refundar la república*. México, D.F.: Grijalbo, 2010.

Navarrete, Federico. *México racista. Una denuncia*. México, D.F.: Penguin Random House Grupo Editorial, 2016.

Nichter, Simeon and Brian Palmer-Rubin. "Clientelism, Declared Support, and Mexico's 2012 Campaign." In *Mexico's Evolving Democracy: A Comparative Study of the 2012 Elections*, eds. Jorge I. Domínguez, Kenneth

F. Greene, and Alejandro Moreno. Baltimore: Johns Hopkins University Press, 2015, 200–225.

Nolasco Armas, Margarita. "La antropología aplicada y su destino final, el indigenismo." In *De eso que llaman antropología mexicana,* eds. Arturo Warman, Margarita Nolasco Armas, Guillermo Bonfil Batalla, Mercedes Olivera de Vázquez, and Enrique Valencia. México, DF: Editorial Nuestro Tiempo, 1970, 66–93.

Olcott, Jocelyn. *International Women's Year: The Greatest Consciousness-Raising Event in History.* New York: Oxford, 2017.

Olcott, Jocelyn. *Revolutionary Women in Postrevolutionary Mexico.* Durham: Duke University Press, 2005.

Olvera, Alberto J. "The Elusive Democracy: Political Parties, Democratic Institutions, and Civil Society in Mexico." *Latin American Research Review,* Special Issue: Living in Actually Existing Democracies (2010): 78–107.

Ortiz-Ortega, Adrianna and Mercedes Barquet. "Gendering Transition to Democracy in Mexico." *Latin American Research Review* Special Issue 45 (2010): 108–137.

Ovalle Fernández, Ignacio. "Bases programáticas de la política indigenista." In *INI, 30 años después: revisión crítica.* México, DF: INI, 1978, 9–21.

Padilla, Tanalís. "Rural Education, Political Radicalism, and *Normalista* Identity in Mexico after 1940." In *Dictablanda: Politics, Work, and Culture in Mexico, 1938-1968,* eds. Paul Gillingham and Benjamin T. Smith. Durham: Duke University Press, 2014, 341–359.

Padilla, Tanalís. *Rural Resistance in the Land of Zapata: The Jaramillista Movement and the Myth of the Pax Priísta, 1940-1962.* Durham: Duke University Press, 2008.

Padilla, Tanalís. *Unintended Lessons of Revolution: Student Teachers and Political Radicalism in Twentieth-Century Mexico.* Durham: Duke University Press, 2021.

Pansters, Wil. "La Santa Muerte: History, Devotion, and Societal Context." In *La Santa Muerte in Mexico: History, Devotion, and Society,* ed. Wil Pansters. Albuquerque: University of New Mexico Press, 2019.

Pensado, Jaime M. "'To Assault with the Truth': The Revitalization of Conservative Militancy in Mexico During the Global Sixties." *The Americas* 70:3 (January 2014): 489–521.

Pensado, Jaime M. *Rebel Mexico: Student Unrest and Authoritarian Political Culture During the Long Sixties.* Stanford: Stanford University Press, 2013.

Pérez Vejo, Tomás. "Raza y construcción nacional. México, 1810–1910." In *Raza y política en Hispanoamérica*, eds. Tomás Pérez Vejo and Pablo Yankelevich. Madrid y Ciudad de México: Iberoamericana/Bonilla Artigas Editores/El Colegio de México, 2018, 61–100.

Pitarch, Pedro. "Los Zapatistas y arte de la ventriloquia." *Istor* 17 (2004): 95–132.

Poniatowska, Elena. *La noche de Tlatelolco: testimonios de historia oral.* México D.F.: Ediciones Era, 1971.

Poole, C.M., Stafford. *The Guadalupan Controversies in Mexico.* Stanford: Stanford University Press, 2006.

Preston, Julia and Samuel Dillon. *Opening Mexico: The Making of a Democracy.* New York: Farrar, Straus and Giroux, 2004.

Rath, Thomas. *Myths of Demilitarization in Postrevolutionary Mexico, 1920-1960.* Chapel Hill: University of North Carolina Press, 2013.

Restall, Matthew. *Seven Myths of the Conquest.* New York: Oxford, 2003.

Restall, Matthew and Kris Lane. *Latin America in Colonial Times.* New York: Cambridge University Press, 2011.

Reyes, Alfonso. *Cartilla Moral.* 2nd ed. Ciudad de México: Secretaría de Educación Pública, 2018 [1992].

Rodríguez, Victoria Elizabeth. *Women in Contemporary Mexican Politics.* Austin: University of Texas Press, 2003.

Rosemblatt, Karin Alejandra. *The Science and Politics of Race in Mexico and the United States, 1910-1950.* Chapel Hill: The University of North Carolina Press, 2018.

Ruiz, Ramón. *The Great Rebellion: Mexico, 1905-1924.* New York: Norton, 1980.

Rus, Jan. "Rereading Tzotzil Ethnography: Recent Scholarship from Chiapas, Mexico." In *Pluralizing Ethnography: Comparison and Representation in Maya Cultures, Histories, and Identities*, eds. John M. Watanabe and Edward F. Fischer. Santa Fe: School of American Research Press, 2004, 199–230.

Schell, Patience A. *Church and State Education in Revolutionary Mexico City.* Tucson: University of Arizona Press, 2003.

Scheper Hughes, Jennifer. "The Niño Jesús Doctor: Novelty and Innovation in Mexican Religion." *Nova Religio: The Journal of Alternative and Emergent Religions* 16:2 (2012): 4–28.

Schulenburg Prado, Monseñor Guillermo. *Memorias del "último Abad de Guadalupe."* México, D.F.: Miguel Ángel Porrúa, 2003.

Sherman, John W. "The Mexican Miracle and its Collapse." In *The Oxford History of Mexico*, 2nd ed., eds. William H. Beezley and Michael C. Meyer. New York: Oxford University Press, 2010, 552–554.

Smith, Benjamin T. "Building a State on the Cheap: Taxation, Social Movements, and Politics." In *Dictablanda: Politics, Work, and Culture in Mexico, 1938-1968*, eds. Paul Gillingham and Benjamin T. Smith. Durham: Duke University Press, 2014, 255–275.

Smith, Benjamin T. *The Dope: The Real History of the Mexican Drug Trade.* New York: W.W. Norton and Company, 2021.

Smith, Benjamin T. *The Mexican Press and Civil Society: Stories from the Newsroom, Stories from the Street.* Chapel Hill: The University of North Carolina Press, 2018.

Smith, Benjamin T. "Saints and Demons: Putting La Santa Muerte in Historical Perspective." In *La Santa Muerte in Mexico: History, Devotion, and Society*, ed. Wil Pansters. Albuquerque: University of New Mexico Press, 2019, 58–83.

Snodgrass, Michael. "The Golden Age of Charrismo: Workers, Braceros, and the Political Machinery of Postrevolutionary Mexico." In *Dictablanda: Politics, Work, and Culture in Mexico, 1938-1968*, eds. Paul Gillingham and Benjamin T. Smith. Durham: Duke University Press, 2014, 175–195.

Soto Laveaga, Gabriela. *Jungle Laboratories: Mexican Peasants, National Projects, and the Making of the Pill.* Durham: Duke University Press, 2009.

Soto Laveaga, Gabriela. "'Let's Become Fewer': Soap Operas, Contraception, and Nationalizing the Mexican Family in an Overpopulated World." *Sexuality Research & Social Policy* 4:3 (Sept. 2007): 19–33.

Soto Laveaga, Gabriela. "Médicos, hospitales y servicios de inteligencia: el movimiento médico mexicano de 1964-1965." *Salud Colectiva* 7:1 (Jan.–April 2011): 87–97.

Staudt, Kathleen and Gabriela Montoya. "Violence and Activism at the Mexico-United States Border." In *Feminist Agendas and Democracy in Latin America*, ed. Jane S. Jaquette. Durham: Duke University Press, 2009, 186-207.

Toledo Tello, Sonia and Anna María Garza Caligaris. "Gender and Stereotypes in the Social Movements of Chiapas." In *Dissident Women: Gender and Cultural Politics in Chiapas*, eds. Shannon Speed, R. Aída Hernández Castillo, and Lynn M. Stephen. Austin: University of Texas Press, 2006, 97–114.

Trejo, Guillermo. "Las calles, las montañas y las urnas (notas sobre la participación social y la transición a la democracia)." In *Los retos de la democracia:*

Estado de derecho, corrupción, sociedad civil, eds. Alberto Ortega Venzor et al. México: Editorial Porrúa, 2004, 519–529.

Trejo, Guillermo and Sandra Ley. *Votes, Drugs, and Violence: The Political Logic of Criminal Wars in Mexico*. New York: Cambridge University Press, 2020.

Trejo, Guillermo and Sandra Ley. "Why Did Drug Cartels Go to War in Mexico? Subnational Party Alternation, the Breakdown of Criminal Protection, and the Onset of Large-Scale Violence." *Comparative Political Studies* 51:7 (2017): 900–937.

Vasconcelos, José. *La Raza Cósmica: Misión de la raza iberoamericana. Notas de viajes a la América del Sur*. Madrid: Agencia Mundial de Librería, 1925.

Vaughan, Mary Kay. *Cultural Politics in Revolution: Teachers, Peasants, and Schools in Mexico, 1930-1940*. Tucson: University of Arizona Press, 1997.

Vaughan, Mary Kay. *Portrait of a Young Painter: Pepe Zúñiga and Mexico City's Rebel Generation*. Durham: Duke University Press, 2015.

Vaughan, Mary Kay and Stephen E. Lewis, eds. *The Eagle and the Virgin: Nation and Cultural Revolution in Mexico, 1920-1940*. Durham: Duke University Press, 2006.

Villarreal, Andrés. "Stratification by Skin Color in Contemporary Mexico." *American Sociological Review* 75:5 (2010): 652–678.

Viqueira, Juan Pedro. *Encrucijadas chiapanecas: economía, religión e identidades*. México, D.F.: Tusquets Editores, 2002.

Walker, Louise. *Waking from the Dream: Mexico's Middle Classes after 1968*. Stanford: Stanford University Press, 2013.

Woldenberg, José. *Historia mínima de la transición democrática en México*. México, D.F.: El Colegio de México, 2012.

Womack, Jr., John, ed. *Rebellion in Chiapas: An Historical Reader*. New York: The New Press, 1999.

Yankelevich, Pablo. "Nuestra raza y las otras. A propósito de la inmigración en el México revolucionario." In *Raza y política en Hispanoamérica*, eds. Tomás Pérez Vejo and Pablo Yankelevich. Madrid y Ciudad de México: Iberoamericana/Bonilla Artigas/El Colegio de México, 2018, 317–354.

Zolov, Eric. *The Last Good Neighbor: Mexico in the Global Sixties*. Durham: Duke University Press, 2020.

Zolov, Eric. *Refried Elvis: The Rise of the Mexican Counterculture*. Berkeley: University of California Press, 1999.

Websites

Animal Político: https://www.animalpolitico.com
Aristegui Noticias: www.aristeguinoticias.com
Instituto Nacional de Estadística y Geografía (INEGI): https://www.inegi.org.mx
International Institute for Democracy and Electoral Assistance (IDEA): https://www.idea.int/data-tools/data/gender-quotas
Latinobarómetro: https://www.latinobarometro.org/lat.jsp
Mediático: https://reframe.sussex.ac.uk/mediatico/
National Security Archive: https://nsarchive.gwu.edu
Reporters Without Borders: www.rsf.org

Index

Mexico's Unscripted Revolutions: Political and Social Change since 1958, First Edition. Stephen E. Lewis.